COMPUTER
BOOK SERIES
FROM IDG

Photoshop® 5 For Macs®
For Dummies®

Cheat Sheet

P9-CQL-743

Selection Tricks

Note: *All selection tricks performed with selection tools. (There's a shocker.)*

Draw straight lines	Option-click with lasso tool
Add to selection outline	Shift-drag
Deselect specific area	Option-drag
Deselect all but intersected area	Shift-Option-drag
Deselect entire image	⌘-D
Reselect last selection	⌘-Shift-D
Select everything	⌘-A
Hide selection outlines	⌘-H
Move selection outline only	Drag or press an arrow key

Moving Selections

Note: *Use the move tool to perform the following tricks. Or press ⌘ and use any other tool except the hand or pen tool.*

Nudge selection one pixel	arrow key
Nudge selection ten pixels	Shift-arrow key
Clone selection	Option-drag

Layer Tricks

New layer	⌘-Shift-N
Clone selection to a new layer	⌘-J
Cut selection to a new layer	⌘-Shift-J
Change opacity of layer	1, ... , 9, 0
Activate layer that contains specific image	Control-Option-click with move tool
Activate next layer up	Option-]
Activate next layer down	Option-[
Hide all layers but one	Option-click on eyeball
Show all layers	⌘-Option-click on eyeball
Select the contents of active layer	⌘-click on layer name in Layers palette

Toolbox Shortcuts

Note: *To access the tools, press the key(s) listed beside the tool.*

M—		—V
Shift-M—		—W
None —		—B
None —		—Y
C—		—N
L—		—Shift-N
Shift-L—		—O
Shift-L—		—Shift-O
J—		—Shift-O
S—		—T
Shift-S—		—Shift-T
E—		—Shift-T
R—		—Shift-T
Shift-R—		—G
Shift-R—		—Shift-G
P—		—Shift-G
Shift-P—		—Shift-G
Shift-P—		—Shift-G
+—		—I
-—		—Shift-I
A—		—Z
U—		—X
K—		—D
H—		—F

Photoshop® 5 For Macs® For Dummies®

Cheat Sheet

Palette Shortcuts

Brushes palette	F5
Color palette	F6
Layers palette	F7
Info palette	F8
Actions palette	F9
Options palette	Return
Step forward in History palette	⌘-Shift-Z
Step backward in History palette	⌘-Option-Z
All palettes and toolbox	Tab
Just palettes	Shift-Tab
Raise value in option box	up arrow
Lower value in option box	down arrow

More Fun with Selections

Fill selection with foreground color	Option-Delete
Fill selection with background color	⌘-Delete
Display Fill dialog box	Shift-Delete
Cut selection	⌘-X
Copy selection	⌘-C
Paste image last cut or copied	⌘-V
Reapply last filter	⌘-F
Reapply filter and change settings	⌘-Option-F
Adjust brightness and contrast	⌘-L
Free transform	⌘-T
Transform again	⌘-Shift-T

Navigation Tricks

Scroll image	spacebar-drag
Zoom in	⌘-spacebar-click
Zoom in and change window size	⌘-plus
Zoom out	Option-spacebar-click
Zoom out and change window size	⌘-minus
Scroll up or down one screen	Page Up/Page Down
Scroll up or down by a few pixels	Shift-PageUp/PageDown
Scroll left or right	Ctrl-Page Up/Page Down
Scroll left or right by a few pixels	⌘-Shift-PageUp/PageDown
Move to upper-left corner of image	Home
Move to lower-right corner of image	End
Zoom to 100%	Double-click on zoom tool

Daily Activities

Cancel operation	⌘-period or Esc
Close image	⌘-W
General preferences	⌘-K
Display last preferences panel used	⌘-Option-K
Open image	⌘-O
Print image	⌘-P
Page setup	⌘-Shift-P
Quit Photoshop	⌘-Q
Save image to disk	⌘-S
Undo last operation	⌘-Z

Painting and Editing Tricks

Increase brush size	]
Select largest brush size	Shift-]
Decrease brush size	[
Select smallest brush size	Shift-[
Change opacity of tool in 10% increments	1, ... , 9, 0
Paint or edit in straight lines	click, Shift-click
Change eraser style	Shift-E
Erase to History	Option-drag
Finger paint with smudge tool	Option-drag

...For Dummies: #1 Computer Book Series for Beginners

Readers Rave about Previous Editions of Photoshop For Dummies:

"Thanks so much for your most enjoyable book, *Photoshop For Dummies*. Not only has it helped me to get through everything, it is even funny."
— Zelia Rosenfeld, Hollis, New Hampshire

"This is the first *...For Dummies* book I've owned, and it is definitely the most enjoyable and easy to read manual I've ever encountered to date. Thanks for the most useful tool I will probably ever own!"
— Carolyn Deckert, Uniontown, Ohio

"Thank you so much for *Photoshop For Macs For Dummies* — it has changed my life — I now don't go out much, have constant eyestrain, and reams of strangely distorted images clog up my hard drive!"
— Sarah Witherby, East Sussex, England

"A quick note to thank you for *Photoshop 4 For Dummies*. You've made me look good even to my all-powerful service bureau."
— Sherra Picketts, Gabriola Island, British Columbia, Canada

"Easy to use, simple language, starts from scratch. Not just tips and tricks. I bought it to have on hand for those I train."
— Carolyn Boyle, Orlando, Florida

"Great book to start learning a complex program . . . I laughed, I cried."
— Robert G. Kopp, Plano, Illinois

"It broke down all of the complicated jargon into simple English. It allowed me to use my program to the fullest extent."
— Jesse Stenbak, Keene, New Hampshire

"This is fun and easy enough to read that I can read it on its own rather than using it only as a reference to solve problems while at the computer."
— Roberta Brenner, Van Nuys, California

"I loved it being so down to earth, and no 'nerd speak'."
— Caron Green, Campbell, California

PHOTOSHOP® 5
FOR MACS®
FOR
DUMMIES®

PHOTOSHOP® 5 FOR MACS® FOR DUMMIES®

by Deke McClelland

Revised by
Barbara Obermeier

IDG Books Worldwide, Inc.
An International Data Group Company

Foster City, CA ♦ Chicago, IL ♦ Indianapolis, IN ♦ New York, NY

Photoshop® 5 For Macs® For Dummies®

Published by
IDG Books Worldwide, Inc.
An International Data Group Company
919 E. Hillsdale Blvd.
Suite 400
Foster City, CA 94404
www.idgbooks.com (IDG Books Worldwide Web site)
www.dummies.com (Dummies Press Web site)

Library of Congress Catalog Card No.: 98-85844

ISBN: 0-7645-0391-X

Printed in the United States of America

10 9 8 7 6 5 4 3 2 1

1B/SZ/QW/ZY/IN

Distributed in the United States by IDG Books Worldwide, Inc.

Distributed by Macmillan Canada for Canada; by Transworld Publishers Limited in the United Kingdom; by IDG Norge Books for Norway; by IDG Sweden Books for Sweden; by Woodslane Pty. Ltd. for Australia; by Woodslane (NZ) Ltd. for New Zealand; by Addison Wesley Longman Singapore Pte Ltd. for Singapore, Malaysia, Thailand, Indonesia and Korea; by Norma Comunicaciones S.A. for Colombia; by Intersoft for South Africa; by International Thomson Publishing for Germany, Austria and Switzerland; by Toppan Company Ltd. for Japan; by Distribuidora Cuspide for Argentina; by Livraria Cultura for Brazil; by Ediciencia S.A. for Ecuador; by Ediciones ZETA S.C.R. Ltda. for Peru; by WS Computer Publishing Corporation, Inc., for the Philippines; by Unalis Corporation for Taiwan; by Contemporanea de Ediciones for Venezuela; by Computer Book & Magazine Store for Puerto Rico; by Express Computer Distributors for the Caribbean and West Indies. Authorized Sales Agent: Anthony Rudkin Associates for the Middle East and North Africa.

For general information on IDG Books Worldwide's books in the U.S., please call our Consumer Customer Service department at 800-762-2974. For reseller information, including discounts and premium sales, please call our Reseller Customer Service department at 800-434-3422.

For information on where to purchase IDG Books Worldwide's books outside the U.S., please contact our International Sales department at 650-655-3200 or fax 650-655-3297.

For information on foreign language translations, please contact our Foreign & Subsidiary Rights department at 650-655-3021 or fax 650-655-3281.

For sales inquiries and special prices for bulk quantities, please contact our Sales department at 650-655-3200 or write to the address above.

For information on using IDG Books Worldwide's books in the classroom or for ordering examination copies, please contact our Educational Sales department at 800-434-2086 or fax 317-596-5499.

For press review copies, author interviews, or other publicity information, please contact our Public Relations department at 650-655-3000 or fax 650-655-3299.

For authorization to photocopy items for corporate, personal, or educational use, please contact Copyright Clearance Center, 222 Rosewood Drive, Danvers, MA 01923, or fax 978-750-4470.

is a trademark under exclusive license to IDG Books Worldwide, Inc., from International Data Group, Inc.

About the Author

In 1985, **Deke McClelland** oversaw the implementation of the first Macintosh-based production department in Boulder, Colorado. He later graduated to be artistic director for Publishing Resources, one of the earliest all-PostScript service bureaus in the United States.

These days, Deke is the author of the best-selling computer titles *Macworld Photoshop 5 Bible* and *Photoshop 5 For Windows 95 Bible* (both published by IDG Books Worldwide, Inc.), which have combined sales worldwide of more than 500,000 copies, making them the best-selling guides of any kind on computer graphics. Other best-selling titles include *CorelDraw 8 For Dummies, PageMill 2 For Dummies* (both IDG Books), and *Real World Illustrator 7* (Peachpit Press). His newest title, *Photoshop Studio Secrets* (IDG Books), chronicles the work of 16 of the world's most prominent computer artists.

When not writing books, Deke serves as contributing editor for *Macworld* and *Publish* magazines and hosts the cable TV computer series "Digital Gurus" (now in its fourth season). Deke has written over 40 books and hundreds of magazine articles about graphics, electronic publishing, and multimedia. His work has been translated into more than 20 languages, including Portuguese, Slovenian, and Thai.

In 1989, Deke won the Benjamin Franklin Award for Best Computer Book. Since then, he has received honors from the Society for Technical Communication (1994), the American Society of Business Press Editors (1995), and the Computer Press Association (1990, 1992, 1994, and 1995). Other recent titles include *FreeHand 8 Bible, Photoshop 5 For Windows For Dummies,* and *Web Design Studio Secrets* (all published by IDG Books).

ABOUT IDG BOOKS WORLDWIDE

Welcome to the world of IDG Books Worldwide.

IDG Books Worldwide, Inc., is a subsidiary of International Data Group, the world's largest publisher of computer-related information and the leading global provider of information services on information technology. IDG was founded more than 25 years ago and now employs more than 8,500 people worldwide. IDG publishes more than 275 computer publications in over 75 countries (see listing below). More than 90 million people read one or more IDG publications each month.

Launched in 1990, IDG Books Worldwide is today the #1 publisher of best-selling computer books in the United States. We are proud to have received eight awards from the Computer Press Association in recognition of editorial excellence and three from *Computer Currents'* First Annual Readers' Choice Awards. Our best-selling *...For Dummies*® series has more than 50 million copies in print with translations in 38 languages. IDG Books Worldwide, through a joint venture with IDG's Hi-Tech Beijing, became the first U.S. publisher to publish a computer book in the People's Republic of China. In record time, IDG Books Worldwide has become the first choice for millions of readers around the world who want to learn how to better manage their businesses.

Our mission is simple: Every one of our books is designed to bring extra value and skill-building instructions to the reader. Our books are written by experts who understand and care about our readers. The knowledge base of our editorial staff comes from years of experience in publishing, education, and journalism — experience we use to produce books for the '90s. In short, we care about books, so we attract the best people. We devote special attention to details such as audience, interior design, use of icons, and illustrations. And because we use an efficient process of authoring, editing, and desktop publishing our books electronically, we can spend more time ensuring superior content and spend less time on the technicalities of making books.

You can count on our commitment to deliver high-quality books at competitive prices on topics you want to read about. At IDG Books Worldwide, we continue in the IDG tradition of delivering quality for more than 25 years. You'll find no better book on a subject than one from IDG Books Worldwide.

John Kilcullen
John Kilcullen
CEO
IDG Books Worldwide, Inc.

Steven Berkowitz
Steven Berkowitz
President and Publisher
IDG Books Worldwide, Inc.

*Eighth Annual
Computer Press
Awards ≥1992*

*Ninth Annual
Computer Press
Awards ≥1993*

*Tenth Annual
Computer Press
Awards ≥1994*

*Eleventh Annual
Computer Press
Awards ≥1995*

IDG Books Worldwide, Inc., is a subsidiary of International Data Group, the world's largest publisher of computer-related information and the leading global provider of information services on information technology. International Data Group publishes over 275 computer publications in over 75 countries. More than 90 million people read one or more International Data Group publications each month. International Data Group's publications include: **ARGENTINA:** Buyer's Guide, Computerworld Argentina, PC World Argentina; **AUSTRALIA:** Australian Macworld, Australian PC World, Australian Reseller News, Computerworld, IT Casebook, Network World, Publish, Webmaster; **AUSTRIA:** Computerwelt Osterreich, Networks Austria, PC Tip Austria; **BANGLADESH:** PC World Bangladesh; **BELARUS:** PC World Belarus; **BELGIUM:** Data News; **BRAZIL:** Annuário de Informática, Computerworld, Connections, Macworld, PC Player, PC World, Publish, Reseller News, Supergamepower; **BULGARIA:** Computerworld Bulgaria, Network World Bulgaria, PC & MacWorld Bulgaria; **CANADA:** CIO Canada, Client/Server World, ComputerWorld Canada, InfoWorld Canada, NetworkWorld Canada, WebWorld; **CHILE:** Computerworld Chile, PC World Chile; **COLOMBIA:** Computerworld Colombia, PC World Colombia; **COSTA RICA:** PC World Centro America; **THE CZECH AND SLOVAK REPUBLICS:** Computerworld Czechoslovakia, Macworld Czech Republic, PC World Czechoslovakia; **DENMARK:** Communications World Danmark, Computerworld Danmark, Macworld Danmark, PC World Danmark, Techworld Danmark; **DOMINICAN REPUBLIC:** PC World Republica Dominicana; **ECUADOR:** PC World Ecuador; **EGYPT:** Computerworld Middle East, PC World Middle East; **EL SALVADOR:** PC World Centro America; **FINLAND:** MikroPC, Tietoverkko, Tietoviikko; **FRANCE:** Distributique, Hebdo, Info PC, Le Monde Informatique, Macworld, Reseaux & Telecoms, WebMaster France; **GERMANY:** Computer Partner, Computerwoche, Computerwoche Extra, Computerwoche FOCUS, Global Online, Macwelt, PC Welt; **GREECE:** Amiga Computing, GamePro Greece, Multimedia World; **GUATEMALA:** PC World Centro America; **HONDURAS:** PC World Centro America; **HONG KONG:** Computerworld Hong Kong, PC World Hong Kong, Publish in Asia; **HUNGARY:** ABCD CD-ROM, Computerworld Szamitastechnika, Internetto online Magazine, PC World Hungary, PC-X Magazin Hungary; **ICELAND:** Tolvuheimur PC World Island; **INDIA:** Information Communications World, Information Systems Computerworld, PC World India, Publish in Asia; **INDONESIA:** InfoKomputer PC World, Komputek Computerworld, Publish in Asia; **IRELAND:** ComputerScope, PC Live!; **ISRAEL:** Macworld Israel, People & Computers/Computerworld; **ITALY:** Computerworld Italia, Macworld Italia, Networking Italia, PC World Italia; **JAPAN:** DTP World, Macworld Japan, Nikkei Personal Computing, OS/2 World Japan, SunWorld Japan, Windows NT World, Windows World Japan; **KENYA:** PC World East African; **KOREA:** Hi-Tech Information, Macworld Korea, PC World Korea; **MACEDONIA:** PC World Macedonia; **MALAYSIA:** Computerworld Malaysia, PC World Malaysia, Publish in Asia; **MALTA:** PC World Malta; **MEXICO:** Computerworld Mexico, PC World Mexico; **MYANMAR:** PC World Myanmar; **NETHERLANDS:** Computer! Totaal, LAN Internetworking Magazine, LAN World Buyers Guide, Macworld Netherlands, Net, WebWereld; **NEW ZEALAND:** Absolute Beginners Guide and Plain & Simple Series, Computer Buyer, Computer Industry Directory, Computerworld New Zealand, MTB, Network World, PC World New Zealand; **NICARAGUA:** PC World Centro America; **NORWAY:** Computerworld Norge, CW Rapport, Datamagasinet, Financial Rapport, Kursguide Norge, Macworld Norge, Multimediaworld Norge, PC World Ekspress Norge, PC World Nettverk, PC World Norge, PC World ProduktGuide Norge; **PAKISTAN:** Computerworld Pakistan; **PANAMA:** PC World Panama; **PEOPLE'S REPUBLIC OF CHINA:** China Computer Users, China Computerworld, China InfoWorld, China Telecom World Weekly, Computer & Communication, Electronic Design China, Electronics Today, Electronics Weekly, Game Software, PC World China, Popular Computer Week, Software Weekly, Software World, Telecom World; **PERU:** Computerworld Peru, PC World Profesional Peru, PC World SoHo Peru; **PHILIPPINES:** Click!, Computerworld Philippines, PC World Philippines, Publish in Asia; **POLAND:** Computerworld Poland, Computerworld Special Report Poland, Cyber, Macworld Poland, Networld Poland, PC World Komputer; **PORTUGAL:** Cerebro/PC World, Computerworld/Correio Informático, Dealer World Portugal, Mac*In/PC*In Portugal, Multimedia World; **PUERTO RICO:** PC World Puerto Rico; **ROMANIA:** Computerworld Romania, PC World Romania, Telecom Romania; **RUSSIA:** Computerworld Russia, Mir PK, Publish, Seti; **SINGAPORE:** Computerworld Singapore, PC World Singapore, Publish in Asia; **SLOVENIA:** Monitor; **SOUTH AFRICA:** Computing SA, Network World SA, Software World SA; **SPAIN:** Communicaciones World España, Computerworld España, Dealer World España, Macworld España, PC World España; **SRI LANKA:** Infolink PC World; **SWEDEN:** CAP&Design, Computer Sweden, Corporate Computing Sweden, Internetworld Sweden, it.branschen, Macworld Sweden, MaxiData Sweden, MikroDatorn, Natverk & Kommunikation, PC World Sweden, PCaktiv, Windows World Sweden; **SWITZERLAND:** Computerworld Schweiz, Macworld Schweiz, PCtip; **TAIWAN:** Computerworld Taiwan, Macworld Taiwan, NEW ViSiON/Publish, PC World Taiwan, Windows World Taiwan; **THAILAND:** Publish in Asia, Thai Computerworld; **TURKEY:** Computerworld Turkiye, Macworld Turkiye, Network World Turkiye, PC World Turkiye; **UKRAINE:** Computerworld Kiev, Multimedia World Ukraine, PC World Ukraine; **UNITED KINGDOM:** Acorn User UK, Amiga Action UK, Amiga Computing UK, Apple Talk UK, Computing, Macworld, Parents and Computers UK, PC Advisor, PC Home, PSX Pro, The WEB; **UNITED STATES:** Cable in the Classroom, CIO Magazine, Computerworld, DOS World, Federal Computer Week, GamePro Magazine, InfoWorld, I-Way, Macworld, Network World, PC Games, PC World, Publish, Video Event, THE WEB Magazine, and WebMaster; online webzines: JavaWorld, NetscapeWorld, and SunWorld Online; **URUGUAY:** InfoWorld Uruguay; **VENEZUELA:** Computerworld Venezuela, PC World Venezuela; and **VIETNAM:** PC World Vietnam.   5/7/98

Dedication

To Elizabeth, who came home from a low-brow evening of bingo to cart her klutz of a husband off to the hospital. That's just the kind of loving person she is.

Author's Acknowledgments

Thanks to the many folks who loaned me products and support, including Marc Pawliger at Adobe, Charles Smith at Digital Stock, Tom Hughes at PhotoDisc, and the helpful folks at Palmer's.

Thanks also to Michael Kelly for providing advice and support, to Karen York and the folks at IDG's production and art departments for their expertise and cooperation, to Daniel McClelland for keeping an eye out for the technical foibles, and to Melba Hopper for keeping the whole shebang on track and in good shape. Finally, special thanks to Barbara Obermeier for her excellent job of updating this book to Photoshop 5.

Publisher's Acknowledgments

We're proud of this book; please register your comments through our IDG Books Worldwide Online Registration Form located at http://my2cents.dummies.com.

Some of the people who helped bring this book to market include the following:

*Acquisitions, Editorial, and
Media Development*

Project Editor: Melba D. Hopper

Acquisitions Editor: Michael Kelly

Technical Editor: Daniel McClelland

Editorial Manager: Mary C. Corder

Editorial Assistant: Paul Kuzmic

Production

Project Coordinator: Karen York

Layout and Graphics: Lou Boudreau, Linda M. Boyer, Angela F. Hunckler, Heather Pearson, Brent Savage, Kate Snell, Michael A. Sullivan

Proofreaders: Christine Berman, Kelli Botta, Michelle Croninger, Sally Burton, Rebecca Senninger, Robert Springer

Indexer: Liz Cunningham

General and Administrative

IDG Books Worldwide, Inc.: John Kilcullen, CEO; Steven Berkowitz, President and Publisher

IDG Books Technology Publishing: Brenda McLaughlin, Senior Vice President and Group Publisher

Dummies Technology Press and Dummies Editorial: Diane Graves Steele, Vice President and Associate Publisher; Mary Bednarek, Director of Acquisitions and Product Development; Kristin A. Cocks, Editorial Director

Dummies Trade Press: Kathleen A. Welton, Vice President and Publisher; Kevin Thornton, Acquisitions Manager

IDG Books Production for Dummies Press: Michael R. Britton, Vice President of Production; Beth Jenkins Roberts, Production Director; Cindy L. Phipps, Manager of Project Coordination, Production Proofreading, and Indexing; Kathie S. Schutte, Supervisor of Page Layout; Shelley Lea, Supervisor of Graphics and Design; Debbie J. Gates, Production Systems Specialist; Robert Springer, Supervisor of Proofreading; Debbie Stailey, Special Projects Coordinator; Tony Augsburger, Supervisor of Reprints and Bluelines

Dummies Packaging and Book Design: Robin Seaman, Creative Director; Jocelyn Kelaita, Product Packaging Coordinator; Kavish + Kavish, Cover Design

♦

The publisher would like to give special thanks to Patrick J. McGovern, without whom this book would not have been possible.

♦

Contents at a Glance

Cartoons at a Glance

By Rich Tennant

The 5th Wave By Rich Tennant

"...AND TO ACCESS THE PROGRAM'S 'HOT KEY,' YOU JUST DEPRESS THESE ELEVEN KEYS SIMULTANEOUSLY. HERB OVER THERE HAS A KNACK FOR DOING THIS THAT I THINK YOU'LL ENJOY—HERB! GOT A MINUTE?"

page 7

The 5th Wave By Rich Tennant

"I THINK YOU'VE MADE A MISTAKE. WE DO PHOTO RETOUCHING, NOT FAMILY PORTRAI...OOOH, WAIT A MINUTE—I THINK I GET IT!"

page 51

The 5th Wave By Rich Tennant

"Remember, your Elvis should appear bald and slightly hunched—nice Big Foot, Brad—keep your two-headed animals in the shadows and your alien spacecrafts crisp and defined."

page 115

The 5th Wave By Rich Tennant

"I'VE GOT SOME IMAGE EDITING SOFTWARE, SO I TOOK THE LIBERTY OF ERASING SOME OF THE SMUDGES THAT KEPT SHOWING UP AROUND THE CLOUDS. NO NEED TO THANK ME."

page 175

The 5th Wave By Rich Tennant

"...AND THROUGH IMAGE EDITING TECHNOLOGY, WE'RE ABLE TO RE-CREATE THE AWESOME SPECTACLE KNOWN AS TYRANNOSAURUS GWEN."

page 235

The 5th Wave By Rich Tennant

ATTEMPTING TO SAVE MONEY ON FAMILY PHOTOS, THE DILBRANTS SCAN THEIR NEWBORN INTO A PHOTO IMAGING PROGRAM WITH PLANS OF JUST DITHERING THE CHILD INTO ADOLESCENCE.

"Nope! She must have moved again! Run the scanner down her once more."

page 305

Fax: 978-546-7747 • E-mail: the5wave@tiac.net

Table of Contents

Introduction

· ·

*W*hy in the world is Adobe Photoshop such a popular program? Normally, graphics software is about as much of a hit with the general public as a grunge rock band is with the senior-citizen set. And yet Photoshop — a program that lets you correct and modify photographs on your computer screen — has managed to work its way into the hearts and minds of computer users from all walks of life. What gives?

Wouldn't you know it, I just happen to have a couple of theories. First, when you work in Photoshop, you're not drawing from scratch; you're editing photos. Sure, tampering with a photograph can be a little intimidating, but it's nothing like the chilling, abject fear that seizes your soul when you stare at a blank screen and try to figure out how to draw things on it. Simply put, a photograph inspires you to edit it in precisely the same way that an empty piece of paper does not.

Second, after Photoshop hooks you, it keeps you interested with a depth of capabilities that few pieces of software can match. Unlike so many programs that have caught on like wildfire over the years, but are actually a pain in the rear to use — I won't name any, but I bet you can think of a few — Photoshop is both powerful and absorbing. After several years with the program, I am continually discovering new things about it, and I've enjoyed nearly every minute of it. (Okay, so a couple of stinky minutes sneak themselves in every once in a while, but that's to be expected. Photoshop is a computer program, after all, and we all know that computers are cosmic jokes whose only reason for being is to mock us, ignore our requests, and crash at the least opportune moments. In fact, considering that it's a computer program, Photoshop fares remarkably well.)

About This Book

Just because Photoshop is a pleasure to use doesn't mean that the program is easy to learn. In fact, it's kind of a bear. A big, ornery, grizzly bear with about 17 rows of teeth and claws to match. This program contains so much that it honestly takes months of earnest endeavor to sift through it all. By yourself, that is.

When you go into battle armed with this book, however, Photoshop sucks in its teeth, retracts its claws, and lies down like a lamb. In fact, studies show that if you just hold the book up to the computer screen, Photoshop behaves 50 percent better, even if you never read a single page.

If you do read a page or two, Photoshop not only behaves, it also makes sense. The truth is, I wrote this book with the following specific goals in mind:

- ✔ To show you what you need to know at the precise pace you need to know it.
- ✔ To show you how to do the right things in the right way, right off the bat.
- ✔ To distract you and shove little facts into your head when you're not looking.
- ✔ To make the process not only less painful, but also a real adventure that you'll look back on during your Golden Years with a wistful tear in your eye. "Oh, how I'd like to learn Photoshop all over again," you'll sigh. "Nothing I've done since — whether it was winning the lottery that one time or flying on the inaugural commuter shuttle to the moon with the original cast of *Star Trek* — seemed quite so thrilling as sifting through Photoshop with that crazy old *...For Dummies* book."

Okay, maybe that's an exaggeration, but prepare yourself for a fun time. In a matter of days, you'll be doing things that'll make your jaw hang down and dangle from its hinges. And don't worry, it's all perfectly legal throughout the 50 states as well as Puerto Rico, the Virgin Islands, and Guam.

Don't You Have Another Photoshop Book?

While you were browsing the bookstore shelves deciding which book on Photoshop to buy, you may have noticed another book by yours truly: *Macworld Photoshop 5 Bible.* That 800-page tome covers just about everything there is to know about Photoshop.

Some folks, though, look forward to reading the 800 pages with the same dread they normally reserve for eating 800 pieces of dry toast. As people who have read the *Bible* know, the pages are anything but dry and laborious; in fact, they're more like 800 tasty cookies. "Make it fatter and throw in a free forklift so that I can tote it around my house" is the typical response I get. But even so, the *Bible* is something that this book is not. It's exhaustive.

Photoshop 5 For Macs For Dummies looks at things from a different angle. It points out the features you need to know and shows you exactly how to use them. You don't want to make Photoshop your life — not yet, anyway — but you don't want the thing to just sit there and beep at you in between completely destroying your photograph, either. You'd like to reach a certain satisfying level of comfort, like the one you've recently achieved with your cat now that he's no longer clawing the furniture apart. Becoming comfortable and productive with Photoshop is what this book is all about.

What's in This Book?

This book comprises a bunch of independent sections designed to answer your questions as they occur. Oh, sure, you can read the book cover-to-cover, and it will make perfect sense. But you can also read any section completely out of context and know exactly what's going on.

To help you slog through the information, I've broken the book into six parts. Each of these parts contains three or four chapters, and these chapters are divided into sections and subsections. Graphics abound to illustrate things that would take 1,000 words to explain, and you'll even find glorious color plates — 16 pages in all — to show off special issues related to color.

To give you an overview of the kind of information you're likely to find in these pages, here's a quick rundown of the six parts.

Part I: What the . . . ? Aagh, Help Me!

The first stage of using any computer program is the worst. You don't know what you can do, you don't know how good the program is, you don't even know how to ask a reasonably intelligent question. These first three chapters get you up and running in record time.

Chapter 1 introduces you to image editing, explains where to find images to edit, and provides a quick glimpse of what's new in Version 5 of Photoshop. Chapters 2 and 3 take you on a grand tour of the Photoshop interface and image window and give you all the information you need to navigate both.

Part II: The Care and Feeding of Pixels

Before you can edit a digital photograph, you have to know a few things about the nature of the beast. What's a pixel, for example, and why is getting rid of one so dangerous? What's the difference between a color image and a grayscale image — other than the obvious? And how do you save or print your image after you finish editing it? All these questions and many more are answered in Chapters 4 through 7.

Part III: Tiptoe through the Toolbox

Photoshop offers fewer tools — pencils, paintbrushes, and the like — than most graphics programs. But these tools are remarkably capable, allowing you to perform pages and pages of tricks while expending minimum effort. Find out how to smear colors, get rid of dust specks, erase mistakes, and do a whole lot more in Chapters 8 through 11.

Part IV: Select Before You Correct

The selection tools let you cordon off the portion of the photograph you want to edit. Select the face, for example, and Photoshop protects the body, no matter how randomly you drag or how spastic your brushstrokes. Chapters 12 through 14 help you understand how selections work and how to use them to your advantage.

Part V: So, You Say You're Serious about Image Editing

Now you step into the really incredible part of the Photoshop playground. In Chapter 15, I introduce you to layers, a Photoshop feature that adds flexibility, creative opportunity, and security to your image-editing life. In Chapter 16, you find out how to create text effects and add them to your image. And in Chapters 17 and 18, I show you the commands that professionals use to sharpen focus, change brightness and contrast, correct colors, and generally make an image look three times better than it did when you started.

Part VI: The Part of Tens

Chapters 19 through 21 contain the ultimate Photoshop Top Ten lists. Find out the most essential Photoshop shortcuts, the most amazing special effects tricks, and the answer to that age-old question, "Now that I've finished mucking up my image in Photoshop, what do I do with it?"

Icons Used in This Book

When you're driving, road signs are always warning you about bad things. Slow, Detour, Stop, Dip — these are all signs that I, for one, hate to see. I mean, you never see good signs like Go Ahead and Speed, No Traffic This Way, or Free Money Up Ahead. This book isn't like that. Using friendly little margin icons, I highlight good things and bad things, and the good things outnumber the bad. So don't shy away from the road signs in this book; welcome them into your reading ritual with open arms. Here's your field guide to icons:

I hate computer jargon as much as the next red-blooded American. But sometimes, I have to use it because there's no word for this stuff in normal, everyday, conversational English. It's a crying shame, I know, but at least I warn you that something nerdy is coming your way with this icon.

Photoshop has very few obvious shortcuts and a ton of hidden ones. That's where the Tip icon comes in. It says, "Hey, whoa there; here's a juicy one!"

This icon calls your attention to special little reminders of things I've mentioned in the past or things I want you to bear in mind for the future.

Photoshop is a kind and gentle program. But every once in a while, it pays to be careful. The Warning icon tells you when to keep an eye out for trouble.

This icon points out features or commands that have changed or are new in Version 5. If you're upgrading to Version 5 from an earlier version of Photoshop, pay attention to this road sign because lots of things are different now.

Now and then, I feel compelled to share something with you that has nothing whatsoever to do with your learning Photoshop or any other computer program. It's just my way of showing that I care.

How to Use This Book

When I was in grade school, I don't think that a year went by that our teacher didn't show us how to handle our new books. Open the book once in the center and then open the first quarter and the last quarter, each time gently creasing the spine. Never fold the pages or roll them so that they won't lie flat. And be sure to read the words from the beginning to end, just as the author meant them to be read. A book, after all, is a Special Thing to Be Treasured. Here are a couple of thoughts:

✔ Break the spine first thing out. The pages lie flatter that way.

✔ When you have a question, look it up in the Index. Feel free to shut the book and get on with your life when you're done (though I do my best to snag you and make you read longer).

✔ If you're just curious about what the book has to offer, look up whatever topic interests you in the Table of Contents and read a few pages.

✔ If you want to learn everything the book has to offer in what I consider the optimum order, turn the next page and start reading at your own pace.

✔ If you come across something important, don't hesitate to fold the page, slap a sticky note on it, circle the text with a highlighter pen, or rip out the page and tack it to the wall.

✔ And when you've gleaned everything there is to glean, house-train your new puppy with the pages or use them for kindling.

Feedback, Please

Want to send me a line of congratulations or a complaint? If so, please feel free to visit my Web site at www.dekemc.com, and then click on the Contact Deke button to drop me a line. I get a ton of mail these days — a hundred or more reader letters a week — so I can't begin to respond to them all. But I do read and appreciate them.

You can also contact the publisher or authors of other ...*For Dummies* books by visiting the publisher's Web site at www.dummies.com, sending an e-mail to info@idgbooks.com, or sending paper mail to IDG Books Worldwide, Inc., 7260 Shadeland Station, Suite 100, Indianapolis, IN 46256.

Part I

What the . . . ?
Aagh, Help Me!

The 5th Wave   **By Rich Tennant**

"...AND TO ACCESS THE PROGRAM'S 'HOT KEY,' YOU JUST DEPRESS THESE ELEVEN KEYS SIMULTANEOUSLY. HERB OVER THERE HAS A KNACK FOR DOING THIS THAT I THINK YOU'LL ENJOY — HERB! GOT A MINUTE?"

In this part . . .

A lot has been written, spoken, and tapped out in Morse code about the value of information. To hear some folks tell it, information is now the top commodity in the industrialized world. Well, I don't know if that's true or not — personally, you can give me money over information any day of the week. "There's always more room in my billfold than my head," is my saying. But being, shall I say, "unlettered," on any subject is no fun.

But if you're not sure how to ask an intelligent question about Photoshop, take heart. These first three chapters answer that most impossible of all questions to express, "What the . . . ? I mean . . . ? You know, if the . . . ? Aagh, help me!" For example, you find out what Photoshop is, take a quick, all-expenses-paid jaunt through its tools and commands, and discover how to open and view images.

By the end of Chapter 3, you won't know everything there is to know about Photoshop — otherwise, I could have dispensed with the 18 chapters that follow it — but you will know enough to phrase a few intelligent questions. And please remember that as you read these chapters, there's no shame in being as yet uninformed. I mean, it must be more than coincidental that the initials for *Photoshop For Dummies* are Ph.D.

Chapter 1

Meet Dr. Photo and Mr. Shop

. . . .

In This Chapter

▶ An introduction to the dual world of Photoshop

▶ The difference between painting and image editing

▶ A few common methods for adjusting photographs

▶ What's new in Version 5

▶ Where to find images to edit

. . . .

Adobe Photoshop is arguably the most comprehensive and most popular photo editor around. In fact, I don't know a single computer artist who doesn't use Photoshop on an almost daily basis, regardless of what other programs he or she may use.

I assume that you've at least seen, if not used, Photoshop and that you have a vague idea of what it's all about. But just so that we're all clear on the subject, the primary purpose of Photoshop is to make changes to photographic images that you somehow managed to get on disk. (For some clever ideas on acquiring such images, see the sidebar "Where do I find images to abuse?" later in this chapter.)

If you've only used Photoshop for a week or so, you may have mistaken it for a fairly straightforward package. Certainly, on the surface of the program, Photoshop comes off as rather friendly. But lurking a few fathoms deep is another, darker program, one that is distinctly unfriendly for the uninitiated but wildly capable for the stout of heart. My analyst would no doubt declare Photoshop a classic case of a split personality. It's half man, half monster; half mild-mannered shoeshine boy, half blonde-grabbing, airplane-swatting King Kong; half kindly old gent with white whiskers chewing on a pipe, half green-gilled invader from another planet chewing on your . . . well, perhaps you don't want to know. In short, Photoshop has a Dr. Jekyll-and-Mr. Hyde thing going — only it's way scarier.

As you may recall from the last time you saw *Abbott and Costello Meet Dr. Jekyll and Mr. Hyde* — indisputably the foremost resource of information on this famous tale — this Jekyll character (not to be confused with the similarly named cartoon crow) is normally your everyday, average, nice-guy scientist. Then one day, he drinks some potion or gets cut off in traffic or something and changes into his ornery alter ego, known at every dive bar in town by the surname Hyde. Photoshop behaves just the same way, except that no magical transformation is required to shift between the program's Jekyll half and its Hyde half. Both personalities coexist simultaneously in what you might call harmony.

This chapter explores both sides of the Photoshop brain. It also introduces you to the personality changes found in the latest incarnation of the program, Version 5. Finally, I get you started on the road to image-editing bliss by explaining where to find images to edit in the first place.

The Bland but Kindly Dr. Photo

To discover the benevolent Dr. Jekyll half of Photoshop, you need look no farther than the standard painting and editing tools. Shown in Figure 1-1, these tools are so simple, they're practically pastoral, the kind of household appliances your great-grandmother would have been comfortable with. The eraser erases, the pencil draws hard-edged lines, the airbrush sprays a fine mist of color, and so on. These incredibly straightforward tools attract new users just as surely as a light attracts miller moths (except new users don't give off quite so much dust when you squish them).

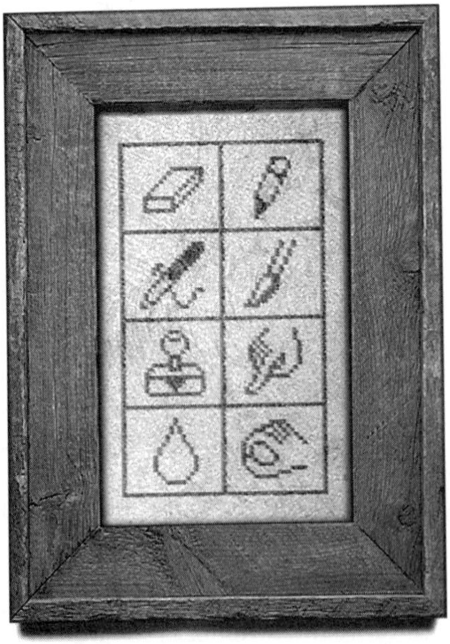

Figure 1-1: Many of the Photoshop tools have an old-world rustic charm that's sure to warm the cockles of the most timid technophobe.

But you quickly discover that, on their own, these tools aren't super-duper exciting, just like the boring Dr. Jekyll. They don't work much like their traditional counterparts — a line drawn with the pencil tool, for example, doesn't look anything like a line drawn with a real pencil — and they don't seem to be particularly applicable to the job of editing images. Generally speaking, you have to be blessed with pretty major hand-eye coordination to achieve good results using these tools.

The Ghastly but Dynamic Mr. Shop

When the standard paint and editing tools don't fit the bill, you try to adjust the performance of the tools and experiment with the other image controls of Photoshop. Unfortunately, that's when you discover the Mr. Hyde half of the program. You encounter options that have meaningless names such as Dissolve, Multiply, and Difference. Commands such as Image Size and Canvas Size — both of which sound harmless enough — seem to damage your image. And clicking on icons frequently produces no result. It's enough to drive a reticent computer artist stark raving insane, as illustrated in Figure 1-2.

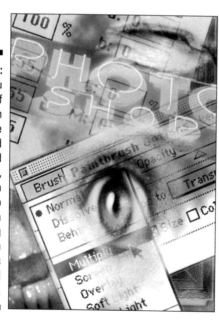

Figure 1-2: When you tire of playing with the standard paint and edit tools, you run smack dab into a terrifying collection of options and commands.

The net result is that many folks return broken and frustrated to the under-equipped and boring but nonthreatening painting and editing tools that they've come to know. It's sad, really. Especially when you consider all the wonderful things that the more complex Photoshop controls can do. Oh sure, the controls have weird names, and they may not respond as you think they should at first, but after you come to terms with these slick puppies, they perform like you wouldn't believe.

In fact, the dreaded Mr. Hyde side of Photoshop represents the core of this powerful program. Without its sinister half, Photoshop is just another rinky-dink piece of painting software whose most remarkable capability is keeping the kids out of mischief on a rainy day.

The Two Phunctions of Photoshop

Generally speaking, the two halves of Photoshop serve different purposes. The straightforward Jekyll tools mostly concentrate on *painting,* and the more complex Hyde capabilities are devoted to *image editing.* Therefore, to tackle this great program, you may find it helpful to understand the difference between the two terms.

Painting without the mess

Painting is just what it sounds like: You take a brush loaded with color and smear it all over your on-screen image. You can paint from scratch on a blank canvas, or you can paint directly on top of a photograph. The first option requires lots of talent, planning, and a few dashes of artistic genius; the second option requires an opposable thumb. Okay, that's a slight exaggeration — some lemurs have been known to have problems with the second option — but most people find painting on an existing image much easier than creating an image from scratch.

Take Figure 1-3, for example. Here's a rather drab fellow drinking a rather drab beverage. (Though you may guess this man to be Dr. Jekyll armed with the secret potion, most scholars consider it highly doubtful that even Jekyll was this goofy.) I introduce this silly person solely to demonstrate the amazing functions of Photoshop.

Were you to paint on our unsuspecting saphead, you might arrive at something on the order of the image shown in Figure 1-4. I invoked all these changes using a single tool — the paintbrush — and just two colors — black and white. Suddenly, a singularly cool dude emerges. No planning or real

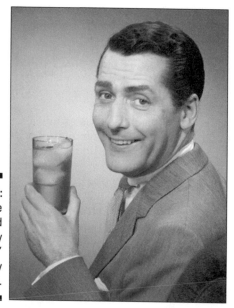

Figure 1-3:
The
unadorned
"I Love My
Libation"
poster boy
of 1948.

talent was involved; I simply traced over some existing details in the image. Better yet, I haven't permanently damaged the image, as I would if I tried the same thing using a real-life paintbrush. Because I saved the original image to disk (as explained in Chapter 6), I can restore details from the original image at whim (the subject of Chapter 11).

Figure 1-4:
A few
hundred
strokes of
the
paintbrush
result in a
party
animal to
rival
Carmen
Miranda.

Editing existing image detail

The remade man in Figure 1-4 is the life of the party, but he's nothing compared to what he could be with the aid of some image editing. When you edit an image, you distort and enhance its existing details. So rather than paint with color, you paint with the image itself.

Figure 1-5 demonstrates what I mean. To achieve this grotesque turn of the visual phrase, I was obliged to indulge in a liberal amount of distortion. First, I flipped the guy's head and stretched it a little bit. Well, actually, I stretched it a lot. Then, I further exaggerated the eyes and mouth. I rotated the arm and distorted the glass to make the glass meet the ear. Finally, I cloned a background from a different image to cover up where the head and arm used to be. The only thing I painted was the straw (the one coming out of the guy's ear). Otherwise, I lifted every detail from one of two photographs. And yet, this man's very own mother wouldn't recognize him, were she still alive today.

Figure 1-5:
Image editing has no respect for composition, form, or underlying skeletal structure.

Mind you, you don't have to go quite so hog-wild with the image editing. If you're a photographer, for example, you may not care to mess with your work to the point that it becomes completely unrecognizable. Call you weird, but you like reality the way you see it. Figure 1-6 shows a few subtle adjustments that affect neither the form nor composition of the original image. These changes merely accentuate details or downplay defects in the image.

Figure 1-6:
If Figure 1-5 is a little too disgusting for your tastes, you can apply more moderate edits to your image.

Just for the record, here are a few common ways to edit photographs in Photoshop:

✔ You can *sharpen* an image to make it appear in better focus, as in the first image in Figure 1-6. Generally, sharpening is used to account for focus problems in the scanning process, but you can sometimes sharpen a photograph that was shot out of focus.

✔ If you want to accentuate a foreground image, you can blur the focus of the background. The image on the right side of Figure 1-6 is an example.

✔ If a photograph is too light or too dark, you can fix it in a flash through the miracle of color correction. You can change the contrast, brighten or dim colors, and actually replace one color with another. Both of the images in Figure 1-6 have been color-corrected.

✔ Using the Photoshop selection and move tools, you can grab a chunk of your image and physically move it around. You can also clone the selection, stretch it, rotate it, or copy it to a different image.

And that's only the tip of the iceberg. The remaining chapters of this book explore Photoshop as both a painting program and an image editor. Most chapters contain a little bit of information on both topics, but as a general rule, the first half of the book stresses painting, and the second half spends more time on image editing. Rip the book in half and you may very well have the makings of a late-night horror flick.

It's New! It's Improved!

Someday, the folks at Adobe may come out with an upgrade to Photoshop that completely tames the Mr. Hyde half of the program. But Version 5 isn't the upgrade to do it, which is good for me because it allows me to continue with my colorful dual-personality analogy. Version 5, it turns out, is one part helpful, unbelievably great upgrade and one part exercise in frustration.

On one hand, Version 5 includes many incredibly useful new features. On the other, Version 5 trashes some time-honored shortcuts and techniques used in earlier versions of the program, a development that is sure to confuse and annoy veteran Photoshop users. One change that may do more than just annoy users is the fact that Version 5 will work only on PowerPC Macs. Computers with 68K processors are no longer supported.

The good news is that Version 5's good side more than compensates for its bad side. So, in the interest of focusing on the positive, here are just some of the improvements Version 5 brings you:

- **Multiple undos (Chapter 11):** Finally the number one wish-list item comes true! Photoshop remembers your steps in the new History palette. You can return to a previous step by merely selecting it from the list. In addition, the new History Brush allows you to paint or clone back to a previous step.

- **Editable type layer (Chapter 16):** Even though you still have to enter text in a dialog box, at least you can preview it while you are doing it. You can also go back to the text and make changes. Version 5 now allows you to mix fonts and sizes within the same text block. Tracking, kerning, and baseline shift and color settings are available via the dialog box. No more endless typing and deleting!

- **Layer effects (Chapter 15):** Creating effects such as shadows, glows, bevels, and embosses just got easier. Why? Because Photoshop now does them automatically. They can even be edited and put on a separate layer.

- **3D transformation filter (Chapter 17):** This new filter wraps a 2D image around a 3D shape, such as a cube or sphere. There are limitations but it has potential.

- **Magnetic selection tools (Chapter 12):** Photoshop 5 gives you two new selection tools — the magnetic lasso and the magnetic pen. These smart tools hug the edges of a foreground image while you make your selection, and they have settings to control sensitivity.

- **Indexed color preview (Chapter 6):** You can now preview the effect of changing your image to the indexed color mode when creating GIFs. Great for Web designers.

✔ **New saving options (Chapters 3 and 6):** You now have more options with file extensions and thumbnail previews. Version 5 can also open and save the new Flash Pix format.

✔ **Freeform pen tool (Chapter 12):** Eliminates the need for drawing paths the hard way. You can now merely drag and draw — a steady hand being the only requirement.

✔ **Align and distribute layers (Chapter 15):** Version 5 lets you align and distribute linked layers. Another useful tool for Web designers.

✔ **More gradient styles (Chapter 14):** Besides linear and radial gradients, you can also choose from angle, reflected, and diamond.

✔ **Transform paths and selection outlines (Chapter 13):** You are now able to directly transform (scale, rotate) a selection outline without affecting the actual image. Also, paths and parts of paths can be transformed.

✔ **Repeat transformation (Chapters 13 and 15):** After transforming a layer, selection, or path, you can repeat the transformation to another layer, selection, or path.

✔ **Measure tool (Chapter 3):** This new tool is like an on-screen ruler, allowing you to measure height, width, distance, and angles.

✔ **Color sampler tool (Chapter 5):** With this new tool, you can sample colors of four areas anywhere in the image and look at the values in the Info palette.

✔ **Reselect command (Chapter 13):** After you deselect an area, Photoshop remembers your last selection outline, even after you have done other things, allowing you to easily reselect. Great addition!

✔ **Position the transformation origin (Chapters 13 and 15):** A center point, which can be moved anywhere, has been added to the transformation box, allowing for different points of origin for scaling, rotating, and so on.

✔ **Toolbox reorganization (Cheat Sheet):** Some tools have moved, and some have new keyboard equivalents. To toggle through the tools, press Shift along with the particular tool's keyboard equivalent.

✔ **Revised rubber stamp (Chapter 10):** This beloved tool, which has improved cloning for cleaning up images, now shares its space with a cousin — the Pattern rubber stamp.

✔ **Near elimination of floating selections (Chapter 15):** Just say layers, layers, and more layers.

✔ **Wizards/Assistants (Chapters 4, 5, and 12):** Three operations — monitor calibration, image resizing, and exporting a transparent image — are now made easier by using step-by-step guides.

✔ **Vertical type tool and vertical type mask tool (Chapter 16):** Type and type masks (selection outlines) can now be entered vertically.

✔ **Page left and right (Chapter 3):** More navigation goodies — ⌘-PageUp/PageDown scrolls your screen left and right.

If you're used to working in Photoshop 4, some of these changes may confuse you at first, but after you get the hang of things, they make the editing process much easier. Of course, if you've never used Photoshop, you won't even be aware of Version 5's bad side — ignorance is bliss, as they say.

Where do I find images to abuse?

We all know how to turn photographs from our cameras into colorful pieces of paper that we can slap into albums or frames. But few of us have scanned a photograph to disk. However, you can find plenty of affordable options if you look in the right places:

✔ You can purchase photos on CD-ROM (prices range from less than 25 cents to several dollars per image). Some of my favorite image vendors are Adobe Studios (888-502-8393), PhotoDisc (800-528-3475), and Digital Stock (800-545-4514).

✔ You can find zillions of photos to download on the Internet or an online service such as CompuServe or America Online. The problem is, most of these images are of dubious quality or pornographic. If you want high-quality, general-purpose images, you have to subscribe to a specialized services such as PressLink Online/MediaStream (go to www.presslink.com or call 800-888-6195)

and Comstock (go to www.comstock.com or call 800-225-2727/2722).

✔ Also, PhotoDisc (www.photodisc.com), Adobe Studios (www.adobestudios.com), and Digital Stock (www.digitalstock.com) are online. Be sure to check prices before you download. They can be expensive.

✔ You can take your own photo into your local Kinko's or some other copy shop or service bureau and scan the image to disk. Kinko's charges about $10 per image.

✔ A better (and cheaper) method for scanning images is to scan them to a Photo CD, which costs between $1 to $3 a shot, plus the price of the CD itself, which is usually in the neighborhood of $10. One CD can hold about 100 images. Check the Yellow Pages under Photo Finishing — Retail. Prices vary widely from vendor to vendor.

Chapter 2

Canvassing the On-Screen Canvas

* *

In This Chapter

▶ Launching Photoshop

▶ Taking some first, tentative looks at the Photoshop interface

▶ Dealing with mouse terminology

▶ Switching between Photoshop and the Finder

▶ Choosing commands

▶ Using dialog boxes and palettes

▶ Picking up tools from the toolbox

* *

*I*f you're brand new to Photoshop — or to computers in general — this is the chapter for you. It explains the basic stuff you need to know before you can begin using the program to distort the faces of all your family members.

Even if you're already familiar with the basic interface of Photoshop, give this chapter the once-over to get acquainted with new features in Version 5 and to make sure that we're speaking the same language. Here is where we calibrate brains, so to speak.

Giving Photoshop the Electronic Breath of Life

Before you can use Photoshop, you have to start up — or launch — the program. Here's how:

1. **Start your Mac.**

   After your computer comes alive, you find yourself at the Mac's central way station, known as the Finder. The Finder is where you can fumble around with the contents of your hard drive.

2. **Locate and activate the Adobe Photoshop 5.0 folder.**

   That famous Adobe eyeball icon is on the folder to let you know what lurks inside the folder. (If you can't find the folder, see the next section for some help.) Use the mouse to move the arrow-shaped cursor over the icon and press the mouse button. Then choose File⇨Open from the menu bar or press ⌘-O. A window labeled Adobe Photoshop should open, containing another eyeball icon and some other icons.

   If choosing File⇨Open requires too much effort, you can launch Photoshop using a couple of shortcuts. Either double-click — press the mouse button twice in rapid-fire succession — on the program icon or press ⌘-↓ (down arrow).

   In case you recently jumped ship from the Microsoft Windows platform — hey, welcome aboard! — you should know that the Enter key does not launch files on the Mac.

3. **Double-click on the eyeball icon in the Adobe Photoshop window.**

   This icon is the one that actually launches the program.

4. **Enter your name, company name, and serial number.**

   You need to take this step only the first time you start Photoshop. You can find the serial number for your copy of Photoshop on your product registration card.

5. **Hope it works.**

   If you see the Photoshop splash screen — a kind of billboard that provides garish graphics and some copyright information — you're in business. If your computer complains that it doesn't have enough memory to open Photoshop or you see some equally discouraging message, scream loudly and hope that the resident computer expert is in close proximity. You need help.

After your computer stops making little shicka-shicka noises and your screen settles down, you arrive at the Photoshop desktop, which is where all the action takes place in this amazing program. You can tell that Photoshop is launched and ready to go by the appearance of a toolbox and one or more palettes, as shown in Figure 2-1. The menu bar at the top of your screen changes to resemble the one in Figure 2-1 as well. (I cover the toolbox, palettes, and menu bar later in this chapter.)

Don't freak out and start running around the room in a frenzy if you're a little fuzzy on what I mean by *menu, dialog box,* and a few other terms. I cover all this stuff in fairly hefty detail, in short order, and in this very same chapter.

Toolbox   Menu bar   Cursor   Palette   Applications menu

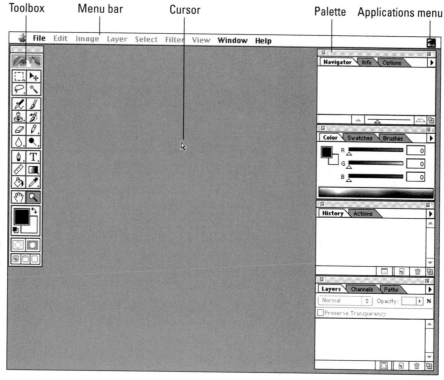

Figure 2-1:
The
Photoshop
desktop
makes its
first
appearance.

Note: As you read, you'll see that you can also use the keyboard and mouse in tandem. For example, in Photoshop, you can draw a perfectly horizontal line by pressing the Shift key while dragging with the line tool. Or you can press Option and click on the rectangular marquee tool in the upper-left corner of the toolbox to switch to the elliptical marquee tool. Such actions are so common that you often see key and mouse combinations joined into compound verbs, such as Shift-dragging, Option-clicking, or Shift-Option-crushing.

Tracking down a lost eyeball

Can't find the Photoshop eyeball icon to start the program? Here are a few suggestions:

✔ If you're not sure where Photoshop is located on your hard drive, choose File⇨Find from the menu bar (or press ⌘-F). Then type the word **Photoshop**, and whack the Return key. If you're using System 7.0 to 7.1.2, a folder opens displaying a file that has *Photoshop* in its name. Or a message appears saying that the file is on the desktop. If the file displayed isn't the program, choose File⇨Find Again, or press ⌘-G to search for the next occurrence of *Photoshop*.

✔ If you're using System 7.5 or higher, your Mac lists every file that contains the word Photoshop in the Items Found dialog box. Click on the Photoshop program in the top list to display the location of the file in the bottom list. Choose File⇨Open Enclosing Folder, or press ⌘-E to open the folder and access the program icon.

✔ If repeated pressing of ⌘-G or thorough searching of the Items Found dialog box doesn't turn up the Photoshop program, cry in anguish and beat your monitor with something soft and squishy.

Switching between Photoshop and the Finder

In back of the myriad desktop elements of Photoshop, you can probably see the icons and open windows from the Finder. (I hid these in Figure 2-1 just to make the picture less confusing.) If you click on a Finder element or on the desktop pattern, you're taken back to the Finder, and the Photoshop toolbox and palettes disappear. If you have an image open, however, the image window remains visible. Here are some tips to help you manage working between the Finder and Photoshop.

✔ If you inadvertently click yourself out of Photoshop, choose Photoshop from the list of running programs in the Applications menu, which is the icon on the far-right side of the menu bar (refer to Figure 2-1). Or just click on the Photoshop image window. The toolbox and palettes return to the screen to show you that Photoshop is back in the game.

✔ You may be wondering why in the heck this program-switching happens. No, it's not just to irritate you. The Finder is a piece of software, just like Photoshop. The only difference is that the Finder has to be running the entire time you use your Mac. This means that all the time you're using Photoshop, the Finder is working away in the background. When you click on the desktop or some other Finder element, the Finder comes to the foreground, and Photoshop goes to the background. But both programs continue to operate until you quit Photoshop or shut down your computer.

✔ When using Photoshop, if the clutter from the Finder gets too distracting, choose the Hide Others command from the Applications menu to hide every Finder element except the icons.

✔ If your Mac is equipped with System 7.5 or higher, you can hide the icons by choosing Apple⇨Control Panels⇨General Controls. (If you don't know how to choose things from menus, see the section, "Maneuvering through Menus," later in this chapter.) Inside the General Controls dialog box, click on the Show Desktop When in Background check box to deselect it. Then close the dialog box. Bye-bye go the icons. (Note that you can't click on the background to switch to the Finder if you choose this option; you have to use the Applications menu to switch between programs.)

✔ Remember that you can always tell where you are just by looking at the Applications menu icon in the upper-right corner of your screen. It always shows a miniature version of the foreground program icon. If you're at the Finder, the icon is a little computer — one of those single-piece computers like the Classic or the old Macintosh Plus. If the icon is some variation on an eyeball, you know you're in Photoshop. Other icons vary. A little W means Microsoft Word. A little X means Excel. A little Krusty the Clown means Bart Simpson has been using your computer (you lucky devil, you).

Maneuvering through Menus

As do all Macintosh programs, Photoshop sports a menu bar (refer to Figure 2-1) at the top of its desktop. Each word in the menu bar — File, Edit, Image, and so on — represents a menu, which is simply a list of commands that you can use to open and close images, manipulate selected portions of a photograph, hide and display palettes, and initiate all kinds of mind-boggling, sophisticated procedures.

Why does Photoshop give your computer Alzheimer's?

If your computer says that it's out of memory, it just means that a part of the machine is filled to capacity. Memory — known in computer dweeb circles as *RAM* (random-access memory, pronounced *ram*, like the goat) — allows your computer to run programs. Photoshop needs lots of RAM — it requires a minimum of 24MB and prefers to have even more.

If you can't launch Photoshop because of a memory error, you have three options:

✔ Free up RAM by quitting all other programs that are currently running.

✔ Restart your computer by choosing Special⇨Restart at the Finder and try to launch Photoshop after the Finder reappears.

✔ Buy and install more RAM.

If you've never tried to upgrade the RAM in your machine, seek out expert advice from your local computer guru.

I explain the most essential Photoshop commands throughout the course of this book. But before I send you off to cope with a single one of them, I feel compelled to provide some background information on how to work with menus:

- To choose a command from a menu, you press on the menu name and hold, drag down to the command name, and release the mouse button at the desired command. (After a few repetitions, it becomes reflexive — I promise.)

- Some commands bring up additional menus called *submenus*. For example, if you choose File⇨Preferences, you display a submenu offering still more commands. If I ask you to choose File⇨Preferences⇨General, you choose the Preferences command under the File menu to display the submenu and then choose the General command from the submenu, all in one, beautiful, continuous movement. When you do it just right, it's like something out of *Swan Lake*.

- In many cases, you can choose a command by using a keyboard equivalent instead of mousing around the menus. For example, to initiate the File⇨Open command, you can press ⌘-O — that is, press and hold the ⌘ key, press the O key, and then release both keys.

- Some keyboard equivalents select tools, and some perform other functions. Either way, I keep you apprised of them throughout this book. If you take the time to memorize a few keyboard shortcuts here and there, you can save yourself a heck of a lot of time and effort. (For the most essential shortcuts, read Chapter 19. Also, tear out the Cheat Sheet at the front of this book, and tape it up somewhere within easy ogling distance.)

- Version 5 offers you yet another way to access some commands. If you press the Control key and hold down the mouse button inside an image window, you display a *context-sensitive menu*. In nongeek-speak, a context-sensitive menu is a mini-menu that contains commands that are related to the current tool, palette, or image, as shown in Figure 2-2.

Talking Back to Dialog Boxes

Photoshop reacts immediately to some menu commands. But for other commands, the program requires you to fill out a few forms before it processes your request. If you see an ellipsis (three dots, like so . . .) next to a command name, that's your clue that you're about to see such a form, known in computer clubs everywhere as a *dialog box*.

Context-sensitive menu

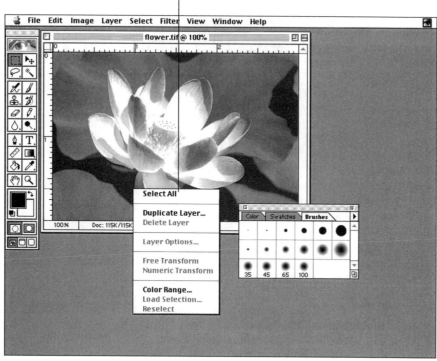

Figure 2-2:
To access
context-
sensitive
menus,
press
Control and
hold down
the mouse
button.

Figure 2-3 shows a sample dialog box. As the figure demonstrates, a dialog box can contain any or all of six basic kinds of options. The options work as follows:

✔ A box in which you can enter numbers or text is called an *option box.* Double-click in an option box to highlight its contents and replace the contents by entering new stuff from the keyboard.

✔ Some option boxes come with *slider bars.* Drag the triangular slider to the left or right to lower or raise the associated numerical value. (All without hydraulics, mind you.)

✔ You can select only one circular *radio button* from any gang of radio buttons. To select a radio button, click on the button or on the option name that follows it. The selected radio button is filled with a black dot; all deselected radio buttons are hollow.

✔ Although you can select only one radio button at a time, you can usually select as many *check boxes* as you want. Really, go nuts. To select a check box, click on the box or on the option name that follows it. An X fills the box to show that it's selected. Clicking on a selected check box turns off the option.

Slider bar   Pop-up menu   Option box   Button

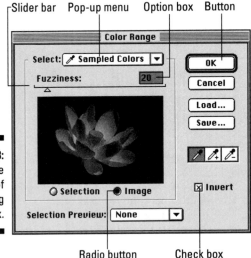

Radio button   Check box

✔ To conserve space, some multiple-choice options appear as *pop-up menus*. Press and hold the ↑ and ↓ (up and down arrows) to display a menu of option choices. Drag to the desired option in the menu to choose it, just as if you were choosing a command from a standard menu. As with radio buttons, you can select only one option at a time from a pop-up menu.

✔ Not to be confused with the radio button, the normal, everyday variety of *button* allows you to close the current dialog box or display others. For example, click on the Cancel button to close the dialog box and cancel the command. Click on OK to close the dialog box and execute the command according to the current settings. Clicking on a button with an ellipsis (such as Load . . . and Save . . .) displays yet another dialog box.

As you can with menus, you can select options and perform other feats of magic inside dialog boxes from the keyboard. The following shortcuts work in most dialog boxes:

✔ To advance from one option box to the next, press the Tab key. To back up, press Shift-Tab.

✔ Press Return to select the button surrounded by a heavy outline (such as OK in Figure 2-3). Press ⌘-. (period) or Esc to select the Cancel button.

✔ Press ↑ to raise an option box value by one; press ↓ to decrease the value by one. Pressing Shift-↑ and Shift-↓ raise and lower the value by ten, respectively.

✔ If you change your mind about choices you make in a dialog box, you can quickly return things to the settings that were in force when you opened the dialog box. In most dialog boxes, pressing the Option key magically changes the Cancel button to a Reset button. Click on the Reset button to bring back the original values.

If a dialog box gets in the way of your view of an image, you can reposition the box by dragging its title bar.

Playing Around with Palettes

Photoshop 5 offers free-floating *palettes* that you can hide or leave on-screen at whim. The palettes, which are basically dialog boxes that can remain on-screen while you work, provide access to options that affect the performance of tools, change the appearance of images, and otherwise assist you in your editing adventures. I cover the specifics of using the options in the most popular palettes in chapters to come, but here's a brief introductory tour of how palettes work:

✔ As illustrated by the palette shown in Figure 2-4, palettes may contain the same kinds of options as dialog boxes — pop-up menus, option boxes, and so on. For information on using these options, see the preceding section.

✔ Each of the palettes is actually a collection of palettes sharing the same palette window. For example, the Layers, Channels, and Paths palettes are all housed in the same palette window (see Figure 2-4). To switch to a different palette in a palette window, click on its tab.

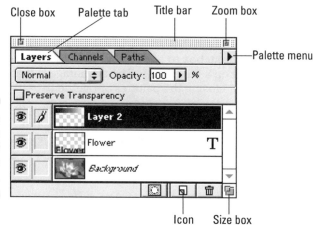

Figure 2-4: The many elements of a healthy palette.

✔ Click on the Close box on the left side of the title bar to — guess what — close the palette. (To make the palette come back, choose the desired palette from the Window menu.)

✔ Press Tab to hide or display the currently open palettes and the toolbox (covered in Chapter 3). Press Shift-Tab if you want to hide or display all the palettes but leave the toolbox as is. Note that this trick doesn't work if an option box inside a palette is active — that is, if the option box is highlighted or if the cursor is blinking inside it. In this case, pressing Tab and Shift-Tab moves you from option to option throughout all open palettes. To deactivate the option box, just click outside it or press Return to make the option box value take effect. You can then use the Tab/Shift-Tab shortcuts to hide and display palettes.

✔ To hide and display individual palettes, press their keyboard shortcuts: F5 for the Brushes palette, F6 for the Color palette, F7 for the Layers palette, F8 for the Info palette, and Return for the Options palette.

✔ Some palettes contain icons, just like the toolbox does. Click on an icon to perform a function, such as changing the brush size or deleting a selected image.

✔ Drag the title bar at the top of the palette to move the palette around on-screen.

✔ Shift-click on a title bar to snap the palette to the nearest edge of the screen. For example, if the palette is near the right side of the screen, Shift-clicking on its title bar moves it all the way over to the right, giving you more space to view your image on-screen.

✔ Click on the zoom box on the right side of the title bar to collapse the palette so that only the most essential options at the top of the palette are visible. Click on the zoom box again to bring all of the options into full view.

✔ Some palettes have a size box, as labeled in Figure 2-4. Drag the size box to resize the palette. Click on the zoom box to return to the default palette size.

✔ Option-click on the zoom box to hide all but the title bar and the palette tabs. Or double-click on a palette tab. The advantage is that you free up screen space without closing the palettes altogether.

✔ You can break any palette into its own window by dragging the palette tab out of the current window, as shown in Figure 2-5. You can also combine palettes into a single palette window by dragging a tab from one palette into another.

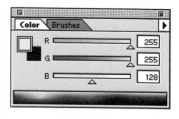

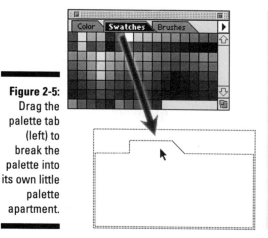

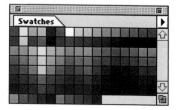

Figure 2-5:
Drag the
palette tab
(left) to
break the
palette into
its own little
palette
apartment.

🎯 *TIP*

✔ Want to know my favorite application of this technique? Drag the Swatches palette out of the Color/Swatches/Brushes palette window to create a separate Swatches palette. Then close the Swatches palette altogether. See, the Swatches palette isn't very useful, so you may as well get it off the screen. Now you can drag the Options palette into the same palette window as the Color and Brushes palette, enabling you to access all three of these very vital palettes quickly while using up a minimum of on-screen space.

✔ Press and hold on the right-pointing arrowhead on the right side of the palette, just below the title bar — phew, I need a breather! — to display the palette menu. Here's yet another place to find commands, just in case you manage to master all of the others. Yeah, right.

✊ *REMEMBER*

✔ As you can in a dialog box, you can raise or lower the value in a palette option box by pressing the arrow keys. Press the ↑ to raise the value by one; press the ↓ to lower the value by one; press Shift-↑ and Shift-↓ to raise or lower the value by ten, respectively.

Opening Up Your Toolbox

I think that you're ready to move on to the tempestuous world of the toolbox. As shown in Figure 2-6, the items in the toolbox fall into three basic categories — tools, color controls, and icons. Future chapters explain in detail how to use the various gizmos in the toolbox, but here's a basic overview of what's in store:

Tools   Color controls   Icons

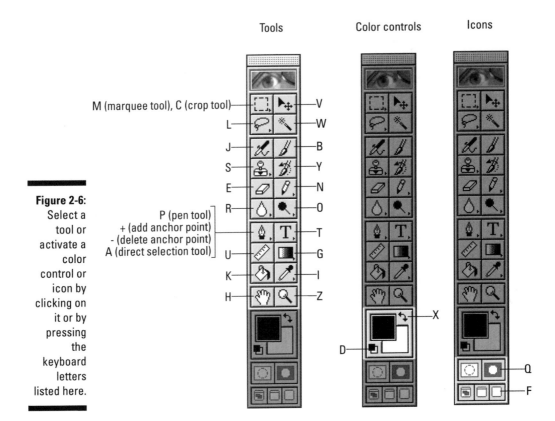

M (marquee tool), C (crop tool) — V
L — W
J — B
S — Y
E — N
R — O

P (pen tool)
+ (add anchor point)
- (delete anchor point) — T
A (direct selection tool) U — G

K — I
H — Z

— X

D —

— Q
— F

Figure 2-6:
Select a tool or activate a color control or icon by clicking on it or by pressing the keyboard letters listed here.

✔ Photoshop 5 adds a whopping 13 new tools with this version! All will be discussed in detail throughout the book.

✔ The top two-thirds or so of the toolbox (refer to Figure 2-1) is devoted to an assortment of tools that you can use to edit images, just as you might use an assortment of pencils and paintbrushes to paint a picture. To select one of these tools, click on its icon. Then use the tool by clicking on or dragging it inside your image.

✔ A tiny, right-pointing triangle in the bottom-right corner of a tool icon indicates that more tools are hidden behind that icon on a flyout menu. To display the flyout menu and reveal the hidden tools, press and hold the mouse button on the icon. Drag across the row of tools until your cursor is hovering over the tool you want to use and release the mouse button.

- ✔ You can also Option-click on a tool icon to cycle through all the tools hidden beneath it, except for the marquee/crop tool and the pen tool.

- ✔ The bottom third of the toolbox contains color selection options and other icons. These icons respond immediately when you click on them.

- ✔ If you've been clicking away on the toolbox icons and haven't seen any results, don't panic. Your copy of Photoshop isn't broken; the icons just don't do anything unless you have an image open. To find out how to open images, see Chapter 3.

- ✔ Actually, one of the icons in the toolbox does do something with no image on-screen. If you click on the very top icon in the toolbox — the one with the ghostly looking eyeball — you will bring up the new Adobe Online dialog window. If you have access to the Internet, clicking on the Refresh button will connect your modem, and files will be downloaded from the Adobe servers. After the download, the Adobe Studio's splash screen will appear. Clicking on a button under the graphic will launch your Web browser and take you to the Adobe Web site, where tons of great info can be found, such as tips and techniques, tech support, and news on products and events.

- ✔ You can also access all the tools and icons and two of the color controls from the keyboard. For example, to select the blur tool, you just press the R key. To select the sharpen tool, which shares the flyout menu with the blur tool, you press Shift-R. Other keyboard equivalents are shown in Figure 2-6.

- ✔ A couple of exceptions to the previous tip: Choosing tools from the flyout menu in the upper-left corner of the toolbox, which contains marquee tools and the crop tool, actually involves two shortcut keys. Press Shift-M to switch between the rectangular and elliptical marquee tools, but press C to select the crop tool. The single column and single row marquees have no shortcut keys and can only be accessed by using the mouse. The pen tool, as well, involves multiple shortcut keys. Press Shift-P to cycle through the pen, magnetic pen, and freeform pen; but press + (plus) for the add anchor point tool, press – (minus) for the delete anchor point tool, and press A for the direct selection tool. The remaining tool — convert point — does not have a keyboard equivalent.

- ✔ If you can't remember the name of a particular tool, pause your cursor over its icon for a second or two. A little label appears telling you the name of the tool and its keyboard equivalent. If this gets annoying, the feature can be turned off in the General panel in the Preferences dialog box under the File menu.

Chapter 3

Now the Fun Really Begins

*W*hen you first start Photoshop, you're presented with a plethora of tools, menus, and palettes, as illustrated in Chapter 2. Until you open up an image, those contraptions are intriguing, yet ultimately worthless — it's like having an easel, a full set of brushes, and a whole paintbox full of paints, but no canvas. And with Photoshop, you can't even amuse yourself by creating a political mural on your neighbor's garage door, as you can with traditional paint. No, if you want to become a digital Picasso (or Rembrandt, or Monet, or whatever artistic legend you choose), you need to open an image.

This chapter explains how to open existing images and also how to create a new, blank canvas for an image you want to paint from scratch. Then the chapter explains the myriad ways you can display your image on-screen in order to view your masterpiece from just the right perspective.

Don't Just Sit There, Open Something

If you're a longtime computer buff, you might expect opening an image to be a relatively straightforward process. You just choose File⇨Open or press ⌘-O and select the image file you want to display, right?

Well, opening files in Photoshop involves a little complication: The steps for opening a Photo CD image are different than the steps for opening images saved in other file formats. The following sections give you the lowdown on opening both types of images.

The term *Photo CD image* can be a bit confusing; it refers to images saved in the Kodak Photo CD file format, not simply to images that come from a CD. A Photo CD image has the letters PCD tagged onto the end of its filename.

Opening a non-Photo CD image

To open an image that's stored in any format except the Kodak Photo CD format, walk this way:

1. Choose File⇨Open.

If choosing the commands from the menu is too much work — and it is — just press ⌘-O. The Open dialog box rears its useful head, as shown in Figure 3-1.

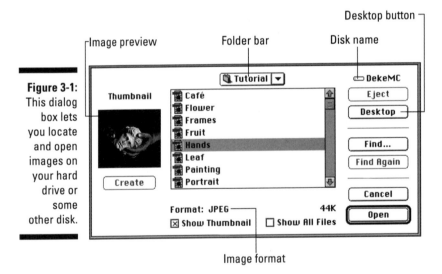

Figure 3-1: This dialog box lets you locate and open images on your hard drive or some other disk.

Desktop button

Image preview   Folder bar   Disk name

Thumbnail

Image format

2. Go to the Desktop level.

Click on the Desktop button or press ⌘-D to see everything that you can see at the Finder. The scrolling list in the center of the dialog box shows you all the folders and images that are strewn loose on the desktop. At the top of the list are the names of the hard drives, floppy disks, and other disks currently available to you.

3. **Select the disk that contains your image.**

   Assuming that your image isn't lying about on the desktop, select the disk name that contains the image you want to open. (It's also possible that the image is inside a folder on the desktop, in which case you should stay at the desktop level.)

4. **Open the desired folder in the central list.**

   Double-click on a folder name to open the folder. The list then displays all folders and images inside that folder. Double-click on another folder if you need to open it, and so on.

5. **Click on the image you want to open.**

   After you locate your image, click on its name in the list to select it. A preview of the image appears on the left side of the dialog box so that you can see what it looks like. (If no preview appears, make sure that the Show Thumbnail check box is selected.)

6. **Click on the Open button.**

   Or press the Return key or press ⌘-O. Alternatively, you can simply double-click on the image to open it.

That's all there is to it. Your image is now open and ready to abuse. But before you have at it in earnest, here are a few additional notes on opening images:

✔ To close a particular folder and view the contents of the folder that contains that particular folder, click on the disk name in the upper-right corner of the Open dialog box (disk name is DekeMC in Figure 3-1).

✔ You can also press ⌘-up arrow to advance up a folder. Or you can drag on the folder bar to display a pop-up menu of folders that contains the current folder. For example, if the items in the pop-up menu read Elephant, Digestive Systems, Food-Processing Enzymes, then the Food-Processing Enzymes folder resides inside the Digestive Systems folder, which is on the Elephant disk.

✔ In addition to double-clicking on a folder to open it, you can press ⌘-down arrow.

✔ Use the preview to help identify images. For example, if you or someone you work with name an image TRX33.Feb24-William (or something equally meaningless), you can click on it and view a small version of the image that may or may not be identifiable. But, hey, it's better than nothing.

✔ If you can't find a file in a certain folder, it may be because Photoshop doesn't think it can open the file. To see all files in a folder, whether Photoshop can open them or not, select the Show All Files check box. If the file appears, go ahead and try to open it. It may not work, but it's worth a try.

✔ If you can't find an image, you can use the Find button to hunt it down. Click on the Find button (or press ⌘-F) to display another dialog box that contains a single option box. Enter the name of the image and press Return. You don't have to enter the complete filename — a partial name will do. For example, if you enter **super**, your computer finds any files that have super in them, including Super Bowl, supersonic, Superman, and others.

✔ If the first search doesn't find the file, click on the Find Again button or press ⌘-G to keep looking.

Opening a Kodak Photo CD image

As mentioned earlier, opening a Kodak Photo CD image involves a different process than opening other types of images. Here's the scoop:

1. **Choose File⇨Open or press ⌘-O.**

   Be sure to choose this command from inside Photoshop.

2. **Locate the Photo CD disc.**

   This task will probably involve a press or two of the ⌘-right arrow. The disk will have some meaningless machine-assigned name like PCD0196.

3. **Open the Photo_CD folder.**

   Inside, you find several weirdly named files.

4. **Open the Images folder.**

   Here's where the real images live. They all have dumb names like IMG0001.PCD;1, and so on. Luckily, every Photo CD disk comes with two or three sheets of tiny thumbnail printouts so that you know which image is associated with each file number.

5. **Double-click on the image you want to open.**

   After what may seem like an interminable amount of time — don't give up and think that your computer has crashed — the dialog box shown in Figure 3-2 appears.

6. **Click on the Source button.**

   Here's the tricky part. The Photo CD interpreter built into Photoshop wants more than anything to make sure that the colors in the image are correctly converted from the disk to your screen. Therefore, you have to tell Photoshop a source and destination for the image. It's kind of weird, but just do as I tell you, and you can't go wrong.

Figure 3-2:
This dialog
box rears
its pesky
head when
you try to
open a
Photo CD
file from the
Images
folder.

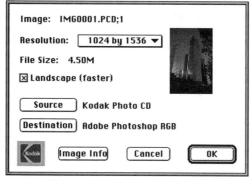

Image: IMG0001.PCD;1

Resolution: [1024 by 1536 ▼]

File Size: 4.50M

☒ Landscape (faster)

[Source]   Kodak Photo CD

[Destination]   Adobe Photoshop RGB

[Kodak]   [Image Info]   [Cancel]   [OK]

7. Select the proper film type.

If the image you want to open was scanned from a 35mm slide, select
the Universal Ektachrome or Universal Kodachrome option, depending
on the film used to shoot the photo. If the image came from a film
negative, select the Color Negative option. (If you're opening an image
from a commercial CD, such as one from Digital Stock, you can assume
that the Source option should be set to Universal Ektachrome.)

Press Return to go back to the dialog box shown in Figure 3-2.

8. Click on the Destination button.

It's right there below Source.

9. Select Adobe Photoshop RGB from the pop-up menu.

This choice converts the scan to a standard color Photoshop image.
Press Return when you finish.

10. Select an option from the Resolution pop-up menu.

The option you select depends on the amount of memory available to
your computer. I suggest starting with 1024 x 1536. If that gives your
computer fits, try selecting the 512 x 768 option, which creates an
image that's roughly big enough to fill a 17-inch monitor. The smallest
option, 128 x 192, results in an image that's too tiny for even an ant
to edit.

11. Press Return or click on OK.

Photoshop opens the Photo CD image. If you get an out-of-memory
error, try opening the image again and selecting a smaller resolution
option, as described in the preceding step.

Version 5 supports a new format called FlashPix. You can open and save in this format. The FlashPix format saves an image in multiple resolutions starting at full, then $^1/_2$, then $^1/_4$, until it reaches a height and width of 100 pixels or less, creating a kind of pyramid structure. This structure is *supposed* to be allow you to quickly edit large, high resolution files by doing the editing on the small, low resolution screen version. (The edits are recorded and applied to the large file when you save.) Photoshop 5, however, doesn't yet take advantage of this process. This will, no doubt, change in time.

If an image opens up lying on its side, you can shift it to an upright position by rotating it. Choose Image⇨Rotate Canvas⇨90° CW (clockwise) if the image is resting on its left side; choose Image⇨Rotate Canvas⇨90° CCW (counter-clockwise) if the image is taking a nap on its right side. (The latter is more common.) If the image turns upside down, choose Edit⇨Undo and then choose the command that you didn't choose the first time.

After you open an image for the first time, the Source and Destination options remain set. This means that you can skip Steps 6 through 9 when opening future Photo CD images.

Note: To create a new image instead of opening an existing one, choose File⇨New or press ⌘-N. Photoshop displays the New dialog box. There, you can name your file; specify the width, height, and resolution (as discussed in Chapter 4); and set the color mode (as discussed in Chapter 5). However, you'll probably have little reason to create a new image unless you just want to play around with the painting tools. Photoshop is, after all, made primarily for editing existing images.

Behold the Image Window

After you open up an image, Photoshop displays the image on-screen inside a new image window. Several new elements appear when you open an image, as labeled in Figure 3-3.

Windows are a staple of the Macintosh working environment. In fact, every element labeled in the figure except the page preview box, magnification box, and collapse box (and the odd-looking creature with the goggles, of course) is found in all windows across the board. Here's your chance to check out everything about windows — that's windows with a small *w* — in one convenient bulleted list:

The following list explains all:

> ✔ The title bar lists the title of your image, hence the name. The added bonus of the title bar is that you can drag it to move the window to a different location on-screen. Easy stuff.

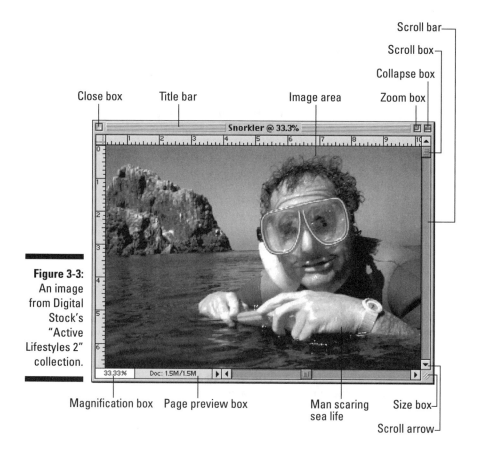

Figure 3-3:
An image
from Digital
Stock's
"Active
Lifestyles 2"
collection.

Close box   Title bar   Image area   Zoom box

Scroll bar
Scroll box
Collapse box

Magnification box   Page preview box   Man scaring   Size box
                                            sea life
                                                        Scroll arrow

✔ Click on the close box to close the image window. Alternatively, you can choose File⇨Close or press ⌘-W to close an image. You know, W as in *hasta la vista, window.* (If you've made some changes to the image, Photoshop asks you whether you want to save the new and improved image, a process explained in great detail in Chapter 6.)

✔ To change the size of the image window, place your cursor over the size box in the lower-right corner of the window and drag. The image remains the same; you're just changing the size of the window that holds the image. Give it a try and see what I mean.

✔ Click on the zoom box to collapse or expand the window to match the exact size of the image. If the image is too big for the screen, the window expands to include as much of the image as possible.

✔ In the lower-left corner of the window is the magnification box, which lets you zoom in and out on your image, as explained later in this chapter.

✔ Next to the magnification box is the page preview box, which shows how much memory your image is consuming, measured in digital chunks called *bytes*. The first number is the size of the image as the image will be sent to the printer; the second number reflects the size of the image with layer information included. I discuss file size and resolution and all those other thorny issues in Chapter 4 and explain layers in Chapter 15. For the time being, don't worry about the preview box too much. I just didn't want to leave you wondering, "What in the Sam Hill is this thingie here?"

✔ If you click and hold the mouse button down on the page preview box, Photoshop displays a window that shows you where the image will appear on the page when you print the image. The big X indicates the image in the preview.

✔ Hold down Option as you click on the page preview box, and Photoshop displays a box showing the height, width, resolution, and number of channels in the image. (Channels are discussed in Chapter 5.)

✔ The scroll bars let you navigate around and display hidden portions of the image inside the window. Photoshop offers two scroll bars, one vertical bar along the right side of the image and one horizontal bar along the bottom.

✔ If you click on a scroll arrow, you nudge your view of the image slightly in that direction. For example, if you click on the right-pointing scroll arrow, an item that was hidden on the right side of the photograph slides into view. Click in the gray area of a scroll bar to scroll the window more dramatically. Drag a scroll box to manually specify the distance scrolled.

✔ Using the scroll arrows isn't the only way to move around your image; in fact, it's probably the least efficient method. For some better options, check out the techniques presented in the section, "The Screen Is Your Digital Oyster," coming up next.

✔ The area inside the title bar and scroll bars is the image area. The image area is where you paint and edit and select details and, otherwise, have at your image. Obviously, you look at the image area a lot throughout the many pages of this book.

You can open as many images on-screen as your computer's memory and screen size allow. But only one image is active at a time. To make a different window active, just click on it or choose its name from the bottom of the Window menu.

The Screen Is Your Digital Oyster

The Photoshop toolbox includes two navigation tools: the hand tool, which lets you scroll the image inside the window with much more ease than the silly scroll bars afford, and the zoom tool, which lets you move closer to or farther away from your image. The hand tool and the zoom tool are called navigation tools because they don't change the image; they merely move your view of the image so that you can get a better look-see.

In addition to these tools, there is another navigation aid, appropriately called the Navigator palette. The palette gives you a super-convenient way to zoom and scroll your image; in fact, after you are familiar with the palette, you may not use the hand and zoom tools at all. But in the interest of fair play, I present all of your various options for moving around in your image in the upcoming sections.

Using the hand tool

If you're familiar with other Macintosh programs, you need to know something about Photoshop: The scroll bars are useless. Keep away from them. I want you to promise me you'll always use the hand tool or the new Navigator palette (explained shortly) instead. Promise? Good. As for you new users, I don't worry about you because I'm going to show you the right way.

Consider the following example: Figure 3-4 shows another Digital Stock image — this time from the "Children and Teens" collection. The top view in the figure shows a young lad in obvious distress. The problem is that the picture is wider than my screen, so I can't see what's causing him such grief.

To view the rest of the scene, I select the hand tool by clicking on its icon in the toolbox. Then I position my Photoshop hand over the hand in the picture, as shown in the top example in Figure 3-4, and drag to the left. The image moves with the hand cursor, as shown in the bottom example, and reveals the source of the boy's torment.

Dragging with the hand tool is like turning your head to view a new part of your surroundings. You can drag at any angle you please — up, down, sideways, or diagonally.

You can also select the hand tool by pressing the H key. To temporarily access the hand tool when another tool is selected, press the spacebar. As long as the spacebar is down, the hand tool is available. Releasing the spacebar returns you to the selected tool.

Using keyboard shortcuts

As in most other programs, you can also use keyboard shortcuts to move about your image. Press Page Up or Page Down to scroll up or down an entire screen. Press Shift-Page Up or Shift-Page Down to scroll in smaller increments. Press Home to go to the upper-left corner of the image, and press End to move to the lower-right corner.

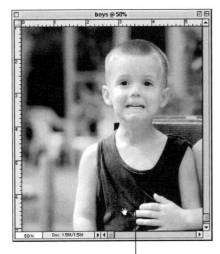

Hand cursor

Figure 3-4:
Dragging
with the
hand tool
reveals that
a bad
haircut isn't
the only
thing a kid
has to
worry
about.

Version 5 offers new keyboard shortcuts for moving right and left. Press ⌘-Page Up or Page Down to scroll left or right an entire screen. Press ⌘-Shift-Page Up or Page Down to scroll left and right in smaller increments.

Zooming in and out on your work

When you first open an image, Photoshop displays the entire image so that it fits on-screen. But you may not be seeing the details in the image as clearly as you want. The first view is sort of like being far away from the image. If you want to inspect it in more detail, you have to step closer.

Photoshop gives you several ways to zoom in and out on your work, as described in these next few sections.

Zooming doesn't change the size at which your image prints. It just affects the size at which you see the image on-screen. Zooming is like looking at some eentsey-teentsey life-form under a microscope. The creature doesn't actually grow and shrink as you vary the degree of magnification, and neither does your image.

The zoom tool

Using the zoom tool is one avenue for changing your view of an image. Every time you click on your image with the tool, you magnify the image to a larger size. Here's an example of how it works:

1. **Select the zoom tool.**

   Click on the zoom tool in the toolbox. It's the one that looks like a magnifying glass. You can also press the Z key to grab the zoom tool.

2. **Click in the image area.**

   Photoshop magnifies the image to the next preset zoom size (the increments are set by Photoshop), as demonstrated in the second example of Figure 3-5. The program centers the magnified view about the point at which you click. In Figure 3-5, for example, I clicked between the girl's eyes.

3. **Repeat.**

   To zoom in still more, click again with the zoom tool, as demonstrated in the bottom example of Figure 3-5.

A setting in the Zoom Tool Options palette determines whether Photoshop resizes your image window to match the image when you zoom with the zoom tool. To display the palette, select the zoom tool and press Return. If you want your image windows to be resized when you zoom, select the Resize Windows to Fit option. The only hitch comes when the window bumps into a palette — when the window hits a palette that's anchored to the side of the screen (as opposed to floating in the middle of the screen), Photoshop thinks that it's hit some sort of wall and stops zooming. To get around the problem, press Tab to hide all the palettes and the toolbox and then zoom. Press Tab again to bring back the palettes and the toolbox.

Figure 3-5: Clicking with the zoom tool magnifies your image in preset increments.

Here's some other zoom-tool stuff to tuck away for future reference:

✔ Option-click with the zoom tool to zoom out on your image.

✔ You can also zoom in and out from the keyboard: Press ⌘-+ (the ⌘ key followed by the plus key) to zoom in; press ⌘-– (⌘ followed by the minus key) to zoom out. Note that Photoshop zooms your window in and out to match the image size when you use this shortcut, regardless of the setting in the Zoom Tool Options palette. If you don't want the window itself to resize, press ⌘-Option-+or ⌘-Option-– to do your zooming from the keyboard.

✔ As you zoom, Photoshop displays the *zoom factor* in the title bar. A zoom factor of 100% shows you one screen pixel for every pixel in your image. (Pixels are explained thoroughly in Chapter 4.)

Keep in mind that a 100% zoom ratio doesn't necessarily correspond to the printed size of your image, contrary to what you might expect. If you want to view your image at its printed size, use the Print Size command (explained in the next section).

✔ To magnify just one section of an image, drag with the zoom tool to surround the area with a dotted outline. Photoshop fills the image window with the area that you surrounded.

✔ To temporarily access the zoom tool while another tool is selected, press ⌘-spacebar. Press ⌘-Option-spacebar to get the zoom out cursor. In either case, releasing the keys returns you to the previously selected tool.

The View commands

The View menu offers some more ways to change the magnification of your image. The first two zoom commands on the menu, Zoom In and Zoom Out, aren't of much interest; they do the same thing as clicking and Option-clicking with the zoom tool, except that you can't specify the center of the new view as you can with the zoom tool. But you may find the other View commands helpful at times:

✔ Choose View⇨Actual Pixels or press ⌘-Option-0 (zero) to return to the 100% zoom ratio. This view size shows you one pixel on your monitor for every pixel in the image, which is the most accurate way to view your image.

✔ Choose View⇨Fit on Screen or press ⌘-0 (zero) to display your image at the largest size that allows the entire image to fit on-screen.

✔ You can also choose the Actual Pixels view by double-clicking on the zoom tool icon in the toolbox. Double-click on the hand tool icon to change to the Fit on Screen view.

✔ Choose View⇨Print Size to display your image on-screen at the same size that it will print. Note that Photoshop provides only an approximation of the print size; your actual printed piece may be slightly smaller or larger.

✔ You can choose View⇨to New View to create a second view of your image. Don't confuse this with duplicating an image, which creates a new file. New View simply creates a second way of looking at the same file. This can be useful when you are editing an image in a magnified view, yet want to see the overall results on your entire image without having to continuously zoom in and out.

The magnification box

The zoom tool and View commands are great when you want to zoom in or out to one of the preset Photoshop zoom ratios. But what if you want more control over your zooming? The answer awaits in the magnification box in the lower-left corner of the image window (labeled earlier in Figure 3-3).

To enter a zoom ratio, just double-click on the magnification box and type the zoom ratio you want to use. If you know exactly what zoom ratio you want, press Return to make Photoshop do your bidding. But if you want to play around with different zoom ratios, press Shift-Return instead. That way, Photoshop zooms your image, but keeps the magnification box active so that you can quickly enter a new ratio if the first one doesn't work out. When you're satisfied, press Return.

When you use the magnification box, the image window size doesn't change as you zoom, regardless of whether the Resize Windows to Fit option is selected in the Zoom Tool Options palette.

Navigating by palette

The Navigator palette, shown in Figure 3-6, is the best navigational aid because it actually combines the functions of the zoom and hand tools in one location. To display the palette, choose Window➪Show Navigator. Or press F8 to display the Info palette and click on the Navigator palette tab. To make the palette smaller or larger, drag on the size box in the palette's lower-right corner.

View box

Figure 3-6:
The
Navigator
palette
provides a
nifty way to
zoom and
scroll your
image.

Zoom out⏘   Zoom in⏘

Magnification box   Zoom slider   Size box

The palette provides a handy, all-in-one tool for scrolling and zooming. It's especially useful when you're working on a large image that doesn't fit entirely on-screen when you're zoomed in for detail work. Here are the how-tos for using the palette:

✔ In the center of the palette, you see a thumbnail view of your image, as in Figure 3-6. The palette shows your entire image, even if it's not all visible in the main image window.

✔ See the box that surrounds a portion of the thumbnail? That's called the view box. The area within the box corresponds to the portion of your image that's visible in the main image window. As you drag the box, Photoshop scrolls your image in the main image window to display the area that's surrounded by the box. You can also click on an area in the thumbnail to move the view box over that portion of the image.

✔ Press and hold ⌘, and the cursor in the palette changes to a zoom cursor. If you drag with the cursor while pressing ⌘, you resize the view box, which, in turn, zooms the image in the image window.

✔ The palette also contains a magnification box, as labeled in Figure 3-6. The box works just like the one in the image window; just enter a zoom factor, and press Return.

✔ To zoom in or out in the preset Photoshop increments (as with the zoom tool), click on the Zoom in or Zoom out buttons, labeled in Figure 3-6.

✔ You can also zoom by dragging the Zoom slider — drag left to zoom out, and drag right to zoom in.

If you don't like the color of the view box, you can change it. Click on the right-pointing arrow in the upper-right corner of the palette, and choose the Palette Options command. Then choose a new color from the Color pop-up menu.

Filling up the screen with your image

The three icons at the bottom of the toolbox let you change the way the window fills the screen. These icons appear labeled in Figure 3-7.

✔ Click on the far-left icon to view the window normally, with scroll bars and title bar and all that stuff. This is the default setting.

✔ Click on the center icon to eliminate the scroll bars and title bar and fill the screen with your image. Any portions of the screen that aren't consumed by the image appear gray. The toolbox, palettes, status bar, and menu bar remain visible.

✔ If you want to take over still more screen real estate, click on the far-right icon to hide the menu bar. Now any portions of the screen that don't contain the image are black. The only desktop elements that remain available are the palettes, toolbox, and status bar.

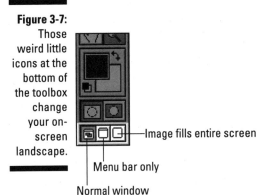

Figure 3-7:
Those weird little icons at the bottom of the toolbox change your on-screen landscape.

Image fills entire screen

Menu bar only

Normal window

You can cycle through the different screen modes by pressing the F key instead of clicking on the toolbox icons, if you prefer. Press F once to select the second icon, press F again to select the third icon, and press F a third time to return to the first icon.

Tools for the Terribly Precise

If you've used a page layout program such as PageMaker or QuarkXPress, you're no doubt familiar with the concept of *grids and guides.* Shown in Figure 3-8, grids and guides are on-screen devices that help you align elements in your image. For example, in the figure, I use a horizontal guide to position my text exactly 2 inches from the left edge of the image and 5.5 inches from the top of the image.

In addition to grids and guides, Photoshop offers rulers that run across the top and left sides of the image window. Grids, guides, and rulers come in handy when you're feeling the urge to be especially precise with your work.

Switching on the rulers

To display rulers, choose View⇨Show Rulers or press ⌘-R. To hide the rulers, choose View⇨Hide Rulers or press ⌘-R again.

By default, the rulers use inches as their unit of measurement. But if you want to use some other unit, say picas instead of inches, choose File⇨ Preferences⇨Units & Rulers. Or just double-click on a ruler. In the Rulers section of the dialog box that appears, select a new unit of measure from the Units pop-up menu.

Guide   Move guide cursor   Ruler   Grid line

Figure 3-8:
Our furry
friend isn't
really
fenced in;
he's just
covered
with grid
lines and
guides.

Using guides

Guides are horizontal and vertical lines that you create to help you align
elements in your image. Guides don't print; they're creatures of the on-
screen world only. You can create as many guides as you need.

Before you can create a guide, you have to display the rulers by choosing
View➪Show Rulers or pressing ⌘-R. Then drag from one of the rulers to
"pull out" a guide. Drag from any point on the horizontal ruler to create a
horizontal guide; drag from the vertical ruler to create a vertical guide.
Release the mouse button at the spot where you want to place the guide.

Here are some more guides to using guides:

> ✔ After you create a guide, you can reposition it. First, select the move
> tool (it's the upper-right tool in the toolbox) by clicking on its icon in
> the toolbox. Then place the cursor over the guide until you see the
> double-headed arrow, as in Figure 3-8, and drag the guide to its new
> home. Alternatively, you can ⌘-drag the guide with any other tool
> except the hand or pen tool. (The ⌘ key temporarily accesses the
> move tool when any tool but the hand or pen tool is selected.)

> ✔ To remove a guide, drag it out of the image window using the move tool
> or ⌘-drag with any other tool but the pen or hand tool. To get rid of all
> guides, choose View➪Clear Guides.

✔ To lock a guide in place, choose View➪Lock Guides or press ⌘-Option-;. To unlock the guides so that you can move them again, choose View➪Lock Guides or press ⌘-Option-; again.

✔ When you drag an image element near a guide, the element "snaps" into alignment with the guide — as if the guide had some sort of magnetic pull. If you don't want stuff to snap to guides, choose View➪Snap To Guides or press ⌘-Shift-;. Choose the command again to turn snapping back on. (A check mark next to the command name means that the feature is turned on.)

✔ To change the color of the guides, choose File➪Preferences➪Guides & Grid, double-click on a guide with the move tool or ⌘-double-click on the guide with any other tool but the hand or pen tool. In the Guides section of the dialog box that appears, you can choose a color and line style for your guides. Press Return to exit the dialog box and make your changes official.

Turning on the grid

Unlike guides, which you can position willy-nilly in the image window, the grid positions lines across your image in preset intervals. You can't move grid lines, but you can change the spacing and color of the lines.

To turn on the grid, choose View➪Show Grid or press ⌘-"(quote). To change the spacing and appearance of the grid lines, choose File➪Preferences➪ Guides & Grid. Photoshop presents you with a dialog box in which you can choose a color and line style for the grid lines, specify how far apart you want to space the lines, and choose whether you want to subdivide the grid with secondary grid lines or not. You can also choose a unit of measurement for the grid.

Like guides, the lines of a grid have "snapping" capabilities — anything you drag near a grid line automatically snaps into alignment with that line. You turn snapping on and off by choosing View➪Snap to Grid or by pressing ⌘-Shift-". A check mark next to the command name in the menu means that snapping is turned on.

Photoshop gives yet another tool for the precision junkies. The new measure tool lets you measure height, width, distance, and angle within your image. All you have to do is drag from one point to another. The numbers are then displayed in your Info palette. The endpoints the measure tool creates can also be dragged to allow for new measurements.

Part II
The Care and Feeding of Pixels

The 5th Wave   **By Rich Tennant**

"I THINK YOU'VE MADE A MISTAKE. WE DO PHOTO RETOUCHING, NOT FAMILY PORTRAI...OOOH, WAIT A MINUTE-I THINK I GET IT!"

In this part . . .

I can't tell you how disappointed I was the first time I dissected a frog. Here we had been looking at all the cool pictures of the animal's colorful innards, and the moment we got the critter open, everything was various shades of pale beige. Where were the blue veins? And the red arteries? And the purple muscles and organs, and the bright yellow fat cells? Was my frog defective?

That's the problem with real life — it's never as interesting as the pictures. But an electronic image is different. It's not some natural miracle that tests the minds of our best scientists and absolutely baffles the brains of junior high school students; it's something designed by humans expressly to be understood by other humans. So, you can be sure that the dissection that takes place in Chapters 4 through 7 will look the same on your computer screen as it does in my figures, except more colorful.

The chapters in this part tell you how to manage the colored specks — called *pixels* — that make up the image, how color and black-and-white images work, and how to save and print the image when you're done editing. These chapters aren't obscure experiments; they're straightforward journeys through features that you use every time you open Photoshop. Even better, you don't have to put up with the nauseating smell of formaldehyde.

Oh, and one more thing: The publisher wants me to tell you that no frogs were killed or inconvenienced in the making of this book. One parrot was made to take notation, but that's it.

Chapter 4

Sizing Up Your Image

· ·

· ·

*I*mages that you create and edit in Photoshop — or in any other image editor, for that matter — are made up of tiny squares called *pixels*. Understanding how pixels work in an image can be enormously confusing to beginning image editors. Unfortunately, managing your pixel population correctly is essential to turning out professional-looking images, so you really do need to come to grips with how pixels work before you can be successful with Photoshop.

This chapter explains everything you need to know to put pixels in perspective, including how the number of pixels in an image affects its quality, printed size, and size on disk. I also show you how to reduce or enlarge the size of the on-screen canvas on which all your pretty pixels perch. In other words, this chapter offers pages of particularly provocative pixel paragraphs, partner.

Welcome to Pixeltown

Imagine, if you will, that you are the victim of a terrifying scientific experiment that has left you 1 millimeter tall. After recovering from the initial shock that such terrifying scientific experiments tend to produce on one's equilibrium, you discover that you are sitting on a square tile that's colored with a uniform shade of blue. Beyond your tile are eight other blue tiles, one to your right and one to your left, one in front and one behind, and four others in diagonal directions. In other words, the tiles are aligned in a perfect grid, just like standard floor tiles. You notice upon further inspection that each of the blue tiles differs slightly in shade and tone. As you slowly turn, it becomes evident that you're surrounded by these colored tiles for as far as your infinitesimally tiny, pin-prick eyes can see.

You cry out in anguish and fling your dust-specked body about in the way that folks always do when plagued by these terrifying scientific experiments. As though in answer to your pitiful squeals, you start to grow. In a matter of moments, you increase in size to almost 5 centimeters tall. A bug that was considering devouring you has a change of mind and runs away. You can now see that you sit in the midst of a huge auditorium and that all the tiles on its vast and unending floor are colored differently, gradually changing from shades of blue to shades of green, red, and yellow. You continue to grow: Ten centimeters, 20, 50, a full meter tall. The tiles start to blend together to form some kind of pattern. Two meters, 5, 10. You've now grown several times beyond your normal height, reaching 20 meters tall. Your massive head bursts through the flimsy ceiling of the room.

When you reach the height of a 50-story building, your growth spurt comes to an end. You look down at the ruined auditorium, whose walls have been shredded to rubble by the great edges of your tremendous feet, and you notice a peculiar thing. You stand not on a floor, but on a picture, as rich in color and detail as any you've seen. The tiles, which now appear dot-sized to you, have merged together to create a seamless blend. You had expected the result to have the rough appearance of a mosaic — requiring a heavy dose of imagination to compensate for occasionally choppy transitions — but, in fact, it looks exactly like a continuous photograph.

The vision inspires you to claw at your temples, fling your arms about in circles, and shriek, "What's happening to me?!" The answer, of course, is nothing. Well, okay, your body may be stretched out of shape, but your eyes are working fine. You see, when you get far enough away from a perfect grid of colored tiles — whether via a terrifying scientific experiment or more conventional means — the tiles disappear, and an overall image takes shape.

What does this little trip down sci-fi lane have to do with Photoshop? Well, a lot, actually. Like the image on the auditorium floor, your Photoshop image is made up of a grid of colored squares. In this case, the squares are called *pixels*.

By now, you're probably thinking, "Fine, images are made up of a bunch of itsy-bitsy square pixels. So what? Who cares? Quit wasting my time, darn you." The truth is, these tiniest of image particles are at the heart of what makes Photoshop and your electronic images tick.

Every single painting and image-editing function in Photoshop is devoted to changing either the quantity or the color of pixels. That's all Photoshop does. I know, it sounds so simple that you figure I must be joking, exaggerating, or just plain lying. But as Salvador Dali is my witness, it's the absolute truth. Photoshop is merely an extremely sophisticated pixel counter and colorer, nothing more.

Screen Pixels versus Image Pixels

Like the tiles in the preceding story, each pixel in a computer image is perfectly square, arranged on a perfect grid, and colored uniformly — that is, each pixel is one color and one color only. Put these pixels together, and your brain perceives them to be an everyday, average photograph.

The display on your computer's monitor is also made up of pixels. Like image pixels, screen pixels are square and arranged on a grid. A typical 13-inch monitor measures 640 screen pixels wide by 480 screen pixels tall. These screen pixels are kind of tiny, so you may not be able to make them out. Each one generally measures $1/72$ inch across.

To understand the relationship between screen and image pixels, open an image. After the image comes up on-screen, double-click on the zoom tool in the toolbox, or choose View⇨Actual Pixels. The title bar on the image window lists the zoom ratio as 100%, which means that you can see one pixel in your image for every pixel displayed by your monitor.

To view the image pixels more closely, enter a value of **200** percent in the magnification box in the lower-left corner of the image window (double-click on the box to activate it). A 200% zoom factor magnifies the image pixels to twice their previous size so that one image pixel measures two screen pixels tall and two screen pixels wide. If you change the zoom factor to 400%, Photoshop displays four screen pixels for every image pixel, giving you a total of 16 screen pixels for every image pixel (4 screen pixels tall by 4 screen pixels wide). Figure 4-1 illustrates how different zoom factors affect the appearance of your image pixels on-screen.

Remember that the zoom factor has nothing to do with the size at which your image will print — it only affects how your image looks on-screen. If you want to see your image on-screen at its approximate print size, choose View⇨Actual Pixels.

100%   200%

400%   800%

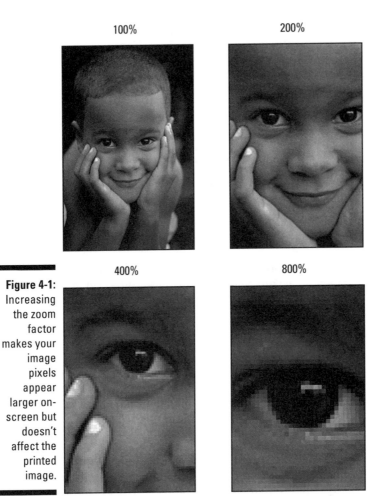

Figure 4-1: Increasing the zoom factor makes your image pixels appear larger on-screen but doesn't affect the printed image.

Image Size, Resolution, and Other Tricky Pixel Stuff

A Photoshop image has three primary attributes related to pixels: *file size, physical dimensions, and resolution,* as explained in the following list. You control these attributes through the Image Size dialog box, shown in Figure 4-2. To display the dialog box, choose Image➪Image Size.

Link icon

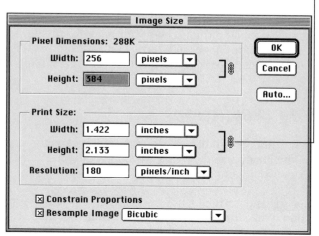

Figure 4-2:
You control
file size,
image
dimensions,
and
resolution
through the
Image Size
dialog box.

If you just want to get a quick look at the dimensions and resolution of an image, press Option as you press and hold the mouse button on the page preview box in the lower-left corner of the Photoshop window (next to the magnification box). Photoshop displays a little box listing the dimensions, resolution, and other scary stuff.

✔ The *file size* of the image is a measure of how many pixels the image contains. (Photoshop refers to file size as *pixel dimensions.*) The image in Figure 4-1 is 256 pixels wide and 384 pixels tall, for a total of 98,304 pixels. Most of the images you create will contain hundreds of thousands or even millions of pixels.

✔ The *resolution* of an image refers to the number of pixels that print per inch. For example, the resolution of the first image in Figure 4-1 is 180 pixels per inch (ppi). That may sound like an awful lot of pixels squished into a small space, but it's about average.

✔ Not to be confused with file size, the *dimensions* of an image are its physical width and height when printed, as measured in inches, centimeters, or your unit of choice. You can calculate the dimensions by dividing the number of pixels by the resolution. For example, the little boy in Figure 4-1 measures 256 pixels ÷ 180 pixels per inch = $1^3/8$ inches wide and 384 pixels ÷ 180 ppi = $2^1/8$ inches tall. Measure him with a ruler, and you see that this is indeed the case.

No problem, right? I mean, okay, this stuff is a little technical, but it's not like it requires an advanced degree in cold fusion to figure out what's going on. And yet, the Image Size dialog box may well be the most confusing Photoshop dialog box. You can even damage your image if you're not careful. So be extremely careful before you make changes in the Image Size dialog box. (The upcoming sections tell you everything you need to know to stay out of trouble.)

Depending on your printer, you may be able to simply reduce or enlarge your image for printing by simply entering a percentage value into the Reduce or Enlarge option box in the Page Setup dialog box. Choose File⇨Page Setup. Photoshop then scales your image to the new size during only the print cycle. Your image isn't permanently altered as it is when you use the Image Size dialog box. For more information, see Chapter 7.

Resolving resolution

Although the Resolution option box is positioned unceremoniously toward the bottom of the Image Size dialog box, it's one of the most critical values to consider if you want your images to look good.

The Resolution value determines how tightly the pixels are packed when printed. It's kind of like the population density of one of those ridiculously large urban areas cropping up all over the modern world. Take Lagos, Nigeria, for example, which is a city of nearly 10 million souls — more than London, Paris, or Shanghai. Lagos, in case you're curious, is the fastest-growing major metropolitan area in the world, with an annual population explosion of 5 percent. (If that doesn't sound so bad, consider that it would put Lagos at 33 million people in the year 2020, which would be more than Tokyo, the current topper.) The population density of Lagos is second only to Hong Kong, at roughly 150,000 people packed into each square mile (on average, that's 15 times as crowded as New York City).

In order to increase the population density, you have to either increase the number of people in a city or decrease the physical boundaries of the city and scrunch everyone closer together. The same goes for resolution. If you want a higher resolution (more pixels per inch), you can either decrease the physical dimensions of the image or increase the file size (pixel dimensions) by adding pixels to the image. For example, the two images in Figure 4-3 have the same file size, but the smaller image has twice the resolution of the larger image — 180 pixels per inch versus 90 ppi.

Conversely, population density goes down as people die off or as the boundaries of the city grow. For example, if we were to mandate that Lagos spread out evenly over the entire 360,000 square miles of Nigeria, the population density would temporarily drop to 28 people per square mile (assuming, of course, that the other 110 million Nigerian residents happened to be on vacation at the time). Likewise, when you increase the dimensions of an image or delete some of its pixels, the resolution goes down.

Before you get the mistaken idea that this analogy is completely airtight, I should in all fairness mention a few key differences between a typical image and Lagos:

Figure 4-3:
Two images
with the
exact same
number of
pixels but
subject to
two
different
resolutions.

- Although I've never been there, I imagine that Lagos has its crowded spots and its relatively sparse areas. An image, by contrast, is equally dense at all points. Unlike population density, therefore, resolution is constant across the board.

- An image is always rectangular. Having misplaced my aerial map of Lagos, I can't swear to its shape, but I imagine that it's rather free-form.

- Population density is measured in terms of area — you know, so many folks per square mile. Resolution, on the other hand, is measured in a line — pixels per linear inch. So an image with a resolution of 180 pixels per inch contains 32,400 pixels per square inch. (That's 180 squared, in case you're wondering where I got the number.)

- The pixels in an image are absolutely square. The people in Lagos are shaped rather arbitrarily, with undulating arms and legs jutting out at irregular and unpredictable angles.

- You have total control over the size and resolution of an image. Like it or not, Lagos is entirely out of your hands.

Changing pixel dimensions

The top two option boxes in the Image Size dialog box enable you to change your *image's pixel dimensions* — the number of pixels wide by the number of pixels tall. (The number of pixels in your image is also known as the *file size*.) Unless you want to risk ruining your image — or you really, really know what you're doing when it comes to pixels — avoid these option boxes like the plague.

Lowering the Pixel Dimensions values can be dangerous because what you're really doing is throwing away pixels, and when you delete pixels, you delete detail. Figure 4-4 shows what I mean. The physical size of all three images is the same, but the detail drops off from one image to the next. The first image contains 64,000 pixels and is printed at a resolution of 140 ppi; the second contains $1/4$ as many pixels and is printed at 70 ppi. The third contains only 4,000 pixels and has a resolution of 35 ppi. Notice how details such as the shadows from the girl's eyelashes and the distinction between individual hairs in her eyebrows become less pronounced and more generalized as the pixel population decreases.

Increasing the file size (by raising the Pixel Dimensions values) isn't such a hot idea, either, because Photoshop can't generate image elements out of thin air. When you raise the Pixel Dimensions values, Photoshop adds pixels by averaging the preexisting pixels (a process computer nerds call *interpolation*) in a way that may result in image softening and never results in the miraculous reconstruction of detail.

If changing the pixel dimensions is so dangerous, you may wonder why Photoshop gives you the option to do so at all. Well, although I don't recommend ever adding pixels to an image, you may need to lower the pixel dimensions on occasion. If your file size is really large — that is, your image contains a ton of pixels — you may want to toss some of the pixels overboard.

In an ideal world, you'd want as many pixels as possible because more pixels means greater image detail. But the more pixels you have, the more disk space the image consumes, which can be a problem if you're working with limited computing resources. Large file sizes can also slow Photoshop down substantially. Also, if you're publishing your image on the Internet, you may want to reduce your file size so that users can download the image more quickly. Finally, you may need to lower the pixel dimensions in order to make an image print at the size you want.

Even when you dump pixels from an image, however, you shouldn't attack the job from the Pixel Dimensions options boxes; I show you a better way in the section, "Using the Image Size dialog box safely," later in this chapter.

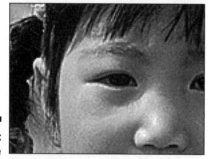

Figure 4-4:
Three
images,
each
containing
fewer pixels
and printed
at a lower
resolution
than the
image
above it.

In some particularly nerdy circles, changing the number of pixels in an image is called *resampling*. The idea is that you sample the photograph when you scan it — as if that makes a lick of sense — so any adjustment to the quantity of pixels after scanning is resampling. Photoshop uses the term resampling, but I prefer to call it *resizing*, because this gives folks a fighting chance of understanding what I'm talking about. But just be aware that there are computer aficionados out there who will gladly stick their noses high in the air, trade shocked stares with one another, and mutter pronouncements such as "Don't tell me she has mouse privileges," or "Gad, did you hear what it said?" These things must be endured.

Yeah, okay, but what resolution should I use?

The Auto button in the Image Size dialog box is supposed to generate a perfect Resolution value based on the line screen that your printer will use. The only problem is, no one knows what a line screen setting is. Rather than bother with trying to explain this arcane bit of printing technology to you at this point — what with your head already spinning with Lagos population data — I decided to come up with both ideal and acceptable values for certain kinds of print jobs. See whether these work for you.

Type of Job Setting	Ideal Resolution	Acceptable
Full-color image for magazine or professional publication	300 ppi	225 ppi
Full-color slides	300 ppi	200 ppi
Color image for laser printing or overhead projections	180 ppi	120 ppi
Color images for multimedia productions and World Wide Web pages	72 ppi	72 ppi
Black-and-white images for imageset newsletters, flyers, and so on	180 ppi	120 ppi
Black-and-white images for laser printing	120 ppi	90 ppi

Keep in mind that there are no hard-and-fast rules about resolution settings. You can specify virtually any resolution setting between the ideal and acceptable settings and achieve good results. (If your commercial printer or service bureau tells you that you're getting bad results because your resolution doesn't match some exact ideal, consult a different company; this excuse is an example of a bad carpenter blaming his tools.) Even if you go with a Resolution value that's lower than the suggested acceptable setting, the worst that can happen is that you'll get fuzzy or slightly jagged results. But there is no wrong setting.

Changing the physical dimensions of the image

The Width and Height boxes in the Print Size portion of the Image Size dialog box reflect the actual printed size of your image and the approximate size of your image when distributed over the World Wide Web. (Because monitors can vary from user to user, the actual size of the image may change a little when viewed on different monitors.)

The pop-up menus next to the Width and Height options let you change the unit of measure displayed in the option boxes. For example, if you select picas from the Print Size Width pop-up menu, Photoshop converts the Width value from inches to picas. (A pica is an obscure typesetting measurement equal to $^1/_6$ inch.) The percent option in the pop-up menu enables you to enter new Width and Height values as a percentage of the original values. Enter a value higher than 100% to increase the print size; enter a value lower than 100% to reduce the print size.

When you change the print size of the image, either the Resolution value or the number of pixels in the image automatically changes, too, which can affect the quality of your image. For more information, read the section, "Resolving resolution," earlier in this chapter. And for details on how to change the print size without ruining your image, see the section, "Using the Image Size dialog box safely," later in this chapter.

Keeping things proportionate

Both pairs of Width and Height option boxes in the Image Size dialog box list the dimensions of your image in the current unit of measure. If you enter a different value into either option box and click on the OK button (or press Return), Photoshop resizes your image to the dimensions. Pretty obvious, eh?

But strangely, when you change either the Width or Height value, the other value changes, too. Are these twins that were separated at birth? Is there some new cosmic relationship between Width and Height that is known only to outer-space aliens and the checkout clerk at your local grocery store? No, it's nothing more than a function of the Constrain Proportions check box, which is turned on by default. Photoshop is simply maintaining the original proportions of the image.

If you click on the Constrain Proportions box and turn it off, Photoshop permits you — in a very generous spirit, I might add — to adjust the Width and Height values independently. Notice that the little link icon (labeled back in Figure 4-2) disappears, showing that the two options are now maverick independents with reckless disregard for one another. You can now create stretchy effects like the ones shown in Figure 4-5. In the first example, I reduced the Width value by a factor of two and left the Height value unchanged. In the second example, I did the opposite, reducing the Height value and leaving the Width value unaltered.

Figure 4-5:
Known to friends and family as Kid Squishums, this versatile little tyke is the result of deselecting the Constrain Proportions check box.

However, in order to deselect the Constrain Proportions check box, you have to select the Resample Image check box. As explained later, in the section, "Using the Image Size dialog box safely," when the Resample Image check box is selected, Photoshop either adds or deletes pixels from your image to compensate for the changes to the width and height of the image. Because adding pixels can make your image look like mud, never increase the width or height value with Constrain Proportions deselected. It's okay to decrease the width and height values, as long as the Resolution value stays in the acceptable range (see the sidebar, "Yeah, okay, but what resolution should I use?" earlier in this chapter for recommended resolution values).

Matching images to columns

What is the meaning of the Columns option in the Print Size Width pop-up menu? Oh, man, you would ask that. All right (sigh), I suppose I'd better tell you.

You see, Photoshop is capable of precisely matching the width of an image to the columns in a printed document. So, for the sake of argument, say that you're working on an image that you eventually want to place into PageMaker. This specific PageMaker document happens to be a three-column newsletter. Each column is 2 inches wide, and the gutter (space) between each column is 1/4 inch wide.

To match Photoshop column settings to those in PageMaker, you choose File⇨

Preferences⇨Units & Rulers and enter the column specs — in this case, 2 and 0.25 — into the Column Size option boxes, highlighted in the following figure. (Select inches from the pop-up menus if you want to use inches.) From that point on, a column in the Image Size dialog box conforms to your settings. One column, for example, would be 2 inches wide; two columns would be 4 1/4 inches wide — 4 inches for the two columns and the extra 1/4 inch for the gutter.

Columns is not an option in the Height pop-up menu (inside the Image Size dialog box) because columns run up and down, not left to right. In other words, columns make no sense as a system of measurement for height.

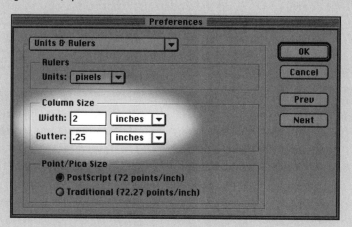

Using the Image Size dialog box safely

As I mentioned earlier in this chapter, you have three image attributes — size, resolution, and dimension — all vying for your attention and all affecting each other. These attributes, in fact, are like three points on a triangle. Change any one of the points, and at least one of the others has to change proportionately. If you decrease the file size (number of pixels), for example, either the physical dimensions (printed size) or resolution (number of pixels per inch) must also decrease. If you want to increase the physical dimensions, you have to increase the file size — add pixels, in other words — or decrease the resolution.

Thinking about all the possible permutations can drive you crazy, and besides, they aren't the least bit important. What is important is that you understand what you can accomplish with the Image Size dialog box and that you know how to avoid mistakes. So, now that I've provided all the background you need, it's finally time for me to offer a modicum of fatherly advice:

✔ Changing the Pixel Dimensions (file size) values can be deadly, as explained in the section, "Changing pixel dimensions." To avoid changes to file size, deselect the Resample Image check box at the bottom of the Image Size dialog box. When you deselect the option, the Image Size dialog box changes, and the Width and Height options in the Pixel Dimensions portion of the dialog box become unavailable to you. A link icon also connects the Print Size's Width, Height, and Resolution option boxes, showing that changes to one value affect the other two values as well.

✔ In order to turn off the Constrain Proportions option box, you have to turn on the Resample Image option box. If you make changes to the image width and height values, Photoshop will resample the image. If you're lowering the width and height values, you'll probably be okay, but if you try to raise the width and height values, you're likely to muck things up.

✔ Want a surefire method to tell whether you've changed the file size? Your image looks different on-screen after you change the Resolution or Print Size values and exit the Image Size dialog box. As long as the file size remains unchanged, you won't see any difference — none, zilch, zippo — on-screen. On-screen, Photoshop just shows your image pixels with respect to screen pixels; resolution and dimension enter into the equation only when you print the image. Therefore, you want the image to look the same on-screen after you get done fiddling around with the Image Size command.

✔ If you manage to mess everything up and change one or more settings in the Image Size dialog box to settings that you don't want to apply, you can return to the original settings by Option-clicking on the Cancel button. Pressing Option changes the word Cancel to Reset; clicking resets the options. Now you have your original settings back in place so that you can muck them up again. If you already pressed Return to exit the Image Size dialog box, choose Edit⇨Undo or press ⌘-Z right away to undo your changes.

✔ If you perform *another* action after you've erroneously resized, you will find, to your dismay, that you can't undo the resize by pressing ⌘-Z. That command lets you undo only your very last action. Now, for the big secret: You can undo your mistakes by using the magnificent new and powerful History palette (see major details in Chapter 11).

✔ Whatever you do, be sure to use the Bicubic setting in the Resample Image pop-up menu. I'd tell you what *bicubic* means, but you don't want to know. Suffice it to say that it keeps Photoshop running smoothly.

✔ If you want to change the unit of measure that displays by default in the Image Size dialog box pop-up menus, choose File⇨Preferences⇨Units & Rulers, and select a different option from the Units pop-up menu.

You may think that changing the image size is something that you never want to do. But you may, in fact, want to reduce the image size on some occasions — to get the image to print at a certain size, to enable your computer to handle the image, or to make the image download faster from the Internet. The following steps show you how to reduce your image size without turning your image into a worthless pile of goo.

Before you follow these steps, choose File⇨Save As to save a backup copy of your image. The steps result in Photoshop tossing away pixels, and after you delete pixels, you can't get them back after you close your file. So always make a copy of the original in case things don't work out or you decide you want to use the original again at a later date.

1. **Open the image at the highest resolution possible.**

   For example, if you're opening a Photo CD image, select the 2048 x 3072 option from the Resolution pop-up menu. If that doesn't work — Photoshop may complain that you don't have enough memory to pull it off — try again and select the 1024 x 1536 option. Whatever works, go for it.

2. **Choose Image⇨Image Size to open the Image Size dialog box.**

3. **Note the values in the Pixel Dimensions Width and Height option boxes.**

   You may want to write 'em down — they're important.

4. **Enter your desired print width and height in the Print Size option boxes.**

   If you want Photoshop to retain the original proportions of your image, make sure that the Constrain Proportions option box is checked.

5. **Enter your desired resolution in the Resolution option box.**

   Check out the sidebar, "Yeah, okay, but what resolution should I use?," earlier in this chapter for some suggestions on acceptable resolution values if you need help.

6. **Check the Pixel Dimensions values.**

   Did either of the values get bigger? If so, you need to reduce your Print Size width and height values or lower the resolution. Otherwise, Photoshop adds pixels to your image, and you won't be happy with the results.

   If the Pixel Dimensions values got smaller, on the other hand, proceed to Step 7.

7. **Make sure that the Resample Image check box is selected.**

8. **Make sure that the Bicubic option is selected in the Resample Image pop-up menu.**

9. **Click on the OK button.**

   Photoshop resizes — or, if you prefer, resamples — your image in accordance with your perfect settings. If you don't like the results, press ⌘-Z or choose Edit➪Undo *immediately* to put things back to the way they were. And, again, if you performed another action after sizing, the History palette is available for undoing.

Okay, now that you patiently let yourself be informed on the dos and don'ts of image sizing, I'll tell you about the Resize Image Assistant.

This Assistant, many other programs refer to them as wizards, is found under Help in the Photoshop menu bar. The Assistant presents a dialog box, as shown in Figure 4-6, that asks you questions regarding your wants and intended use for the image, and then steps you through the resizing process. If you choose options that it feels are unwise, it warns you that you are lowering your image quality. You can then step back and try another setting. The Assistant creates a new file, putting Resize Assistant in front of your filename, thereby not disturbing your original. All in all, the Resize Image Assistant is pretty smart, but like anything, the more *you* know, the better decisions you can make.

Whereas the Resize Image Assistant has some value, the new File➪Automate➪Fit Image command has very little. Based on numbers that you enter for width and height, Photoshop resizes your file as close to the dimensions as possible, while maintaining the same aspect ratio (proportions). The problem is that Photoshop stretches or shrinks your image while leaving the resolution the same. In other words, it *resamples* the image. If you are enlarging your image, this process could reduce image quality drastically. I recommend reading this chapter and using the guidelines presented plus your own brain power to size images.

Figure 4-6:
The Resize
Image
Assistant
steps you
through the
sizing
process.

What Does This Canvas Size Command Do?

You should know about one more command related to the topic of image sizing: Image⇨Canvas Size. Unlike the Image Size command, which stretches or shrinks the photograph, the Canvas Size command changes the size of the page — or canvas — on which the image sits. If you increase the size of the canvas, Photoshop fills the new area outside the image with white, the default color (or the background color). If you make the canvas smaller, Photoshop crops the image.

When you choose Image⇨Canvas Size, the dialog box shown in Figure 4-7 pops up from its virtual hole. You can play with the options found in the dialog box as follows:

Figure 4-7:
Use the
Canvas Size
dialog box
to change
the size of
the page on
which the
image sits.

✔ Enter new values into the Width and Height option boxes as desired. You can also change the unit of measurement by using the pop-up menus, just as in the Image Size dialog box.

✔ You can't constrain the proportions of the canvas the way you can inside the Image Size dialog box. Therefore, the Width and Height values always operate independently.

✔ The Anchor section shows a graphic representation of how the current image sits inside the new canvas. By default, the image is centered in the canvas. But you can click inside any of the other eight squares to move the image to the upper-right corner, center it along the bottom edge, or place it where you like.

✔ If you reduce either the Width or Height value and press Return, Photoshop asks you whether you really want to crop the image. If you click on the Proceed button (or press Return) and decide you don't like the results, you can always choose Edit⇨Undo or press ⌘-Z to restore the original canvas size.

Chapter 5

Auntie Em versus the Munchkins (Death Match)

• •

In This Chapter

▶ Understanding RGB color theory

▶ Viewing independent color channels

▶ Photoshop 5 color management

▶ Defining colors using the Color palette

▶ Selecting colors that will print

▶ Lifting colors from an image with the eyedropper

▶ Converting color images to grayscale

• •

*1*n case you're wondering what the title of this chapter means, it's all about color — the same kind of color that Dorothy encountered when she passed over the weather-beaten threshold of her old Kansas porch onto a path of lemon-yellow bricks in that beloved classic, *The Wizard of Oz.* As you might imagine, Auntie Em represents the world of black and white, and the Munchkins represent the wonderful world of color.

With that in mind, you might think that Auntie Em is pretty well doomed. I mean, how can one woman cope with an entire Oz full of rowdy Munchkins? And how can drab black and white compete with rich, beautiful color?

Well, I'm rather fond of black and white myself. To me, the absence of color offers its own special attractions. It's the mysterious essence of a torch-lit castle on a stormy night. It's the refreshingly personal vision of a 16mm short-subject film you stumble across one evening on Bravo. It's the powerful chiaroscuro of an Ansel Adams photograph or a Rembrandt oil. In an age when every screen, page, and billboard screams with color that's more vivid than real life, black and white can beckon the eye like an old friend.

But on the off chance you think all that's a pretentious load of hooey, I can tell you one area in which Auntie Em kicks major Munchkin keister, and that's cost. Despite the increasing influence of computers in print houses, color printing remains extremely expensive. Major four-color magazines — including the ones I write for — spend more on ink than they do on their writers. The color medium costs more than the message, and that's a sad fact.

Though by no means free, black-and-white images are substantially less expensive to reproduce. Only one ink is involved — black. Other supplies, such as film and plates for the printing press, are kept to a minimum. Black-and-white printing is also incredibly versatile. You can print black-and-white images with any laser printer, you can photocopy black-and-white images using cheap equipment, and you can fax black-and-white images with relatively little loss in quality. And finally, black-and-white images require one-third of the overhead when you're working in Photoshop, meaning that you can edit black-and-white images that contain three times as many pixels as color images without Photoshop complaining that it's out of memory. I'd say that this is one match in which Auntie Em can be counted on to hold her own. No surprise, really. Farm women are well-known troupers, while the Munchkins — to hear Judy Garland tell it — were a bunch of randy booze hounds.

Whether you choose black and white, color, or — like most folks — vacillate between the two, this chapter tells you how it all works. You find out how to use color, create colors that you can apply with the painting tools, and switch between color modes. Not bad for a chapter based on an old MGM musical, eh?

Looking at Color in a Whole New Light

To understand color in Photoshop, you have to understand a little color theory. To this end, I want you to do me a favor and open some random color image that you have sitting around. Chances are that you'll see the telltale initials RGB inside parentheses in the image title bar. (If you don't, try opening a different image.) These initials mean that all colors inside the image are created by blending red, green, and blue light.

Red, green, and blue? That doesn't sound particularly colorful, does it? But, in fact, these colors are the primary colors of light. The red is a vivid scarlet, the green is so bright and tinged with yellow that you might be tempted to call it chartreuse, and the blue is a brilliant Egyptian lapis. It just so happens that these colors correspond to the three kinds of cones inside your eyeball. So, in theory, your monitor projects color in the same way your eyes see color.

Surfing the color channels

To get a hands-on feel for the inner workings of a color image, follow these steps:

1. **Open an RGB image.**

   Oh, you already did that. My mistake.

2. **Choose File⇨Preferences⇨Display & Cursors.**

   The Preferences dialog box shown in Figure 5-1 appears.

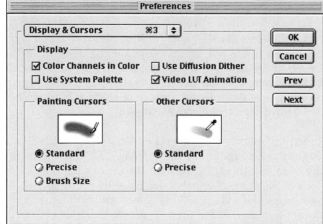

Figure 5-1:
Select the Color Channels in Color option to see how the primary colors work.

The Preferences dialog box actually contains several panels of options. You switch between the panels via the pop-up menu at the top of the dialog box. Another way to display the dialog box is to press ⌘-K, which brings up the Preferences dialog box with the General preferences panel showing. Then press ⌘-3 or choose Display & Cursors from the pop-up menu to display the options shown in Figure 5-1. After you close the dialog box, you can redisplay the last panel you visited by pressing ⌘-Option-K.

3. **Select the Color Channels in Color check box and press Return.**

   Checked in the Figure 5-1, this option makes the individual layers of red, green, and blue color appear in red, green, and blue. These layers of color are called *channels*.

4. **Press ⌘-1 to view the red channel.**

   You see a black-and-red image. Notice that the RGB in the title bar changes to Red to show that you're viewing the red channel. This image is the one being sent to the red cones in your eyes.

5. **Press ⌘-2 to view the green channel and press ⌘-3 to view the blue channel.**

   These images are the ones being sent to your green and blue cones.

6. **Press ⌘-~ (tilde) to return to the full-color RGB view.**

   The tilde key, by the way, is found in the upper-left corner of the keyboard, next to the 1 key. To type an actual tilde, you have to press the Shift key, but you don't need to press Shift to invoke the full-color view shortcut. The shortcut really should be ⌘-` (grave) because pressing the key without Shift accesses the grave mark. But Photoshop prefers to label this shortcut ⌘-~ (tilde), so I follow suit.

   At any rate, when you press ⌘-~ (tilde), you can see the red, green, and blue channels all mixed together.

Pretty nifty, huh? Here's another way to think about it: If you were to take the images you saw in the red, green, and blue channels, print them to slides, put each of the slides in a different projector, and shine all three projectors at the same spot on a screen so that the images precisely overlapped, you would see the full-color image in all its splendor. Check out Color Plate 5-1 for the pictorial representation.

Now try something different. Choose File⇨Preferences⇨Display & Cursors (or press ⌘-Option-K to redisplay the Display & Cursors panel of the Preferences dialog box), but this time, turn off the Color Channels in Color check box. Now look at the color channels once more by pressing ⌘-1, ⌘-2, and ⌘-3. Each channel looks like a standard black-and-white image. Figure 5-2, for example, shows the contents of the red, green, and blue channels as they appear in black and white.

Figure 5-2: The black-and-white channels combine to make a full-color image.

Mixing red, green, and blue to create color

Every channel contains light areas and dark areas, just like a black-and-white image. With the Color Channels in Color check box turned off, you can really see these light and dark areas without a bunch of distracting colors getting in your way (which is why the option is off by default). The light and dark pixels from each channel mix together to form other colors.

The following list explains how corresponding pixels from the different channels mix together to form a single full-color pixel.

- ✔ A light pixel from the one channel mixed with dark pixels from the other two channels produces the color from the first channel. For example, if the red is light, and green and blue are dark, you get a red pixel.

- ✔ Light pixels from the red and green channels plus a dark pixel from the blue channel form yellow. This may sound weird — two colors, red and green, mixing to form a lighter color — but that's exactly how things work in the upside-down world of RGB. Because you're mixing colors projected from a monitor, two colors projected together produce a still lighter color.

- ✔ With me? No? Well, say that you had a flashlight with a red bulb and your friend had one with a green bulb. I don't know, maybe it's Christmas or something. At any rate, if you were to point your flashlight at a spot on the ground, the spot would turn red. No surprise there. But if you then said, "Look, Nancy, it's the missing key from the old Smithers' place," and your friend pointed her green flashlight at the same spot, the spot wouldn't get darker, it would get lighter. In fact, it would turn bright yellow. "Gee wizikers, Ned, do you suppose this means Mrs. Johnson is innocent after all?" I'm afraid we'll never know.

- ✔ Light pixels from the green and blue channels plus a dark pixel from the red channel make a bright turquoise color called cyan. Light red and blue pixels plus a dark green pixel make magenta.

- ✔ By a strange coincidence, cyan, magenta, and yellow just happen to be the main ink colors used in the color printing process. Well, actually, it's not coincidence at all. Color printing is the opposite of color screen display, so the two use complementary collections of primary hues to produce full-color images. The difference is that because cyan, magenta, and yellow are pigments, they become darker as you mix them. Yellow plus cyan, for example, make green. This won't affect how you edit RGB images, but I thought you might find it interesting.

- ✔ Light pixels from all three channels mix to form white. Dark pixels all around form black. Medium pixels make gray.

Although all this is highly stimulating, I have a feeling that it would make more sense if you could see it. If you're the visual type, take a look at Color Plate 5-2. The left side of the figure shows the RGB combinations I just discussed. The right side shows RGB mixes that result in other colors, including orange, purple, and so on. Give it the once-over and see whether you can't feel your brain grow by leaps and bounds.

Using the Channels palette

Keyboard equivalents such as ⌘-1 and ⌘-2 aren't the only way to access different channels. You can also use the Channels palette. Choose Window⇨Show Channels to display the Channels palette, shown in Figure 5-3. Here's how to use the palette:

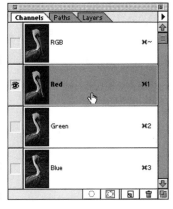

Figure 5-3:
Click on a
channel
name in the
Channels
palette to
view that
channel.

✔ To switch to a different channel in the palette, simply click on its name. Figure 5-3 finds me clicking on the Red channel.

✔ To return to the full-color RGB view, click on the top item in the Channels palette or press ⌘--(tilde).

✔ The Channels palette includes little thumbnails of the contents of each channel. To change the size of these thumbnails, choose Palette Options from the palette menu — click on that little right-pointing arrowhead just beneath the title bar — and select a different Thumbnail Size icon.

Photoshop 5 Color Management

Now that you have basic color theory, it's time for basic color management. Color management seems to be the thorn in every Photoshop user's side. To make matters worse, or better, depending on your point of view, Version 5 comes with some complex color management and color conversion capabilities. Even seasoned users may find some of them baffling and mysterious, so we'll boil it down to the basic essentials and allow you to go on to fun stuff.

People want to be able to have a true WYSIWYG (What You See Is What You Get) world. In other words, they want to be able to look at their monitor and get the exact colors they see come out the other end. This "other end" can be in the form of printouts, or perhaps viewing the image on the Web from another monitor. Getting this exact color is next to impossible. There are devices that help — expensive hardware and software calibrators that come with high end monitors. But most of us average Joes have to try and manage this dilemma on our own. Photoshop 5 does provide some help. The first step is to calibrate your monitor and identify it to Photoshop. The second step is to tell Photoshop if and how you want the colors in your images to convert from one computer to another. Photoshop embeds *color profiles* that identify the source of the image and uses that info to convert colors when it is opened on another computer. Luckily, you have to tell Photoshop all this stuff only once. On to step one — calibrating with the Gamma Assistant (see Figure 5-4).

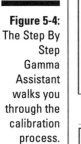

Figure 5-4:
The Step By
Step
Gamma
Assistant
walks you
through the
calibration
process.

1. **At the Finder, open the Photoshop 5 application folder.**

2. **Open the Extras folder and then the Calibration folder.**

3. **Double-click on the Adobe Gamma icon.**

   A dialog box appears.

4. Choose the Step By Step Assistant option, which asks certain questions and walks you through the setup procedure. Answer each question and click on the Next button to move on.

If you aren't sure about a setting, check the documentation that came with your monitor or call the vendor. When you are done, Photoshop knows everything about your monitor.

Now for the second step. First, you need to tell Photoshop what you see on your screen — the RGB environment — so that the program can try and match that environment. Then you need to tell Photoshop how you want to deal with converting colors in files created elsewhere. The Profile Setup dialog box, shown in Figure 5-5, is the color conversion "Command Central." Here are the steps for choosing the right color settings:

1. Choose File⊅Color Settings⊅RGB Setup.

2. Set the RGB setting to Apple RGB.

This step lets you see how an RGB image, like the one you just opened, will look on a typical Mac screen. Check the Preview box so you can see changes on-screen. Leave the rest of the settings at their default.

3. Click on OK.

4. Choose File⊅Color Settings⊅Profile Setup.

Don't panic and run! Just do the following steps.

5. Leave all of the embed profiles checked.

Your files will then be saved with profiles — in simple English, your files will be given an identity according to your computer settings.

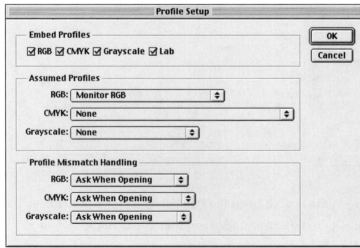

Figure 5-5:
The Profile
Setup
dialog box
gives your
color
conversion
direc-
tions to
Photoshop.

6. **Under Assumed Profiles, set the RGB setting to Monitor RGB and set CMYK and Grayscale to None.**

   Using these settings will prevent any bizarre color changes. Assumed Profiles are meant to provide "identities" to files that have no embedded profiles. Because this profile business is a new feature, most files you open will not have a profile. Think of it as a file with no country, and you are providing it with a name, a purpose — an identity.

7. **For the Profile Mismatch Handling options, select Ask When Opening for all three profiles.**

   These settings tell Photoshop what to do when it opens an image whose profiles, or identities, don't match your settings. Setting the options to Ask When Opening allows you to control any changes you want and not have Photoshop automatically do it for you. For example, say that a friend creates a file in Photoshop on his computer and he has his RGB Setup set to Wide Gamut RGB (remember that yours is Apple RGB). When you open his file, you will be confronted with a Profile Mismatch dialog box that says his embedded profile, Wide Gamut RGB, doesn't match your RGB setup, Apple RGB, and that asks you to specify how it should be converted (see Figure 5-6).

   At this point, you have two choices — Convert or Don't Convert. If you choose Convert, the colors will convert from his profile to yours. If you choose Don't convert, the image opens unchanged. What to do? Simply choose convert, look at the image, and be the judge. If you don't like the results, close the file and reopen — this time choosing Don't Convert.

8. **Click on OK.**

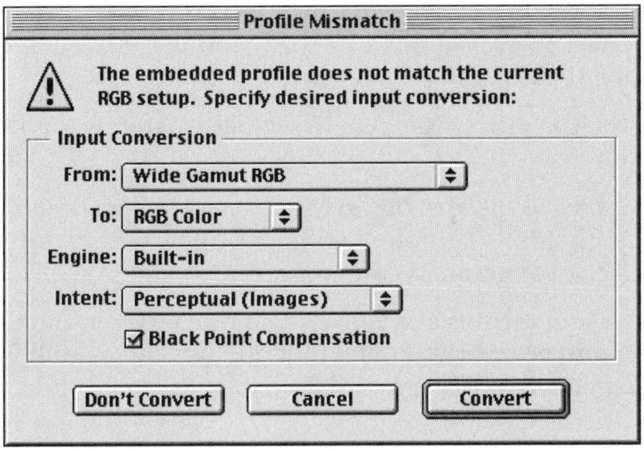

Figure 5-6: When a profile doesn't match yours, you will be alerted with this dialog box.

Being Your Own L.J. Grand Master Funky Glow

In case you're hip-hop impaired, L.J. stands for *Light Jockey,* and that's exactly what you have to be to create colors in Photoshop. In other words, to define a color, you have to specify the quantities of red, green, and blue that go into it.

Uh, just so you don't go and make a fool of yourself the next time your kid's friends come over by saying something painfully embarrassing like, "Hey, check me out, I'm L.J. Grand Master Funky Glow!" I thought that I should admit that L.J. isn't a real hip-hop term. I just made it up. I mean, for all I know, L.J. means lemon juice or lantern jaw in today's imaginative middle-school lingo. "You're what, Dad? A lentil jar?"

Juggling foreground and background colors

In Photoshop, you can work with two colors at a time: a *foreground color* and a *background color.* Some tools and commands paint your image with the foreground color; others splash it with the background color.

The two colors are displayed in the lower portion of the toolbox. As shown in Figure 5-7, the foreground color is on top, and the background color is on the bottom. To get some idea of how these colors work, read the following list. (Skip the following list if you'd like to remain ignorant.)

✔ The foreground color is applied by the painting tools, such as the airbrush, paintbrush, and pencil.

✔ When you use the eraser tool, you're actually painting with the back-ground color.

✔ When you increase the size of the canvas using Image⇨Canvas Size (as explained in Chapter 4), Photoshop fills the new empty portion of the canvas with the background color.

✔ The gradient tool creates a rainbow of colors between the foreground and background colors (assuming that you use the default gradient option, Foreground to Background, as explained in Chapter 14).

The toolbox includes a few icons that enable you to change the foreground and background colors, swap them around, and so on.

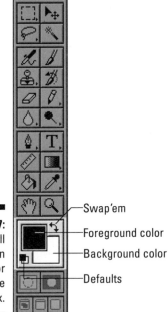

Figure 5-7:
The small
collection
of color
icons in the
toolbox.

Swap'em

Foreground color

Background color

Defaults

✔ Click on the foreground icon to display the intensely complex Color Picker dialog box, which is filled with about 17,000 options you don't need to know anything about.

✔ Press Esc or click Cancel to leave that dialog box. Then pick up a Bible or some other holy relic, and swear that you'll never go back there again. The next section tells you a better option for defining the foreground and background colors.

✔ Click on the background color to go to that same terrible dialog box. Hey, didn't I specifically instruct you to stay out of there?

✔ Click on the defaults icon (refer to Figure 5-7) to restore the foreground color to black and the background color to white.

✔ Click on that little two-way arrow icon — childishly labeled *swap 'em* in the figure — to swap the foreground and background colors with each other.

✔ You can also access the default and swap 'em icons from the keyboard. Press D to restore the default colors, black and white. Press X to swap the foreground and background colors.

Defining colors

You can define the foreground and background colors in Photoshop in three ways:

✔ You can click on the foreground or background color icon in the toolbox and battle your way through the Color Picker. If you read the preceding section, you know that I think that this option is a real stinkeroo and should be avoided at all costs.

✔ You can use the handy-dandy Color palette. The Color palette is pretty much the same thing as the Picker palette found in Version 4.

✔ You can lift colors from your image using the eyedropper tool.

Using the Color palette

To define colors using the Color palette, shown in Figure 5-8, choose Window⇨Show Color or press the F6 key. You should see three slider bars labeled R, G, and B (for Reginald, Gertie, and Bert). If you don't see them, choose RGB Sliders from the palette menu. (Click on the right-pointing arrow in the upper-right corner of the palette to display the menu.)

┌─Background color

┌─Foreground color

Figure 5-8: The Color palette fully adorned with its cheerful RGB slider bars.

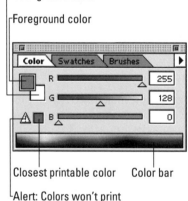

Closest printable color   Color bar

└─Alert: Colors won't print

Here's how you go about changing a color using the Color palette:

1. Decide which color you want to change.

The palette offers its own foreground and background color icons, as labeled in Figure 5-8. Click on the icon for the color you want to change. A double outline surrounds the icon to show that it's selected.

Clicking on the selected icon again, or double-clicking it initially, takes you back to the dreaded Color Picker.

2. Drag the little RGB slider bar triangles to change the color.

Think of red, green, and blue as ingredients in baking the perfect color. You can add 256 levels of each of the primary hues, 0 being the darkest amount of the hue, 255 being the lightest, and 128 being smack dab in the middle. For example, if you set the R slider to 255, the G slider to 128, and the B slider to 0, you get a vibrant orange, just like the one shown in the upper-right corner of Color Plate 5-2.

If you've never mixed colors using red, green, and blue, it can be a little perplexing at first. For example, folks often have a hard time initially accepting that all yellows and oranges are produced by mixing red and green. I encourage you to experiment. Better yet, I order you to experiment.

3. Click on the triangular alert icon if desired.

If a little triangle with an exclamation point appears in the lower-right corner of the palette, Photoshop is pointing out that the color you have mixed will not print exactly as you see it on-screen. The closest print-able color appears inside a little square to the right of the alert icon. Click on either the icon or the square if you want to use the printable color instead.

Isn't the color on-screen the same as a color on the page? No, and the reason is the difference between the principles of colored light and colored pigments. Your monitor creates white by mixing the lightest amounts of red, green, and blue — the opposite of how things work on the printed page. Color printing exploits the fact that sunlight and man-made light (both referred to as "white light") contain the entire spectrum of visible light, including all shades of red, green, and blue. The primary printing inks — cyan, magenta, and yellow — are actually *color filters.* When white light hits cyan ink printed on a page, the cyan ink filters out all traces of red and reflects only green and blue, which mix to form cyan. Similarly, magenta is a green light filter, and yellow is a blue light filter, as illustrated in detail in Color Plate 5-3. This and other factors (such as purity of inks, variation of ink tints, whiteness of paper, and lighting conditions) result in the CMYK world producing fewer and duller colors. Unfortunately, you have to just accept it and go on with life.

Here are just a few other things I want to pass along about the Color palette:

✔ If you can't get the knack of using the RGB slider bars, you can select a color by clicking inside the color bar at the bottom of the palette. By default, all the colors in the bar are printable. (To make sure that this is true, ⌘-click on the color bar, select CMYK Spectrum from the Style pop-up menu, and press Return.)

✔ Option-click in the color bar to change the opposite color. For example, if the foreground color is active, Option-click to select the background color. If the background color is active, Option-click to select the foreground color.

✔ If you want to set the foreground or background color to a shade of gray, you can set all sliders to the same value. Or better yet, choose Grayscale Slider from the palette menu and adjust the single K slider. (K stands for black.)

Lifting colors with the eyedropper tool

You can also change the foreground or background colors by lifting them from the image. Just select the eyedropper tool — on the right side of the toolbox just above the zoom tool — and click inside the image on the color you want to use. If you have more than one image open, you can even click inside an image different from the one you're working on.

Here's some stuff to know about this incredibly easy-to-use tool:

✔ You can press I (for I-dropper) to select the eyedropper tool instead of clicking on its toolbox icon.

✔ The eyedropper affects whatever color is selected in the Color palette. So, if the foreground color icon is selected, the eyedropper tool changes the foreground color, and if the background icon is selected — well, you get the idea.

✔ To select the opposite color — in other words, to select the background color when the foreground color icon is active or the foreground color when the background color icon is active — Option-click with the eyedropper.

✔ You can temporarily access the eyedropper when another tool is selected by pressing the Option key. As long as the key is down, the eyedropper is available. This trick doesn't always work; in fact, it works only when you're using the type, paint bucket, gradient, line, pencil, airbrush, or paintbrush tool. But it can come in handy.

✔ If you use the preceding tip, you can change only the active color in the Color palette. You need the Option key to change the opposite color, so you can't use the key to temporarily access the eyedropper. You have to select the eyedropper for real (click on its icon or press I) and then Option-click. (If your keyboard offers two Option keys, it doesn't help to press both of them.)

Version 5 gives you a new tool that shares the same space as the eyedropper. It's the color sampler tool and looks like an eyedropper with a small target. The tool doesn't lift; it measures only the colors you click on.

Here's how to use this new tool:

✔ Select the color sampler and click on the color you want. Notice the target that's added and labeled #1.

- ✔ Photoshop opens the Info palette and shows you the RGB formula of numbers for that color.

- ✔ You can repeat this procedure three times for a total of four targeted colors.

- ✔ Targets can be moved by dragging with the color sampler tool and deleted by holding down the Option key and clicking on the targets.

- ✔ A fifth color can be measured by just moving the cursor around the image.

Basically, the big use of the color sampler is to monitor changes to your image after you apply things like color correction (explained in Chapter 18) and filters (see Chapter 17).

Going Grayscale

Now that I've wasted most of the chapter on the colorful Munchkins, you may be wondering when I'm ever going to get around to discussing the much-lauded Auntie Em. Friends of Kansas, take heart, the heralded hour of black-and-white images has arrived.

The first thing to understand about black-and-white images is that the black-and-white world offers more colors than just black and white. It includes a total of 256 unique shades of gray and is therefore more properly termed grayscale. Each one of these shades is a color in its own right, which is why the term "black and white" can inspire fisticuffs among some grayscale devotees.

Second, all the stuff I told you about creating colors holds true for grayscale image editing as well. You have a foreground and background color. You can define colors in the Color palette. (Be sure to choose Grayscale Slider from the palette menu so that you have to use just one slider bar.) And you can lift or measure colors from a grayscale image using the eyedropper and color sampler tools.

But some aspects of grayscale editing are different than full-color editing, which is what led me to write the next two sections.

The road to grayscale

Most images that you'll come across will be in color. Most commercial images and all Photo CD images are in color. Scans from a commercial quick-printer or service bureau may be in color or in grayscale, but you never know. My point is that working in grayscale generally requires a conversion inside Photoshop.

Unlike a three-channel RGB image, a grayscale image includes only one channel of imagery. That's why the red, green, and blue channels all appear in black and white — each is its own grayscale image. If you plan on printing in black and white, you should jettison all the extraneous color information, for two reasons. First, it's easier for Photoshop to keep track of one channel than three. In fact, given the same image size and resolution, Photoshop performs faster and with fewer problems when editing a grayscale image than when editing in color. Second, you can better see what your printed image will look like. When you're designing an image to be printed in black and white, color just gets in the way.

To convert a color image to grayscale, just choose Image⇨Mode⇨Grayscale. Photoshop asks you whether you want it to discard color information. You can answer OK or chicken out and cancel. That's all there is to it. You now have a single-channel grayscale image. No matter what color you choose in the Color palette, the color appears gray in the foreground and background color icons. If you don't like the results of your conversion to grayscale, you can go back to the full-color original by choosing Edit⇨Undo or pressing ⌘-Z. However, if you have gone ahead and performed some other actions (⌘-Z will only undo the last operation) and then decide you want to go back to color, you can retrieve the color by using the new History palette (explained in detail in Chapter 11).

Before you change a color image to grayscale, you may want to make a backup copy of the original image, just in case you ever want to have the image available in color in the future. For details on saving images, see Chapter 6.

When you choose Image⇨Mode⇨Grayscale, Photoshop merges all three RGB channels together to create the new colorless image. But what if the contents of any one of the RGB channels strikes you as just right and you want to simply dump the other two? The answer is to go to that channel (press ⌘-1, ⌘-2, or ⌘-3) and choose Image⇨Mode⇨Grayscale. This time, Photoshop asks whether you want it to discard all the other channels. If the channel you see on-screen is the one you want to keep, press Return to give Photoshop the go-ahead. Otherwise, click on Cancel and go back to channel surfing.

Figure 5-9 shows an example of the difference between converting all channels in an image and retaining just one. In the first image, I chose Image⇨Mode⇨Grayscale in the RGB view to merge all channels. The result is washed out, with little distinction between lights and darks. I didn't like it, so I chose Edit⇨Undo to restore my RGB image. Then I tiptoed through the channels to find something better, and wouldn't you know, the red channel looked just right. So, after pressing ⌘-1, I again chose Image⇨Mode⇨ Grayscale to toss out the green and blue channels, thus arriving at the second image in Figure 5-9.

Figure 5-9: The difference between converting a color image to grayscale (left) and throwing away all but the red channel.

More grayscale tips from Auntie Em

That's basically all there is to tell about grayscale images. Future chapters explain how to edit color and grayscale images, and Chapter 18 explains how to make automated adjustments, such as changing brightness and contrast. So, I'll wrap things up with four last-minute grayscale tidbits:

✔ If you decide to convert a single channel from an RGB image to grayscale, you'll almost always want to use either the red or green channel. The red channel is generally lighter than the other two because skin tones gravitate toward red. The green channel is the detail channel, full of nice edges. Blue is the dark and dank channel. Except for skies and oceans, not much in this world is blue. Also, your eye contains fewer blue cones than red or green ones. Many scanners generate some pretty cruddy detail in the blue channel — knowing that you won't be able to see it.

✔ To add color to a grayscale image, convert back to RGB by choosing Image⇨Mode⇨RGB Color. Photoshop won't add a bunch of colors to the image, but it will allow you to add colors of your own.

✔ If you use the Image➪Mode➪Grayscale conversion method and your color image contains more than one layer (as explained in Chapter 15), Photoshop asks whether you want to flatten (merge) your image. If you want to keep your layers, click on the Don't Flatten button. If you use the single channel conversion method and your image contains more than one layer, the layers are flattened when you convert to grayscale. So, before you go ahead with the conversion, do all editing that involves layers and also make a backup copy of the layered image.

✔ If you're using an 8-bit monitor — that is, a monitor that can display only 256 colors — you're better off editing grayscale images. When you edit full-color RGB images, Photoshop shows only 256 of the 16 million possible colors at a time, resulting in *dithering,* an effect in which a random pattern of pixels is used to emulate lots more colors. When you edit a grayscale image, however, you can see every shade just right. Don't worry that Photoshop converts your entire screen to grays, including Finder icons and all other background items. This is a normal effect of editing in grayscale on an inexpensive computer system.

Chapter 6

Save Before You Say Good Night

*1*f you've used a computer before, you may be wondering why I devote an entire chapter to saving files. After all, you just press ⌘-S, and you're done, right? Well, if we were talking about any other program, I'd have to agree with you. If this book were about Microsoft Word, for example, I'd say, "Not to worry, Dear Reader, saving a file is so simple, a newborn lemur could pull it off with the most cursory supervision from a parent or older sibling." If this book were about PageMaker, I'd add, "Saving makes tying your shoes look like a supreme feat of civil engineering," all the while gently smiling and donning a cardigan sweater in a manner not unlike Mr. Rogers.

But this book is about Photoshop. And Photoshop, as you may or may not be aware, enables you to save images in more flavors than Willy Wonka manages to squeeze into an Everlasting Gobstopper. In the software world, these flavors are called *file formats,* and each one has a different purpose.

This chapter offers a thorough explanation of the saving process, including an exhaustive — well, okay, pretty decent review of the various file formats you can use. With this chapter by your side, ⌘-S can be a pretty easy command, after all.

Save an Image, Save a Life

I don't know you from Adam — or Eve for that matter — but I'm guessing that you're the kind of person who doesn't like to spend hours editing an image only to see your work vanish in a poof of on-screen smoke as the result of some inexplicable and unforeseen computer malfunction. If you are indeed that kind of person, finding out how to save your image is essential. By saving your image early and often, you improve your chances of weathering any digital storm that may come your way.

Saving for the very first time

After applying the first few edits to your image, save it under a new name and — if necessary — specify where you want to store it on disk. If you do this, the original image remains untouched, allowing you to return to it at a later date for inclusion in a different project. Here's how to save your customized image without harming the original:

1. **Choose File⇨Save As.**

   The dialog box shown in Figure 6-1 appears.

   You can also open the dialog box by pressing ⌘-Shift-S.

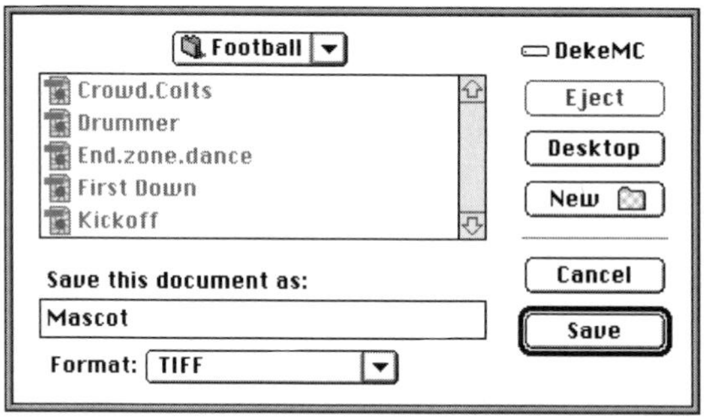

Figure 6-1:
Use this
dialog box
to name
your image
and decide
where you
want the
image to
hang out on
disk.

```
┌──────────────────────────────────────────────┐
│    📁 Football ▼          ⊂ DekeMC             │
│  📄 Crowd.Colts        ⬆     ┌──────────┐      │
│  📄 Drummer                  │  Eject   │      │
│  📄 End.zone.dance           └──────────┘      │
│  📄 First Down               ┌──────────┐      │
│  📄 Kickoff            ⬇     │ Desktop  │      │
│                              └──────────┘      │
│                              ┌──────────┐      │
│                              │  New 📁  │      │
│                              └──────────┘      │
│  Save this document as:      ┌──────────┐      │
│  ┌──────────────────────┐    │  Cancel  │      │
│  │ Mascot               │    └──────────┘      │
│  └──────────────────────┘    ┌──────────┐      │
│  Format: [ TIFF      ] ▼     │  Save    │      │
│                              └──────────┘      │
└──────────────────────────────────────────────┘
```

2. **Enter a name into the Save this Document as option box.**

   You can enter any name up to 31 characters long, putting periods and spaces anywhere you want them. Personally, I like to keep my filenames below 20 characters so that I can see them in their entirety at the Finder level. Longer filenames become abbreviated when viewed by name. For example, FamilyReunion.UnpleasantBrawl may appear as FamilyReunion.Unpleasan... at the Finder. You also have the option of adding a three-character file extension (such as TIF) that indicates the file format (explained shortly). This option is located in the Preferences dialog box under the Saving Files panel. You can choose Never, Always, or Ask When Saving.

Photoshop now lets you save a file with a lowercase extension. If Always is selected, a lowercase extension is automatically added, regardless of whether the lowercase option is checked in the Preferences dialog box. If Ask When Saving is selected, when you go to save the file, the Save dialog box shows check boxes for both Append and Use Lower Case. I recommend always using a lowercase extension. It makes for fewer problems when creating images for the Web. In addition, it allows you to share images with PC people or use the images on a PC yourself. Never in a zillion years, you say? Never say never.

3. **Select a format from the Format pop-up menu.**

   This is the point at which you have to deal with the image flavors I touch on in the introduction to this chapter. The pop-up menu provides all kinds of options, such as TIFF, JPEG, PICT, and others. I discuss the ramifications of the important formats later in this chapter.

   Some formats are restricted to certain kinds of images. For example, you can save only images that contain layers (as explained in Chapter 15) in the Photoshop format. If a format is grayed out in the Save As pop-up menu, that format isn't available for the kind of image you're trying to save.

4. **Use the Desktop button, folder bar, and any other controls to hunt down the folder in which you want to save the image.**

   These controls are explained in Chapter 3.

5. **Click on the Save button or press Return.**

   Watch out. If the button with the heavy outline reads Open instead of Save, Photoshop selects a folder in the central list. If you press the Tab key to activate the filename, the button automatically changes back to Save. Then you can press Return.

6. **If another dialog box appears, fill out the options and press Return.**

   Most formats present additional dialog boxes that enable you to modify the way the image is saved. I explain this later in more detail.

Your image is now saved! Come heck or high water, you're protected.

Version 5 gives you the option to save thumbnails in Windows format as well as Macintosh format. I recommend saving both Macintosh and Windows thumbnail options. Again, it allows for easier use on the PC. Remember, never say never.

To make sure Photoshop always saves thumbnail previews of your images to be viewed in the Open dialog box, select the Always option in the Saving Files panel in the Preferences dialog box under File. If you choose the Ask When Saving option, check boxes appear in the Save and Save As dialog boxes allowing you to make your decision then. The only time not to save a preview is when you're extremely limited on disk space; saving images with previews requires a bit more disk space than saving them without previews. The file-saving process also takes longer when you save with previews.

Joining the frequent-saver program

After you name your image and save it to disk for the first time, press ⌘-S or choose File⇨Save every time you think of it. In either case, Photoshop updates your image on disk, without any dialog boxes or options popping up and demanding your attention. Then, when something goes wrong — notice that I said when, not if — you won't lose hours of work. A few minutes, maybe, but that comes with the territory.

Creating a backup copy

If it takes longer than a day to create an image, you should make backup copies. The reasoning is that if you invest lots of time in an image, you're that much worse off if you lose it. By creating backup copies — Dog1, Dog2, Dog3, and so on, one for each day that you work on the project — you're that much less likely to lose mass quantities of edits. If some disk error occurs or you accidentally delete one or two of the files, one of the backups will probably survive the disaster, further protecting you from developing an ulcer or having to seek therapy.

At the end of the day, choose File⇨Save As. The Save dialog box appears, as when you first saved the image. Change the filename slightly and click on the Save button. Want to be doubly protected? More protection, you say? Save to another disk entirely. If the whole disk goes bad, you've got another. Triple protection!

You can also use the Save a Copy command to make a backup copy of an image, but that command offers a few extra options specifically designed for saving images that have multiple layers. Ignore it for now. For more information on working with layers, see Chapter 15.

Photoshopper's Guide to File Formats

Even though the Format pop-up menu appears at the bottom of the Save As dialog box — as though it were an afterthought or something — selecting a format is a critical decision. So, you need to pay attention to the sections to come, even if the subject is a rather dry one — which it is. Get a Jolt cola if you need one, but don't skip this information.

What is a file format, anyway?

Glad you asked. A *file format* is a way of saving the electronic bits and pieces that make up a computer file. Different formats structure those bits and pieces differently. In Photoshop, you can choose from about a zillion file formats when you save your image to disk, which makes things a tad bit confusing.

Luckily, you can ignore most of the file format options. The Amiga IFF and Raw formats, for example, sacrifice colors and other image information, so avoid them. The Pixar, Targa, and Scitex CT formats are very sophisticated formats used by very sophisticated (and well-funded) creative types, so you can forget about those formats, too. In fact, you probably will have use for only a handful of formats: TIFF, JPEG, EPS, PICT, and the native Photoshop format. If you plan on publishing your image on the World Wide Web, you may also want to use the CompuServe GIF format at times, too.

TIFF: The great communicator

One of the best and most useful formats for saving Photoshop images is TIFF (pronounced *tiph*), which stands for Tagged Image File Format. TIFF was developed to serve as a platform-independent standard so that both Macintosh and Windows programs could take advantage of it. TIFF is an excellent file format to use for printed images. It can be imported into virtually every page layout and most drawing programs.

When you select the TIFF option from the Format pop-up menu and click on the Save button, Photoshop displays the TIFF Options dialog box. In the area labeled Byte Order, you can tell Photoshop whether to save the TIFF image for use on a Macintosh or Windows program. Unless you're going to open your image in a Windows program, select Macintosh. (Why are these options labeled Byte Order? Just to confuse you.)

The TIFF Options dialog box also offers a check box labeled LZW Compression. If you check the box, Photoshop compresses your image file so that it takes up less room on disk. Unlike some types of compression, LZW Compression doesn't sacrifice any data to make your file smaller. It's known as a *lossless compression scheme.*

Most programs that support TIFF also support LZW. For example, you can import a compressed TIFF image into either PageMaker or QuarkXPress. (For more information on these two programs, check out *PageMaker 6 For Macs For Dummies,* 2nd Edition, by Galen Gruman and yours truly; and *QuarkXPress 4 For Dummies,* by Barbara Assadi and Galen Gruman, with John Cruise — both published by IDG Books Worldwide, Inc.)

JPEG: The space saver

Photoshop also supports the JPEG (pronounced *jay peg*) format. JPEG stands for some Joint Photographers convention, but that doesn't really matter. What matters is that the JPEG format uses *lossy compression*. Lossy is the computer nerd's way of saying that stuff is lost during the compression process — namely, some of the data that makes up your image.

The good news, however, is that you probably won't miss what's not around anymore — sort of like when you were a kid and you "lost" your little brother at the park. You may notice a slight difference in your on-screen image after you save the file using JPEG, but when the image is printed, the compression is usually undetectable.

Like LZW compression, JPEG compression saves you lots of disk space. In fact, a JPEG image takes up less space on disk than a compressed TIFF file — half as much space, maybe a tenth as much, depending on your settings. Although JPEG isn't supported by as many programs as TIFF is, it's becoming more and more common.

So should you use JPEG or TIFF? My philosophy is this: Save in TIFF when you're editing an image or when excellent print quality is vital, for example, in high resolution printing (see Chapter 4). Then, when you think you're finished editing and you want to conserve space, save in JPEG at the Maximum setting. You generally won't see the results of JPEG right away. But editing an image can bring out its weaknesses, and JPEG definitely weakens an image. So, it's best to go to JPEG after you finish editing. This is not a hard-and-fast rule — I've edited plenty of JPEG images without incident — but it's good to be aware of the risks.

Also, if you want to distribute your image on the World Wide Web, you have to save it in either the JPEG, GIF, or the new and not yet widely supported PNG format. JPEG works well with Photographic images, especially people, where there is a wide range of colors. TIFF isn't an option for Web publishing.

When you choose the JPEG option in the Format dialog box and press Return, the dialog box shown in Figure 6-2 appears. Here's a rundown of the options you need to worry about:

- ✔ The Quality pop-up menu lets you choose the amount of compression that is applied to your image and therefore the quality of your saved image. The higher the image quality, the less the file is compressed and the more space it takes on disk.

- ✔ The Quality option box and the slider bar beneath the box give you other ways to choose your compression setting. The slider bar and option box give you access to 11 settings (0 through 10), whereas the pop-up menu gives you access to only four. But, unless you're a real control freak like me, you can just select one of the pop-up menu options.

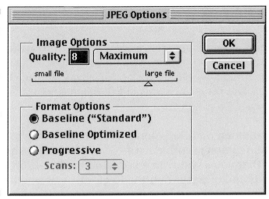

Figure 6-2:
When
saving a
JPEG file,
select the
Maximum
option or, if
space is
limited,
select the
High option.

✔ For print images, choose the Maximum or High option from the Quality pop-up menu. The Maximum option is best because it preserves the most image data, but High is okay if you're really short on disk space.

✔ If you plan to publish your image on the World Wide Web, choose the Medium option from the pop-up menu. The Medium option is the standard because it can retain a fair amount of image data while substantially reducing file size. But, before you save your image using this option, make a backup copy using the Maximum or High setting. Because of the amount of image data that is dumped with the Medium setting, you won't be able to successfully edit the image after you save it using that setting.

✔ Another option for images published on the Web is to save them as progressive JPEG files. A progressive image initially appears on the Web-surfer's monitor at a very low quality and then improves as more and more image data is downloaded. If you want to save your image in this way, select the Progressive radio button at the bottom of the dialog box. The Scans pop-up menu lets you choose the number of intermediate images the browser displays before the image appears in full. Be aware that a few older browsers do not support progressive images.

✔ If you want to save an image for the Web, but you don't want to create a progressive image, choose the Baseline Optimized radio button. For regular print graphics — that is, graphics that aren't going to be distributed over the Web — use the default setting of Baseline ("Standard").

Photoshop recompresses a JPEG image every time you save it. During a single edit session, this won't hurt because JPEG works from the on-screen version. But, if you close, reopen, and resave it in JPEG format, some damage, albeit small, will occur. Repeat this process over and over, however, and the damage increases each time. Some advice — apply all your edited work, save in JPEG format, and leave well enough alone.

GIF: For Webbies only

GIF, which was developed for CompuServe specifically for transferring images via modem, is one of two options you can consider when you want to distribute your image online, whether on CompuServe, America Online, or the World Wide Web. (The other format is JPEG, discussed in the preceding section.)

Computer hacks are divided on how you pronounce GIF. Some folks swear that the proper pronunciation is with a hard "G" — as in one *t* short of a *gift*. Other experts insist that you say it with a soft *g,* so that the word sounds just like that famous brand of peanut butter. Regardless of which camp you decide to join, GIF is best used for high-contrast images, illustrations created in Photoshop or imported from a drawing program, screen shots, and text. The biggest drawback to GIF is that it can save only images with 256 colors or less. However, it is the format you want to use for simple — no computer programming skills required — animations, called *animated GIFs.* These can be easily created using shareware programs that are downloadable from the Web, such as GIF Builder.

If your image contains more than 256 colors, choose Image➪Mode➪ Indexed Color to reduce the number of colors before you save in the GIF format. In the Indexed Color dialog box, choose Adaptive from the Palette pop-up menu. For Color Depth, start with the lowest possible setting (the smallest number of bits per pixel), and see what happens to your image. Use the lowest setting that keeps your image reasonably intact. You may find that photographic images, especially those with a wide range of colors, will require a higher setting than either non-photographic images or photos with a limited color range.

You need to do similar experimentation with the Dither option. The best choice is None, but if that setting wrecks your image, choose Diffusion. You can ignore the Colors setting entirely; Photoshop handles that one for you automatically. Under Color Matching, the Best option ensures that color conversion and dithering are accurate. By choosing the Faster option, color conversion and dithering are a little less accurate, but much faster. Keep Preserve Exact Colors checked on. By doing this, colors in your image that are also in the palette are not dithered; therefore lines, text, and other small details in your Web images have better on-screen quality.

Version 5 now lets you preview the Indexed Color mode change in the dialog box. This allows for experimentation with color depth and dithering and prevents a lot of Edit to Undos.

When you save an image to the GIF format, you're presented with a dialog box containing just two radio buttons, Normal and Interlaced. The Interlaced setting results in an image that appears gradually when it is downloaded, like a progressive JPEG image. If you don't want your image to be downloaded in this way, choose Normal.

The GIF format also enables you to create images that include transparent areas that allow other parts of your Web page to show through. If you want to give this trick a try, see the sidebar, "Meet GIF89a."

EPS: The 10 percent solution

EPS (pronounced *E-P-S*) stands for Encapsulated PostScript. PostScript is a page-description language used by printers such as LaserWriters, Linotronic imagesetters, and hundreds of others. Although TIFF and JPEG can save only images, the EPS format accommodates anything that the printer can print. Unfortunately, an EPS image takes up considerably more disk space than the same image saved in the TIFF format — even more if the TIFF image is compressed.

For the most part, EPS is used by high-end professionals producing high-end projects — for example if you want to create expert color separations (see Chapter 7) from QuarkXPress. Laymen, however, will want to save in EPS format for images with clipping paths, where a selected portion of the image is transparent (explained in Chapter 12). In addition, EPS is the format of choice for importing to and from drawing programs such as Illustrator, FreeHand, and CorelDraw. By and large, however, you can ignore the EPS format 90 percent of the time and use TIFF instead.

PICT: The generic picture format

Apple developed PICT as the primary format for Macintosh graphics. Just as EPS is based on the PostScript printer language, PICT is based on the QuickDraw screen language. Although you may assume that PICT would be the best option for Mac graphics, it can be a rather shaky format. Just about every Macintosh graphics program supports PICT, but support varies. PageMaker, for example, does a terrible job of printing imported PICT images.

I sometimes choose PICT if I am going to be using the image only in Photoshop, however, because it offers JPEG compression. Say that you select the PICT File option from the Format pop-up menu in the Save dialog box and press Return. Assuming that QuickTime is running — Apple's digital video system extension that installs with Photoshop — the dialog box shown in Figure 6-3 appears.

Meet GIF89a

Photoshop 5 includes a command on the File➪Export menu that enables you to create a transparent GIF image for use on the World Wide Web. Using this command — which has the user-friendly name of GIF89a Export — you can make portions of an image transparent so that a background pattern on your Web page can be seen through the image.

After choosing the Indexed Color command to reduce your image to 256 colors, as described in the section, "GIF: For Webbies only," choose File➪Export➪GIF89a Export. In the dialog box that appears, click in the image preview on each color that you want to make transparent (cursor will look like an eyedropper). Or click on the color swatches at the bottom of the dialog box. ⌘-click on a color if you change your mind and want to make the color opaque again. To restore all colors in the image, hold down the Option key, and click on Reset.

Notice the zoom and hand tools to help you navigate through the image. If you choose the Interlace check box, your image is drawn incrementally when a Web surfer downloads it, just like a progressive JPEG image. If you check the Export Caption option, any captions entered via the File Info dialog box under the File menu will appear in the GIF header. (Captions are mainly used by the newspaper folks.)

After you press Return to exit the dialog box, Photoshop prompts you to save the image by displaying a dialog box that looks and works just like the regular Save As dialog box (but has the name Export to GIF File). Give your image a name, specify where you want to store the image on disk, click on Save, and you're done.

PICT-formatted images are mostly used for graphics to be incorporated into slides, screen presentations (like PowerPoint), multimedia projects, and digital video.

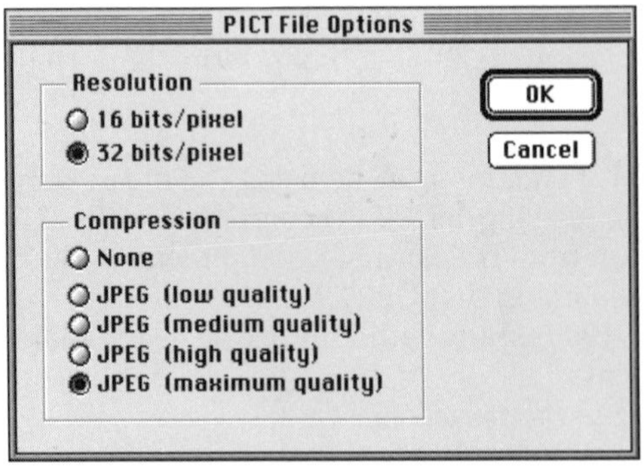

PICT File Options

Resolution
○ 16 bits/pixel
● 32 bits/pixel

[OK]
[Cancel]

Compression
○ None
○ JPEG (low quality)
○ JPEG (medium quality)
○ JPEG (high quality)
● JPEG (maximum quality)

Figure 6-3: The PICT format offers JPEG compression options.

If you're saving a grayscale image, the Resolution options are 2, 4, and 8 bits per pixel rather than the 16 and 32 bit per pixel options shown in Figure 6-4. But regardless of which Resolution options you see in the dialog box, don't change them! Doing so deletes colors from your image and prevents you from accessing the JPEG options.

The JPEG compression options available to PICT files are different than those available to the regular JPEG format. JPEG compression in a PICT file can cause more damage over time — nothing serious, just something to keep in mind. I suggest always selecting the JPEG (Maximum Quality) in the PICT File Options dialog box.

What about the native Photoshop format?

The Save As pop-up menu in the Save As dialog box offers one other important format choice: the native Photoshop format.

The Photoshop format is the only format that saves the layers in your image; all the others "flatten" (merge) the layers together.

If you need to open a Photoshop 5 image in earlier versions of the program, you can use the Photoshop format without worry. Versions 3 and 4 can open files saved in the Version 5 native format.

Like TIFF, the Photoshop formats offer a lossless compression scheme. And Photoshop can open and save images faster in its native format than in any other format. But very few programs other than Photoshop support the native format. So use the native format when you don't plan to import the image into another program and you don't need JPEG compression.

Make sure, really sure, absolutely sure, that you do not check the option Include Composited Image with Layered Files in the Saving Files panel in the Preferences dialog box.

This option inserts a flattened (merged) version of the image in your file, which tremendously increases the file size. The option is supposed to ensure compatibility between Photoshop and programs that support the Photoshop file format, but not layers. However, it is not worth the tremendous increase it creates in the file size. If you want to be able to use the image in other applications, save a copy of the image in a TIFF or JPEG format.

What format to use when

Ooh, you cheated, didn't you? You skipped right over the sections on how formats work and why they were invented. Instead of reading all that juicy background information I offered up — information that would help you make your own decision about which format to use — you want me to make the decision for you.

Okay, fine. You plunked down good money so that I would make things easy for you, so I suppose that I can give you a break just this once. Think of the following list as your Cliff's Notes to File Formats. Just don't blame me when you're standing around at a cocktail party and the discussion turns to JPEG compression versus TIFF, and you don't have an intelligent word to offer.

- ✔ If you are just going to use the image in Photoshop, save it in the Photoshop format. You can open images saved in this format in Versions 3, 4, and 5. You can open images in Version 2.5 as well (if you turn on the Include Composited Image with Layered Files option in the Preferences dialog box, as discussed in the preceding section), but layers, grids, and guides won't be available to you in Version 2.5.

- ✔ If your image contains layers (as explained in Chapter 15) and you want to preserve those layers, choose the Photoshop format.

- ✔ If you want to import your image into another program, use TIFF, as long as you have the available disk space.

- ✔ If you want to import your image into another program and you don't have the available disk space, use JPEG.

- ✔ If you want to import your image into a program that doesn't support either TIFF or JPEG or you have a clipping path, resort to EPS.

- ✔ If you're creating a photograph for online distribution, use JPEG. For high-contrast graphics or partially transparent images, use GIF.

Good Night, Image — Don't Let the Programming Bugs Bite

To put Photoshop to bed for the night, choose File⇨Quit or press ⌘-Q (as in quit). Photoshop may display a message asking you whether you want it to save the changes you made to your image. Unless you have some reason for doing otherwise, press Return to select the Save button. The program quits, leaving you back at the Finder.

If you don't want to save your changes, press the D key, which is the same as clicking on the Cancel button. This not only cancels any saving that may have occurred, but the quitting as well. Photoshop continues to run as though ⌘-Q were nothing more than a bad dream.

Chapter 7

Going to Hard Copy

· ·

In This Chapter

▶ Making sure that your printer is ready to go

▶ Previewing the image on the page

▶ Selecting a printer, paper size, and page orientation

▶ Using the Page Setup command

▶ Printing multiple copies

▶ Printing a contact sheet

▶ Making CMYK color separations

▶ Creating spot color separations

· ·

*I*n case you don't already know, *hard copy* is a term for the printed page. The on-screen image is just a figment of your computer's imagination. The final printed piece is something tangible that you can really sink your teeth into (assuming that you're extremely hungry).

In this chapter, I explain how to go from on-screen, imaginary image to hard copy. But I have to confess that there's a lot that I don't know. For example, I don't know what kind of printer you're using, I don't know what kind of cabling is installed, and I don't even know where the printer is located in your home or office. In other words, I'm suffering from a terrific deficit of knowledge. With this in mind, I ask for your sympathy and understanding as I explain — very briefly — how to print from Photoshop using an everyday, generic printer.

For starters, I am going to be totally rash and assume the following:

▸ **You have a printer.** If I've said it once, I've said it, I don't know, two or three times: You must have a printer to print.

▸ **Your printer is plugged in,** it's turned on, and it doesn't have a 16-ton weight sitting on top of it. In other words, your printer works.

▸ **The printer is properly connected to your computer.** A cable running out of your computer and into your printer is a good sign.

▸ **The proper printer software is installed on your computer.**

> ✔ Your printer is stocked with ribbon, ink, toner, paper, film, chew toys, little bits of felt, spring-like gizmos that go "bazoing," or whatever else is required in the way of raw materials.

If you've used your printer before, everything is probably ready to go. But if something goes wrong, I advise that you call your local printer wizard and ask for assistance. Or you can try walking into the boardroom and wringing your hands and weeping in a cloying but professional way. This strategy has been known to produce the desired effects.

This May Be All You Need to Know

When things are in working order, printing is not a difficult process. Though it involves slightly more than picking up your mouse and saying "print" into it, printing does not require a whole lot of preparation. In fact, a quick perusal of the following steps may be all you need to get up to speed:

1. **Turn on your printer.**

   And don't forget to remove that printer cozy your uncle knitted for you.

2. **Select the printer you want to use with the Chooser.**

   If your Mac is on a network, you may have access to more than one printer. If not, skip this step. (By the way, the following sections in this chapter explain this step and others in more detail, should you need more information.)

3. **Check that the image fits on the page.**

   Press and hold on the page preview box in the lower-left corner of the image window to see a little preview of the printed page. The page preview box is just to the right of the magnification box. (If you can't remember where the preview box is located, see Chapter 3 for a refresher.)

   If the image doesn't fit on the page or if you want to change its size or orientation, move on to Step 4. Otherwise, skip ahead to Step 5.

4. **Choose File⇨Page Setup or choose ⌘-Shift-P.**

   This command lets you change the size and orientation of the printed image. You can also change the printed size and resolution using Image⇨Image Size, as discussed in Chapter 4, but this command affects the image permanently, while the Page Setup command just affects how the image prints.

5. **Choose File⇨Save or press ⌘-S.**

   Although this step is only a precaution, it's always a good idea to save your image immediately before you print it because the print process is one of those ideal opportunities for your computer to crash. Your computer derives a unique kind of satisfaction by delivering works of art from the printer and then locking up at the last minute, all the while knowing that the image on disk is several hours behind the times. If you weren't the brunt of the joke, you'd probably think that it was amusing, too.

6. **Choose File⇨Print or press ⌘-P.**

   The print dialog box lets you request multiple copies of an image or print colors on separate sheets of paper.

7. **Press Return.**

   Experts say that this is the easiest step. Well, one guy got a blister on the end of his finger, but otherwise the vote was unanimous.

Congratulations! You now have what is commonly known as a brand-new, 1-gram-baby piece of output. But on the off chance that you're unclear on how a couple of the preceding steps work or you're simply interested in excavating every possible nugget of information from this book, I encourage you to probe the depths of the rest of this chapter.

Choosing a Printer

If you use the same printer day in and day out to produce pages of text and numbers, you probably don't need to worry about the Chooser. Provided with every Mac, this little program is designed to let you confirm the connection to your printer and select a different printer over a network. So, unless you just want to make sure that everything's A-OK or you want to specify the exact printer you intend to use, skip to the next section.

To access the Chooser dialog box shown in Figure 7-1, select the Chooser command from the Apple menu. The left side of the dialog box contains a bunch of icons that represents the kinds of printer drivers that are available to your system. Not to be confused with the drivers that allow you to knock golf balls into uncooperative printers, these drivers serve as a liaison between your computer and your printer.

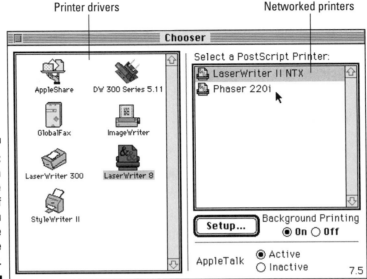

Printer drivers

Networked printers

Figure 7-1:
You can
select the
kind of
printer you
want to use
from the
Chooser.

If you use a PostScript device — meaning a printer that supports the PostScript printer language — select the LaserWriter driver icon. Nearly every printer over $1,000 supports PostScript, which is, without a doubt, the professional printing standard.

If you see a driver icon that matches your specific model of printer, select it. For example, I recently bought a portable HP DeskWriter 320 for use with my PowerBook. Figure 7-1 shows an icon labeled DW 300 Series 5.11, which happens to look just like my little printer. I'd be plum crazy not to select it.

Some fax/modems allow you to print to remote fax machines over the phone lines. If you own a fax/modem and it's cabled up correctly, you may be able to select a driver icon for the modem, such as the GlobalFax icon in Figure 7-1.

After you select a driver from the left-hand list, some additional options appear on the right side of the dialog box.

If you're on a network, you see a list of networked printers, as in Figure 7-1. Select the printer you want to use by clicking on it.

If you're not on a network, you are more likely to see two icons labeled Select a Printer Port. The first icon represents the printer port; the second represents the modem port. Select the port into which the printer cable is plugged. More likely, your printer is hooked up to the printer port, but some people do use the modem port.

After you finish doing all that stuff, click on the close box on the left side of the Chooser title bar. A message may appear telling you to confirm your settings using the Page Setup command. Don't worry, the next section explains how to do exactly that.

If any other message appears — one announcing that the printer is not available or has taken leave of its senses, for example — you very likely have a cabling problem or your printer is not turned on. Otherwise, you're in business.

Getting Image and Paper in Sync

Before you send your image to the printer, you need to make sure that the image you want to print actually fits on a piece of paper. To see whether all is well in this regard, click and hold on the page preview box in the lower-left corner of the image window. As shown in Figure 7-2, Photoshop displays a preview of how your image fits on your chosen paper size.

Figure 7-2: You can preview how the image fits on the page by clicking and holding on the page preview box (hidden by the preview in the figure).

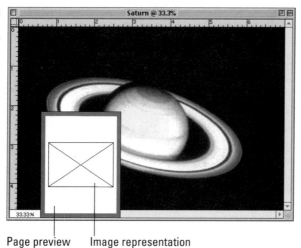

Page preview   Image representation

The white area in the page preview represents the size of the page; the rectangle with an X through it represents the image. (All right, so the image preview isn't particularly accurate when it comes to showing actual images, but it's good enough for showing the dimensions.) If the rectangle with an X fits entirely inside the white area, as in Figure 7-2, your image fits on the page. If the X exceeds the boundaries of the white area, the image is too big for the page and needs to be reduced. After you know whether the image fits or not, you can release your mouse button.

If the image doesn't fit, you have some work to do. One way to get the image to fit the paper is to reduce the image size. Another possibility is to rotate the image on the page. For example, if the image is wider than it is tall, you could print it horizontally by rotating the page 90 degrees. Here's a closer look at these two options:

✔ To rotate the image on the page, choose File⇨Page Setup or press ⌘-Shift-P to display the Page Setup dialog box. Though your dialog box may not look exactly like the one shown in Figure 7-3, you should find two Orientation icons, one with a guy standing up and another with a guy on his side like a felled tree. Select the guy on his side to rotate the image on the page.

Figure 7-3:
Not all Page Setup dialog boxes look the same, but most let you rotate and scale an image for printing purposes.

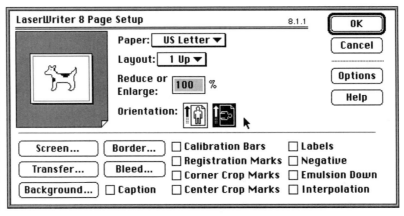

✔ The specific options found inside the Page Setup dialog box vary depending on the kind of printer you're using, but you can generally find a Reduce or Enlarge option box. Enter any percentage below 100% to reduce the dimensions of the printed image. The printer still prints all pixels in the image; the pixels are just smaller.

✔ If you can't find a Reduce or Enlarge option, you have to abandon the Page Setup dialog box and choose Image⇨Image Size instead. Be sure to deselect the Resample Image check box so that you don't affect the number of pixels in the image. Then increase the Resolution value or decrease the values in the Print Size Width and Height option boxes. (You can find a complete explanation of the Image Size dialog box in Chapter 4.)

After trying one of these options, click and hold on the page preview box again to see whether you're making any progress. If the image still doesn't fit, move on to the second option, and give it a try.

Keep in mind that changes made inside the Page Setup dialog box have absolutely no effect on anything except how your image prints. You can't do any permanent damage via this particular dialog box, so feel free to change settings recklessly and without regard to personal safety.

Changes made inside the Image Size dialog box are another story. As I explain in Chapter 4, you can easily do permanent damage if you forget to deselect the Resample Image check box.

Sending the Image to the Printer

After you confirm that the image fits inside the page, choose File⇨Print or press ⌘-P. If the image is still too large for the page, an error message appears, asking whether you want to proceed. If the image fits, the print dialog box appears, much like the one shown in Figure 7-4.

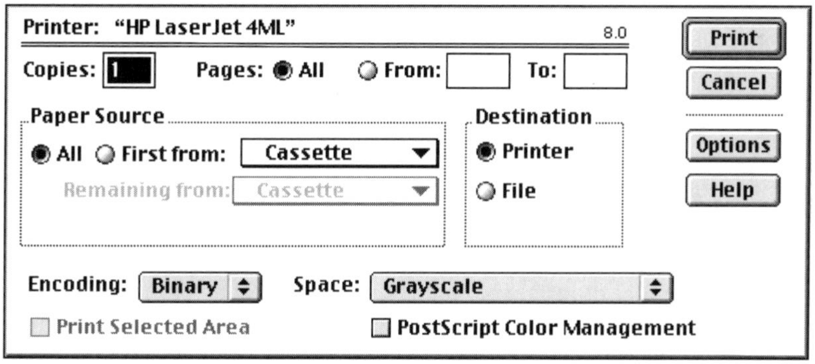

Figure 7-4:
The mostly irrelevant print dialog box.

| Printer: "HP LaserJet 4ML" | 8.0 | Print |

Copies: 1   Pages: ● All   ○ From: [   ] To: [   ]   Cancel

Paper Source
● All ○ First from: [Cassette ▼]
Remaining from: [Cassette ▼]

Destination
● Printer
○ File

Options
Help

Encoding: [Binary ▲▼]   Space: [Grayscale ▲▼]
☐ Print Selected Area   ☐ PostScript Color Management

What I love about the print dialog box is that you can ignore some of it. However, a few of the options are useful:

- ✔ If you want to print more than one copy of the image, enter the number of copies you want into the Copies option box.

- ✔ If you selected a portion of your image by using one of the tools I don't get around to discussing until Chapter 12, you can print the selected area only by selecting the Print Selected Area check box. If you just want to take a quick look at an isolated area, this option can save time.

✔ In Photoshop 4, you had the option of printing to the Grayscale, RGB, or CMYK settings. Due to improved color management, Version 5 gives you a multitude of choices of what it refers to as *color spaces*. In addition to the Grayscale, RGB, or CMYK settings, there are settings for monitors and printers. Your first choice should be the setting for your particular printer. If you can't find it in the list, check the documentation that came with your printer for the manufacturer's recommendation. If you can't find your documentation, stick to RGB. Most desktop color printers will print well in RGB. However, if you don't have anything better to do, experiment with other color spaces, and compare the output results.

✔ The CMYK option doesn't create color separations, incidentally. To accomplish that feat, read the next section.

✔ If you want to print your color image in grayscale, don't choose the Grayscale color space in the print dialog box. Instead, convert the image to grayscale as described in Chapter 5. Your file will print much faster.

That's it. Don't worry about the other options in the dialog box. Just click on the OK button or press Return, and you're off. Depending on the size of the image, it should print in a matter of a few minutes.

Creating and Printing a Contact Sheet

Photoshop 5 has provided the capability for creating a digital version of a traditional contact sheet. This new feature takes a folder of images, creates thumbnails, and arranges them on a single page. This feature is good for record-keeping because it allows you to catalog large quantities of files. It is also useful for merely checking out a big batch of images.

Here are the steps for creating and printing a contact sheet:

1. **Choose File⇨Automate⇨Contact Sheet.**

2. **Click the Choose button in the Contact Sheet dialog box.**

   Locate the folder containing the images you want to print (see Figure 7-5). Count the number of images in your folder.

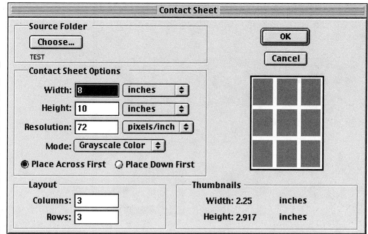

3. **Specify the size and resolution of the contact sheet.**

   Be sure to set the width and height large enough to accommodate all of your images. If you are unsure about the resolution setting, see Chapter 4 for details.

4. **Specify a color mode — Grayscale, CMYK, or RGB.**

   For information on color modes, see Chapter 5.

5. **Specify the order and the number of columns and rows for your layout.**

   Again, make sure the number of thumbnails you create can accommodate (or exceeds) the number of images in your folder.

6. **Press Return or click on OK.**

   An automated process opens, copies, pastes, and positions each file. Depending on the number of images, this process could take a few minutes. When the process is completed, you should see a file similar to the one in Figure 7-6.

7. **Save the contact sheet and print using the guidelines in this chapter.**

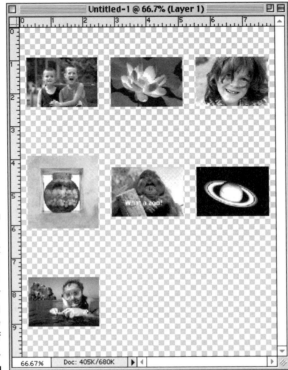

Untitled-1 @ 66.7% (Layer 1)

66.67%   Doc: 405K/680K

Figure 7-6:
Contact
sheets can
be a good
method for
cataloging
a large
quantity of
images.

Printing Color Separations

So far, I've explained how to print *composite* images, in which all colors are combined together on a single page from your desktop printer. Unfortunately, color printing on a desktop printer may not be the best route to go if you intend on having more than 50 copies or so. Although desktop color printers are becoming more economical, they can be very slow, and in some cases, the quality may not be up to par. An increasingly popular intermediate step is short run, on-demand *digital printing,* such as Spontane or Indigo prints. Digital printing takes your file directly from the disk to print, without the use of *color separations* (see following section). The quality is very good, and the cost can be reasonable.

Creating CMYK separations

After the quantity is 500 copies or more, it's wise to look into traditional offset printing. For this, you need to produce color separations. You print four pages, one each for the primary printing colors: cyan, magenta, yellow, and black. Then you let your commercial printer — the person, not the machine — combine the color separations to create mass quantities of colorful pages. This process is the same one used to create magazines, newspapers, and other professional color publications.

To print color separations of a full-color image from Photoshop, you have to go through these steps:

1. **Save your image to disk.**

   Before diving into CMYK, you want to make sure that your RGB image is backed up and safe from harm. If you need help, Chapter 6 provides assistance with the saving process.

2. **Choose the final printer.**

   Click File⇨Color Settings⇨CMYK Setup and tell Photoshop what kind of printer you intend to use. The CMYK Setup dialog box may seem complex and maybe even incomprehensible. I recommend talking to your commercial printer and finding out what settings he recommends. He may even provide a disk with the information that you can load.

3. **Choose Image⇨Mode⇨CMYK Color.**

   Photoshop converts the image from the world of RGB to the world of CMYK. After the conversion, you have a four-channel image with one channel each for cyan, magenta, yellow, and black. You can even view the channels if you want by pressing ⌘-1, ⌘-2, ⌘-3, and ⌘-4. (This channel thing is explained in Chapter 5.)

4. **Choose File⇨Page Setup and check Calibration Bars, Registration Marks, Corner Crop Marks, Center Crop Marks, and Labels, as shown in Figure 7-7. Press Return.**

   These five options print a series of alignment markings that will prove very useful to your commercial printer. (If you're printing to a non-PostScript printer, some of these options may not be available; select the ones that are.)

   Be sure to select all these check boxes. If you miss any of them, your commercial printer may have problems lining up the images on the press, and your pages may come out like a page from the Sunday comics.

5. **Choose File⇨Print and in the Print dialog box, select Separations in the Space option, as shown in Figure 7-7.**

   Selecting this option tells Photoshop to print each of the channels from the image to a separate page.

6. **Click on Print or press Return.**

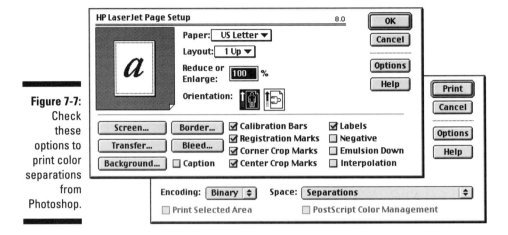

Figure 7-7:
Check
these
options to
print color
separations
from
Photoshop.

When printed, each page looks like a standard black-and-white printout, but don't let that worry you. When you take your file to your commercial printer, a technician prints your file on plastic material, referred to as *film,* which is then transferred onto sheets of metal called *plates.* Each plate is inked with cyan, magenta, yellow, or black ink. The technician prints all the pages with the cyan plate first, then runs the pages by the magenta plate, then the yellow plate, and finally the black plate. The inks mix together to form a rainbow of greens, violets, oranges, and other colors.

For example, Figure 7-8 shows four color separations for the full-color photograph that appears in Color Plate 5-1. (Compare these separations to the red, green, and blue channels I included in Chapter 5, Figure 5-2, to get a feel for the dramatic changes that occur when you convert from RGB to CMYK.) Color Plate 7-1 shows the separations as they appear when inked with cyan, magenta, yellow, and black. I also show a few examples of how the inks look when combined.

Creating spot color separations

Version 5 allows for *spot color separations* (to perform this feat in Version 4 special software was used). Spot, or *custom,* colors are predefined colors — that is, premixed inks made by various ink companies, the most popular in the U.S. being Pantone. A spot color is generally used for a logo, type, or small illustration. To output the additional separation, Photoshop adds a separate channel for the spot color, as shown in Figure 7-9.

Cyan

Magenta

Yellow

Black

Figure 7-8:
The black-
and-white
contents of
the cyan,
magenta,
yellow, and
black
channels as
they appear
when
printed to
separate
sheets of
paper.

To have Photoshop add a spot color to an image:

1. **Select the artwork or type to which you want to apply the spot color.**

   Use one of the selection methods described in Chapter 12. If you are
   applying the spot color to type, flatten the layers before making your
   selection. (See Chapter 15 for details on layers.)

2. **To fill the selection with white, choose Edit⇨Fill.**

   Press the D key to get your default colors. Choose Edit to Fill, and set
   the Use option to Background and the Opacity option to 100%.

   Or Press ⌘-Delete. Make sure that you don't deselect.

3. **Choose Window⇨Show Channels. Choose New Spot Channel from the
   Channels palette pop-up menu or press ⌘-click on the page icon at
   the bottom of the Channels palette.**

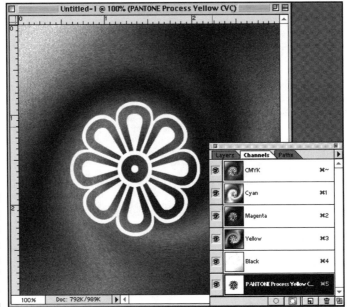

Figure 7-9:
Photoshop
now adds a
separate
channel for
spot colors.

4. Under the Ink Characteristics option, click on the color swatch in the New Spot Channel dialog box and select your Pantone color from the Custom Colors dialog box.

If you get the Color Picker instead, click on the Custom button.

5. Click on OK twice.

A new channel is added for the spot color, and your selection is filled.

6. Save the image as either a native Photoshop or DCS 2.0 (Desktop Color Separations) format.

If you want to import the image into a different program, such as PageMaker or QuarkXPress, save in DCS 2.0 format. For more information on PageMaker and QuarkXpress, check out *PageMaker 6 For Macs For Dummies,* 2nd Edition, by Galen Gruman and yours truly, and *QuarkXPress 4 For Dummies,* by Barbara Assaidi and Galen Gruman, with John Cruise — both published by IDG Books Worldwide, Inc.

If you want to use spot colors, I highly recommend that you choose your color from a printed Pantone swatch book. Remember that your screen can only give you its best match to the printed color. For accuracy, the colors must be selected from the printed material.

Part III
Tiptoe through the Toolbox

The 5th Wave   By Rich Tennant

NATIONAL ENQUIRER
PHOTO IMAGING
WORKSHOP

"Remember, your Elvis should appear bald and slightly
hunched - nice Big Foot, Brad - keep your two-headed animals
in the shadows and your alien spacecrafts crisp and defined."

In this part . . .

In real life, a paintbrush is a fairly static tool. You dip it in paint and drag it across the canvas; in return, it paints a line. The line varies depending on how much you dab onto the brush and how hard you press, but your options are limited. In Photoshop, on the other hand, a single tool is capable of literally hundreds of variations. You can change the size of the brush tip, the angle of the brush, the translucency of the paint, and the way colors mix, all at the drop of a hat. You can even paint straight lines and change the brush strokes from hard-edged to soft.

If painting isn't your primary interest, Photoshop provides an assortment of editing tools for smearing colors, changing their focus, lightening or darkening pixels, and adjusting the intensity of colors. You'll also find a rubber stamp tool for cleaning up dust and hairs on an image and an eraser for eliminating mistakes. All these tools go beyond anything that's available in real life, providing a degree of flexibility and forgiveness that natural media simply do not offer.

But my favorite thing about Photoshop is the convenience. No wiping up spills, no soaking brushes, and no opening windows to clear the fumes. You just paint what you want and erase what you don't want. Everything you do on-screen is imaginary — until you print the image, you haven't changed one scrap of real-life material — so spills, stains, and fumes are a thing of the past. And when it comes time to clean up for the day, you just press ⌘+Q, and you're finished. Who says things aren't better now than they used to be?

Chapter 8

Paint Me Young, Beautiful, and Twisted

. . . .

In This Chapter

▶ Using the pencil, paintbrush, and airbrush

▶ Drawing straight lines with the painting tools

▶ Changing the brush size

▶ Creating your own custom brush

▶ Selecting brushes from the keyboard

▶ Creating translucent brush strokes

▶ Painting with strangely named brush modes

. . . .

*O*kay, here's a big assumption. As a novice or casual Photoshop user, you fall into one of two camps: artist or nonartist. Some people are so comfortable with a pencil or paintbrush that they feel like they were born with the device. But a much larger group of Photoshop users falls into a camp that modern sociologists call "artistically challenged."

Take this quick test to determine where you fall:

✔ After doodling in the phone book, are you so horrified by the results that you rip out the page, pour ketchup on it, and feed it to your dog?

✔ When you're asked to draw a map to your house, do you try to lie your way out of the situation by asserting that you have no idea where your house is located and you doubt very seriously that you live anywhere?

✔ Do you have recurring dreams in which you suddenly remember that today is the day your final project is due in the art class you've forgotten to attend all year? And as you attempt to quickly paint a lounging model, you notice that the model is fully clothed and you're the one who's naked?

If you answered "Yes" to any of the preceding questions, you can safely assume that you belong to the nonartist camp. If you answered "Yes" to any two of the questions, you are so firmly entrenched in the nonartistic tradition that completing a dot-to-dot picture seems like an immense and terrifying project. And if you answered "Yes" to two of the questions and "Oh, wow, I had that exact dream just last night!" to the third, I am obliged by the code of computer ethics to ask you one more question: Are you sure that your analyst isn't overcharging you?

Whatever your level of artistic skill, though, a time will probably come when you'll want to rub a couple of the Photoshop painting tools against an image. Sure, it'll be scary. But you'll be prepared, thanks to this chapter.

Doodling with the Pencil, Paintbrush, and Airbrush

Photoshop offers just three painting tools, the bare minimum for artists and nonartists alike. Shown in Figure 8-1, they work like so:

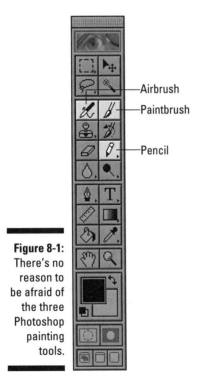

—Airbrush

—Paintbrush

—Pencil

Figure 8-1:
There's no
reason to
be afraid of
the three
Photoshop
painting
tools.

✔ The pencil tool draws hard-edged lines of any thickness.

✔ The paintbrush draws soft lines with slightly blurry edges to create more natural transitions.

✔ The airbrush paints soft lines like the paintbrush. The only difference is that this tool pumps out color continuously even when you hold it in place — as long as the mouse button is down. By contrast, the pencil and paintbrush tools paint only as you drag.

You can select each of the painting tools from the keyboard. Press J to select the airbrush, B to select the paintbrush, and N to select the pencil. In Photoshop 4, the Y key selected the pencil tool and the A key selected the airbrush. The Y key is now assigned to the history brush and the A key now selects the direct selection tool.

The pen tool, by the way, doesn't draw beautiful, flowing lines that look as though they're emanating from a kazillion-dollar status pen. In Photoshop, you use the pen tool to create *paths.* Paths enable you to select a portion of your image by creating a sort of connect-the-dots outline. The pen tool and paths are covered in detail in Chapter 12.

By default, Photoshop displays a little paintbrush, airbrush, or pencil cursor when you select the painting tools. If you press the Caps Lock key, however, the cursor changes to a crosshair cursor that makes it easier to see what you're doing. Use the crosshair when the standard cursor gets in your way. Press Caps Lock again to return to the standard cursor.

If you prefer, you can make your cursor match the brush size exactly. (The upcoming section, "Switching the brush size," explains how to change brush sizes.) To make the cursor reflect the brush size, press ⌘-K to display the Preferences dialog box. Then choose Display & Cursors from the top pop-up menu or press ⌘-3 to get to the cursor options. Select Brush Size from the Painting Cursors radio buttons, and press Return.

The painting tools are small, nonpoisonous, and good with children. So why not take them for a walk and see how you like them? The following steps show you how to use the paintbrush, pencil, and airbrush to create the friendly Mr. Sun image shown in Figure 8-4 (go ahead, flip forward to take a look).

1. **Choose File⇨New (or press ⌘-N) to create a new canvas.**

   Photoshop displays a dialog box that asks what size to make the new canvas. The dialog box offers Width, Height, and Resolution options, just like the Image Size dialog box discussed in Chapter 4.

2. **Make the canvas about 400 pixels wide by 400 pixels tall.**

   That's about 5^1/$_2$ x 5^1/$_2$ inches with a Resolution value of 72 ppi or 4 x 4 inches with a Resolution of 100 ppi. Alternatively, you can select Pixels from the Width and Height pop-up menus, enter **400** into each, and forget about the Resolution value. Also, choose the RGB Color option from the Mode pop-up menu.

3. **Press Return.**

   The new empty canvas appears in a new window.

4. **Select the paintbrush tool.**

   Click on its icon in the toolbox or press the B key. That's B for buff, as in, "Boy howdy, Biff, this brush is beaucoup buff!" That's what the programmers told me, anyway.

5. **Draw a circle in the middle of your new canvas.**

   A rude approximation of a circle is fine. Experts agree that a lumpy circle has more personality.

6. **Now paint some rays coming off the circle.**

   Figure 8-2 shows more or less how your image should look so far.

Figure 8-2:
The beginnings of a sun, drawn exclusively with the paintbrush tool.

Color Plate 5-1:
The red, green, and blue color channels in Photoshop act like slides in separate projectors pointed at the same spot on a screen. You may find it hard to believe that three primary hues could mix together to produce so many colors, but it's true.

Color Plate 7-1:
The cyan, magenta, and yellow channels as they appear when inked in their proper colors (top row). Each color channel takes on new depth and detail when combined with black (middle row). During the commercial printing process, the cyan image is first combined with magenta (bottom left), and then yellow (bottom center), and then black (bottom right).

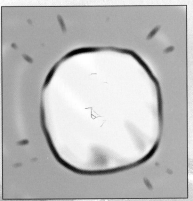

Multiply

Screen

Overlay

Difference

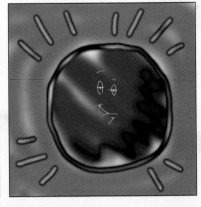

Color Plate 9-1:
Using the smudge tool, I turned a common, household-variety shark into a red-hot shark torpedo. In the Smudge Tool Options palette, I turned on the Finger Painting check box, set the brush mode to Color, and set the Pressure slider bar to 90%.

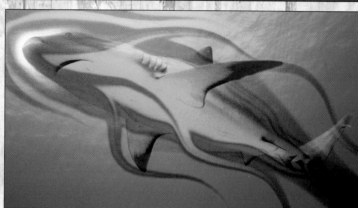

Color Plate 10-1:
By cloning from the top left image onto the bottom left image with the rubber stamp tool, I was able to merge the two images to create the strange but nonetheless believable specimen on the right.

Tolerance: 32

Tolerance: 90

Tolerance: 180

Color Plate 12-1:
By raising the Tolerance value in the Magic Wand Options palette, I instructed
Photoshop to select a wider range of colors around the point at which I clicked (just to
the right of the forward giraffe). In this case, 90 seems to be the best setting.

One base color, Fuzziness: 200

Color Plate 12-2:
The result of clicking just to the right of the monster's nose and applying the Color Range command with a Fuzziness setting of 200. In the right image, I filled the selection with white and then deselected it.

Three base colors, Fuzziness: 60

Color Plate 12-3:
By Shift-clicking in the image while inside the Color Range dialog box and lowering the Fuzziness value, I selected more of the blue sky and made the selection outline less blurry.

Color Plate 14-1:
I filled the area behind the jar with custom gradients created by using the Gradient Editor.

Color Plate 15-1:
To create this composition, I combined eight images and blended them together by using various modes and Opacity settings from the Layers palette. I selected all the images using the Color Range command, tinted the astronaut by using the Variations command, and erased, scaled, and rotated a few others.

7. Now select the pencil tool.

To access the pencil from the keyboard, press N, as in "Number 2 Pencil."

8. Draw a little face inside the sun.

Using the pencil, you get hard-edged lines, as in Figure 8-3.

Figure 8-3:
A face drawn with the pencil tool.

9. Select the airbrush tool.

Press J to access the airbrush from the keyboard.

10. Change the foreground color to orange.

Use the RGB slider bars in the Color palette (press F6 to display the palette). Max out the R slider to 255, set the G slider to 150, and leave the B slider at 0.

11. Click and hold — without moving your mouse — inside the sun.

Notice that the airbrush continuously pumps out paint. Neither the paintbrush nor the pencil do this.

12. Paint some shading in the lower-right region of the sun.

Figure 8-4 shows what I mean. The airbrush is useful for shading images. Of course, the real sun can't possibly have a shadow, but it doesn't have a face either, so I think that we can allow room for some personal expression.

Figure 8-4:
Use the
airbrush to
paint a
highly
unrealistic
shadow on
the sun.

That's good enough for now. You may want to save this image because I come back to it later in this chapter. Then again, if something goes wrong and you don't save the sun, no biggie. You can always re-create it or experiment with a different image.

Remember that at any stage in the previous exercise — or during any other painting mission you may embark on — you can eliminate the last brush stroke by choosing Edit⇨Undo or pressing ⌘-Z. Everyone makes mistakes, and the Undo command is there to correct those errors. If you need to undo back a few steps, you can use the History palette (see Chapter 11 for details).

Performing Special Painting-Tool Tricks

Dragging with a tool inside the image window is obviously the most common way to paint in Photoshop. But it's not the only way, as the following list makes clear:

✔ To create a straight line, click at one point in the image with any of the three painting tools, and Shift-click at another. Photoshop automatically creates a straight line between the two points.

✔ Continue Shift-clicking at various points in the image to create a straight-sided polygon. This method is great for creating triangles, five-pointed stars, and all sorts of other geometric shapes.

✔ To create a straight line that is exactly vertical or horizontal, click and hold with one of the painting tools, press and hold the Shift key, and then drag with the tool while the Shift key remains down. In other words, press Shift immediately after you begin to drag, and hold Shift throughout the length of the drag. If you release the Shift key while dragging, the line returns to its naturally free-form and wiggly ways.

✔ You can also use the line tool to draw straight lines. But using the Shift key in combination with the painting tools is usually a better option because the painting tools give you more flexibility. You can vary the softness of your lines if you use the painting tools, but you can't if you use the line tool. The only time I use the line tool is to create lines with arrowheads at the end. To create this kind of line, double-click on the line tool in the toolbox to display the Line Options palette, which contains options that enable you to specify the placement of the arrowhead, the shape of the arrowhead, and the width of your line. Then drag with the tool to create the line.

✔ Version 5 puts the line tool with the pencil tool. To toggle between the pencil and the line tools, press Shift-N.

✔ Option-click to lift a color from the image. Then drag to start painting with that color. Pressing Option when you're using a painting tool accesses the eyedropper.

Choosing Your Brush

If the preceding two sections covered everything there is to know about the painting tools, Photoshop would be a royal dud. But as we all know, Photoshop is not a dud — far from it — so there must be more to the painting tools than I've shown you so far. (This is classic Sherlock Holmes-style deductive reasoning at work here.)

You can modify all three tools to a degree that no mechanical pencil or conventional paintbrush can match. For starters, you can change the size and shape of the tip of the tool, as explained in the next few sections. You can draw thick strokes one moment and then turn around and draw thin strokes the next, all with the same tool.

Switching the brush size

To change one tool tip — called a brush size or just plain brush — for a different one, choose Window➪Show Brushes or press the F5 key. Photoshop displays the Brushes palette, shown in Figure 8-5. Here you can find a total of 16 brush sizes (assuming default settings), all free for the taking.

Figure 8-5:
The
Brushes
palette lets
you switch
one size
brush for
another.

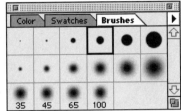

Figure 8-5: The Brushes palette lets you switch one size brush for another.

Most brush size icons are shown at actual size, but the last four are too large to fit inside their little boxes. The numbers below the icons represent the diameters of the brushes. (In case that year of high-school geometry has altogether removed itself from your brain, diameter is merely the width of a circle measured from side to opposite side.)

To change the brush size associated with the pencil, paintbrush, or airbrush tool, select the desired tool and click on an option in the Brushes palette. The left column of Figure 8-6 shows how each of the predefined brushes affects the performance of the paintbrush tool. (In each case, an icon from the Brushes palette is shown directly to the left of a stroke created with that brush.) Notice that the first six brushes have soft edges, whereas the remaining ten have downright blurry edges.

In Photoshop, soft edges are said to be *anti-aliased* (pronounced *an-tie-ay-lee-ast*), whereas blurry edges are *feathered.* Both terms are proof positive that computer professionals actually don't want to be understood by the greater public. They prefer to speak in their own private code.

Figure 8-6 also shows the effect of some of the brushes on the pencil and airbrush tools. As you can see, the pencil tool draws a harsh, jagged line no matter which brush you select. Even the feathered brushes produce jagged lines when used with the pencil. The airbrush generally produces softer lines than the paintbrush.

Making your own brush

You might think that 16 brushes would be enough to keep you happy well into your declining years. But I assure you, one day you'll want a brush size that's a little thicker than Option A and a little thinner than Option B. You'll have to modify one or the other to come up with a custom brush of your own.

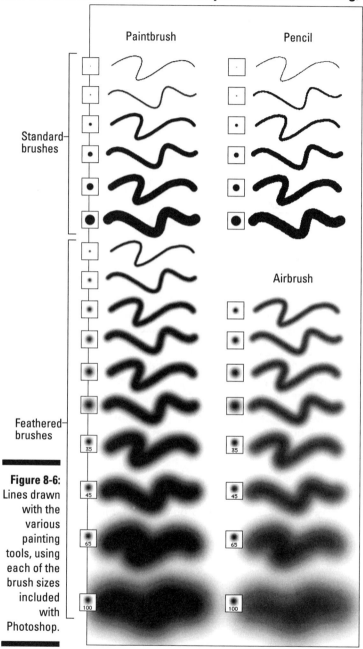

Figure 8-6:
Lines drawn with the various painting tools, using each of the brush sizes included with Photoshop.

To edit a brush, you can select one of the options in the Brushes palette and then choose the Brush Options command from the palette menu. But I recommend that you just double-click on a brush icon and be done with it. In response to your double-click, Photoshop displays the Brush Options dialog box, shown in Figure 8-7. Here's how you modify the brush:

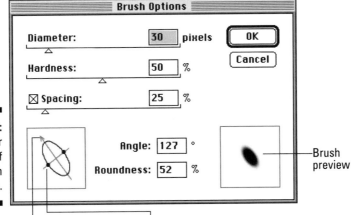

Figure 8-7:
The inner
workings of
a brush
size.

Drag to rotate   Drag to change roundness

✔ Drag the Diameter slider to make the brush bigger or smaller. If you
know the exact width value, enter it into the option box on the right
side of the slider. This value is measured in pixels.

✔ The Hardness value represents the blurriness of the brush size. A value
of 100% is hard, like the first six options in the Brushes palette. Anything else is progressively fuzzier. The ten feathered options in the
Brushes palette have Hardness values of 0%.

✔ Don't change the Spacing value. And don't even think about turning off
the Spacing check box. The Spacing option determines how many
dollops of paint are applied to your canvas and is better left
unmolested.

✔ Before I tell you about the Angle option, which comes next, I need to
explain how Roundness works. (You see, the Angle value doesn't have
any effect unless you first change the Roundness value.) The Roundness option lets you make the brush oval instead of round. A value of
100% is absolutely circular, as are all the predefined brushes; anything
less results in a shape that is shorter than it is wide.

✔ If you want an oval brush to be taller than it is wide or some other
variation on its present state, you can rotate it by changing the Angle
value. Keep in mind that 360° represents one complete counterclockwise
turn, so 90° is a quarter-turn, 180° is a half-turn, -90° is a clockwise
quarter-turn, and so on.

✔ I never use the Angle and Roundness option boxes to change the
values. Instead, I use that diagram in the lower-left corner of the dialog
box. Drag one of the two circular handles on either side of the circle to
make the brush oval. To rotate the brush, either drag the gray arrowhead or just click at the position where you want the arrow to point.
The labels in Figure 8-7 tell the story.

As you change the settings, the preview box in the lower-right corner of the dialog box shows what the brush will look like. If the diameter of the brush is too large for the preview to fit in its box — 74 pixels or larger — Photoshop automatically reduces the preview and displays a zoom ratio above the box. A zoom ratio of 1:2, for example, means that you're seeing the preview at half-size.

When you finish editing the brush, press Return to accept your changes.

Going nuts with the Brushes palette

Whenever I explain some feature or other associated with Photoshop, I'm tempted to say, "But wait, there's more!" like some daft Ginsu Knife salesman. But that's because there always is more. Photoshop is never satisfied to supply you with anything short of everything. You have to admire that in a program.

Here's what I mean:

- ✔ You don't need to manually click on a brush icon in the Brushes palette to select it. You can change the brush size from the keyboard, even when the Brushes palette is hidden. Press the right bracket key ( ]) to select the next brush in the Brushes palette. Press the left bracket key ([ ) to select the previous brush.

- ✔ To select the very first brush size option — something that comes in especially handy when using the pencil tool — press Shift-[. To select the last option, press Shift-].

- ✔ To delete a brush size option from the palette, ⌘-click on it. (When you press the ⌘ key, you get a miniature pair of scissors. That's how Photoshop tells you that you're ready to clip a brush into oblivion.)

- ✔ To add a new brush icon, click in the empty area in the lower-right corner of the Brushes palette. The dialog box in Figure 8-7 appears, though it's titled New Brush instead of Brush Options. Change the settings as desired, and press Return.

- ✔ You can load additional custom brushes from disk by choosing the Load Brushes command from the palette menu. (Click on the right-pointing arrow in the palette to display the menu.) When you choose the command, you see a dialog box similar to the standard Open dialog box. Go to the Photoshop folder, the Goodies folder, and then the Brushes folder, where you find the file Assorted Brushes. That's a fun one. Click on Open to add the custom brushes to the Brushes palette.

- ✔ To get rid of any changes made to the brush size options in the Brushes palette, choose Reset Brushes from the palette menu. After the message appears, click on the OK button or press Return.

Exploring More Painting Options

The Options palette represents the heart and soul of the Photoshop tool modification options. Although the Brushes palette controls only one aspect of a painting tool, the Options palette lets you modify tools in a whole bunch of ways. You can modify nearly every tool in the toolbox to some extent by using the Options palette.

Ogling the Options palette

To get to the Options palette, you can choose Window⇨Show Options. Or you can press F8 and then click on the Options tab in the Info palette. Both of those methods are the sucker's routes for displaying the Options palette. Here are two better ways:

- ✔ Double-click on the toolbox icon for the tool you want to modify.

- ✔ If the tool you want to modify is already selected, just press the Return key. Photoshop not only displays the Options palette, but it also highlights the first option box in the palette so that you can immediately enter the option value without selecting the option box first.

Figure 8-8 shows the Paintbrush Options palette that appears when the paintbrush is active. With a few exceptions, these options are the same ones that appear when the pencil and airbrush tools are selected. Here's how they work:

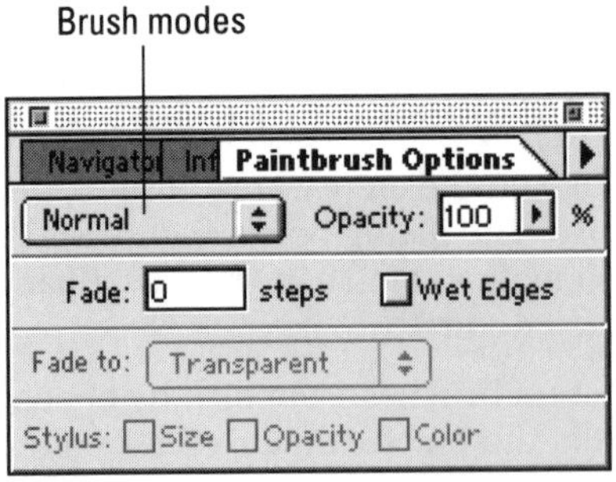

Brush modes

Figure 8-8:
The
Paintbrush
Options
panel is
headquarters
for
modifying
the painting
tools.

✔ The pop-up menu in the upper-left corner of the palette provides access to a bunch of different brush modes that control how the foreground color applied by the tool mixes with the existing colors in the image. The modes have confusing and seemingly meaningless names such as Multiply, Hard Light, and Difference, so beginners tend to avoid them like the plague. I show you some fun tricks you can perform with some of the modes in the next section.

✔ Available when you use the pencil or paintbrush, the Opacity slider bar controls the translucency of the foreground color. In Version 5, the Opacity slider bar can be accessed by pressing on the arrow next to the default setting of 100%. A setting of 100% ensures that the paint is opaque so that you can't see the colors underneath. (When you use a feathered brush, the edges are translucent even at 100%, but the center is opaque.) Any Opacity setting lower than 100% makes the brush translucent.

✔ If you're still a little fuzzy on how the Opacity slider works, it may be because you're a visual learner. Figure 8-9 shows four lines drawn with the paintbrush, two using a standard soft brush and two using a feathered brush. In each case, one line is set to 100% Opacity, and the other is set to 40%.

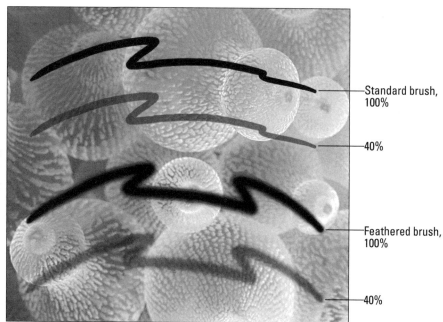

Figure 8-9: Here's what it looks like when you paint over sea anemone at different Opacity settings.

—Standard brush, 100%

—40%

—Feathered brush, 100%

—40%

✔ When the airbrush is selected, the Opacity slider bar changes to the Pressure slider bar. Rather than producing translucent lines at lower settings, the airbrush applies less paint. It's as though you tightened the nozzle on a real airbrush.

✔ You can change the Opacity or Pressure value in 10% increments by pressing a number key. As long as one of the painting tools is selected, pressing 9 changes the Opacity to 90%, 8 changes it to 80%, and so on. Press the 0 key to change the Opacity back to 100%. If you want a more precise setting — say, 75% — just type the value quickly.

✔ Fade does not rank among the most useful Photoshop options. It fades out the line over the course of several "steps" (those dollops of paint I discuss a few pages back) based on the Spacing option in the Brush Options dialog box. Skip it.

✔ The Stylus Pressure check boxes affect how pressure-sensitive tablets work in Photoshop. But if you've never even seen a pressure-sensitive tablet, let alone have one hooked up to your computer, don't give these options another thought.

✔ The Wet Edges check box appears only when the paintbrush tool is selected. When selected, this option makes your lines translucent with dark edges, as though the lines were drawn with a magic marker. Give it a try. For a variation on the effect, choose the Multiply mode from the brush modes pop-up menu.

✔ When the pencil is selected, the check box changes to Auto Erase. This option draws in the background color whenever you click or drag on a pixel painted in the foreground color (the accepted practice in other painting programs). It's very useful for making touch-ups with the single-pixel brush — click to add the foreground color, click again to change it to the background color. I almost always leave this option on because it lets you add and erase color with a single tool.

Experimenting with brush modes

Of all the controls in the Options panel, the brush modes in the pop-up menu make the least sense. Don't worry, I'm not going to list every one of them and explain how it works. That would just fry your brain, and you need your brain for other chapters. Instead, I demonstrate a few specific effects you can achieve using brush modes and let you experiment with the others at your own pace.

For example, consider the sun image shown back in Figure 8-4. Suppose that you want to color in the sun with yellow and the sky with blue.

The problem is, if you try to color in the sun and sky with one of the painting tools — even the airbrush — you end up covering the face inside the sun and the rays outside the sun. You can't fix the problem by lowering the Opacity value because it just results in washed out colors, and you still obscure some of the sun's detail.

The two images in Color Plate 8-1 show what I'm talking about. In the left image, I've painted in the sun and sky with the paintbrush tool at 100% Opacity. Obviously a bad move. In the right image, I changed the Opacity to 40% and tried again. It looks like I smeared chalk all over the image. Yuk.

The solution is to select a brush mode. Change the Opacity back to 100% by pressing the 0 key. Then select Multiply from the brush modes pop-up menu in the Options palette. Miraculously, you can now paint both sky and sun without covering up the rays and the face. This is because the Multiply option darkens colors as though you had painted with watercolors. It mixes the colors together to create darker colors. The upper-left example in Color Plate 8-2 shows the result.

Here are some other brush modes that you may find interesting:

- ✔ The Screen mode is the exact opposite of Multiply. Rather than mixing colors together to create darker colors, you mix them together to create lighter colors. In the upper-right example of Color Plate 8-2, I was able to apply color exclusively inside the black outlines and orange shadow. When I painted over white areas, nothing happened because any color mixed with white just makes more white.

- ✔ Does that make sense? Let me take another stab at it. Multiply mixes colors as though they were pigments, which is why the colors get darker. (You may want to check out my discussion of CMYK colors in Chapter 5.) By contrast, Screen mixes colors as though they were lights — just like RGB colors — which is why they get lighter.

- ✔ The Overlay mode darkens dark colors and lightens light colors, resulting in a heightening of contrast. In the case of our sun, Overlay creates halos around the black lines because it darkens the inside of the lines and lightens the feathered edges. The lower-left example in Color Plate 8-2 shows what I'm talking about.

- ✔ The Difference brush mode is the loopiest mode of them all and the most likely to surprise you. It creates a photo-negative effect by mixing colors and finding their opposites. Check out the final example in Color Plate 8-2 to see the resulting plum sun against a tomato sky. Way cool.

- ✔ You can also have some fun experimenting with Difference's cousin, Exclusion. It sends all blacks to white, all whites to black, and all medium colors to gray.

✔ Use the Color brush mode to colorize grayscale images or change the color of portions of RGB images. Suppose that you want to change the color of the sky in the upper-left example of Color Plate 8-2 from blue to green. You can't use the Normal mode because that would wipe out the rays and the other lines. And you can't use Multiply again because that would further darken the sky. The answer is the Color mode, which replaces a color with the foreground color without harming underlying detail.

✔ The Color Dodge and Color Burn brush modes offer an interesting new twist on the dodge and burn tools discussed in Chapter 9. In case you haven't discovered the dodge and burn tools yet, you drag with the dodge tool to lighten a portion of your image and drag with the burn tool to darken a portion of your image. If you use one of the painting tools and the Color Dodge mode, you can lighten your image and infuse it with color. Using Color Burn, you can darken and infuse with color. For example, to darken your image and give it a greenish tint, you would paint with green using the Color Burn brush mode.

✔ To paint normally again, just select the Normal brush mode.

I'd rate six of the preceding brush modes — Multiply, Screen, Overlay, Difference, Color, and Normal — as super-useful, the kinds of modes you want to get to know on a first-name basis. Exclusion, Color Dodge, and Color Burn are also worth some attention. The others aren't nearly so useful. In fact, they're mostly boring and obscure. With that in mind, I encourage you to freely experiment with the ones discussed here to the exclusion of all the others.

If brush modes seem a little daunting at first, don't give up. Just keep on plugging away. Remember, everything's daunting at some time. Heck, walking upright on two legs once seemed impossible, and yet look how well you do that today. Sure, not as well as some folks, but you're still getting there. Keep your chin up.

Chapter 9

Making a Mockery of Reality

*B*ack in the old days, retouching a photograph was a formidable task. If you wanted to remove the reflection from someone's glasses, sharpen the focus of a detail, or tidy up a wrinkle or two, you had to actually take paint or airbrush to the photo and hope for the best. Anyone short of a trained professional would more often than not make a complete mess of the project and wish to heck it had never been started. Even the pros found it difficult to match flat colors on a palette to the ever-changing landscape of a photograph.

The beauty of Photoshop is that you can paint not only with specific colors — as explained in the previous chapter — but also with colors and details already found in the image. Using the editing tools — smudge, blur, sharpen, dodge, burn, and sponge — you can subtly adjust the appearance of pixels by shifting them around, boosting contrast between them, or lightening and darkening them. The results are edits that blend in with their surroundings.

With the Photoshop crop tool and Image⇨Crop command, you can also snip away unwanted portions of your image. Never before has it been so easy to cut relatives you hate out of your family photos.

Photoshop enables you to retouch images in ways that traditional photographic techniques simply don't allow and also offers a built-in safety net. You can undo any change you make or simply revert to your original image if you don't like how your retouched image turns out. In other words, Photoshop is a real pleasure for modern retouching enthusiasts. After you finish this chapter, you'll be so inspired to enhance and modify photographic details that you'll welcome problem images with open arms.

Trimming Excess Gunk Off the Edges

In Chapter 4, I explain how to change the size of your image without changing the elements therein — in other words, how to turn that 8 x 10 wedding photograph into a nifty wallet-size snapshot without trimming off anyone's vital body parts. But suppose that your spouse up and runs off to Lagos with your next-door neighbor? What do you do then? Why, you use the crop tool to cut the cretin out of the picture, that's what.

The sharp edges of the crop tool

Novice photographers have a habit of worrying about getting too much imagery into their pictures. This can be a dangerous concern. In your effort to cut out background flack, you may overcompensate and cut off Grandma's head or the right half of little Joey's body. The fact is, it's better to have too much stuff in your photos than too little, for the simple reason that excess stuff can be cut away, but missing stuff has to be reshot. Since photography was invented, production artists have been taking knives and scissors to just about every image that passes over their light tables in an effort to clip away the extraneous gook around the edges and home in on the real goods. Called *cropping,* this technique is so pervasive that professional photographers purposely shoot subjects from too far away knowing that someone, somewhere, will slice the image and make it right.

Inside Photoshop, you can cut away the unpalatable parts of an image using the crop tool. The crop tool used to have its own single-family home in the toolbox but now is forced to share a cramped apartment with the marquee tools in the upper-left corner of the toolbox. To select the crop tool without messing with the toolbox, press C.

Here's how to use the crop tool:

1. **Drag with the tool around the portion of the image you want to retain.**

   In Figure 9-1, I dragged around the floating spaceman. A dotted rectangle called a *marquee* follows your drag to clearly show the crop boundaries. Don't worry if you don't surround your image elements just right; you get the chance to edit the boundary in the next step.

Handle   Resize cursor   Crop boundary

Figure 9-1:
Drag the
square
handles to
change the
crop
boundary.

If you press the spacebar during your drag, Photoshop stops resizing the crop boundary and starts moving the entire boundary. This technique can be helpful when you're trying to position the boundary precisely. (You can also move the boundary after you create it, though.)

2. **Drag the crop boundaries as desired.**

   After you release your mouse button, Photoshop displays square handles around the edges of the marquee (refer to Figure 9-1). If the marquee is not the right size, drag a handle to change the crop boundary. Your cursor changes to a double-headed arrow when you place it over a handle, indicating that you have the go-ahead to drag the handle. You can drag as many handles as you please — one at a time, of course — before cropping the image.

   If you move the cursor outside the crop boundary, the cursor changes to a curved, double-headed arrow. Dragging then rotates the crop boundary.

3. **After you get the crop boundary the way you want it, double-click inside the boundary to crop the image.**

   Or just press Return. Photoshop throws away all pixels outside the crop boundary, as shown in Figure 9-2. If you rotated the crop boundary in Step 2, Photoshop rights the rectangular area and thus rotates the image, as illustrated in Figure 9-3.

Figure 9-2:
Up close and personal with a spaceman.

Figure 9-3:
If the photograph isn't straight, you can rotate the crop boundary to match (top), while telling Photoshop to crop and straighten the image at the same time (bottom).

Rotate cursor

When you rotate an image in this way, Photoshop *resamples* your image —
that is, it rearranges the pixels to come up with the rotated image. As I
discuss in Chapter 4, resampling can damage your image. For best results,
don't rotate your image more than once. Also, make sure that the Interpolation option in the General panel of the Preferences dialog box is set to
Bicubic. (Press ⌘-K to display the dialog box.)

More good news about cropping

Cropping is easy and fun for the whole family. You can do it at home or at
work, with friends or by yourself, in the car, or while performing household
chores. Find out how you can make cropping an everyday part of your new
life.

Sorry, I misplaced the real intro to this section and can't seem to find it. But
before I hunt around, I just want to mention briefly that the next few items
explain more cropping techniques that you might find useful.

- ✔ If you change your mind about wanting to crop your image, press Esc
  or ⌘-period to get rid of the cropping boundary.

- ✔ If you try to drag with the crop tool when a portion of the image is
  selected (as discussed in Chapter 12), Photoshop deselects the image
  but doesn't respond to your drag. You have to drag a second time to
  make Photoshop sit up and take notice.

- ✔ To move the cropping boundary in its entirety, just drag inside the
  boundary.

- ✔ In addition to using the crop tool, you can crop an area selected with
  the rectangular marquee tool (see Chapter 12) by choosing
  Image⇨Crop. I take advantage of this alternative quite often because
  Photoshop can slow down and react lethargically when you edit the
  crop marquee.

  The only trick is that the selected area has to be exactly rectangular. If
  one side is even slightly crooked — which might happen if you modify
  the selection outline slightly — the Crop command doesn't work. Also,
  the Feather option in the Marquee Options palette must be set to 0.
  (To display the palette, double-click on the marquee tool icon in the
  toolbox.)

- ✔ The Fixed Target Size option in the Crop Tool Options palette is useful
  for cropping one image so that it's the same size as another image.
  Suppose that you want to make Image A the same size as Image B. First,
  open Image B, turn on the Fixed Target Size option, and click on the
  Front Image button. Next, open Image A and use the crop tool as you
  normally would. When you press Return to execute the crop,
  Photoshop automatically resizes the image to match Image B.

✔ You can also crop an image by using the Canvas Size command, as discussed at the end of Chapter 4. You may want to consider this method if you need to trim your image on one or more sides by a precise number of pixels to get the image to a certain size. The Canvas Size command can also come in handy if you want to crop a very small area — say three pixels worth — along one or more edges of the image and you have trouble selecting the area with the crop marquee. You can reduce the size of the canvas using Image⇨Canvas Size to eliminate the offensive pixels.

Touching Base with Retouching Tools

When push comes to shove, the editing tools are more like than unlike the painting tools. You use an editing tool by dragging with it, just as you do with a painting tool. You change the size of the tool tip by selecting an option from the Brushes palette. You modify the performance of an editing tool from the Options palette. You can even apply brush modes and Opacity settings. (Brush modes, the Brushes palette, and the Options palette are all introduced in Chapter 8, in case your response to these last few sentences was "Huh?")

But the editing tools are sufficiently different from their painting cousins to confuse and perplex the unsuspecting neophyte. Moreover, unlike the pencil, paintbrush, and airbrush, the editing tools don't have any common real-world counterparts. I can't say, "the Photoshop smudge tool works just like the conventional smudge tool that's hanging out in your garage right next to the leaf rake," because almost no one has a smudge tool hanging in the garage or anywhere else.

What do the editing tools do, exactly?

Editing tools would be extremely useful in real life, if only someone would get around to inventing them. Take the task of touching up the walls in your rec room. (Come on, everyone has a rec room!) Using paintbrushes and rollers alone, this job can be a nightmare. The paint on the walls and the paint in the can may no longer exactly match. If you have to scrape away any dry paint, you'll have a heck of a time matching the texture. And knowing you, you may very well trip over something and spill paint all over the carpet.

But scan the walls of the rec room into Photoshop, and your problems are solved. Even if you have to retouch both paint and wallpaper, the editing tools, labeled in Figure 9-4, can handle the job without incident:

✔ The smudge tool, which had its own space in Photoshop 4, now has to share space with the blur and sharpen tools.

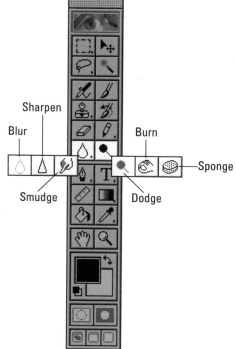

Sharpen

Blur

Burn

Smudge

Dodge

—Sponge

✔ Use the smudge tool to smear colors from a pristine area of the wall over the bare spots and the stains. You can smear the paint as far as you want, just as though it were still wet and in infinite supply. This is the editing tool you'll use most often. It's discussed further in the section, "Smudging Away Imperfections," later in this chapter.

✔ If the transitions between elements in the wallpaper are a little ragged — for example, if the pixels in the little polka-dot mushrooms don't seem to blend naturally with those in the cute little frogs sitting beneath them — you can smooth the pixels out with the blur tool, which looks like a water drop. This tool blurs the edges between colors so that the colors blend together.

✔ To rebuild textures, drag with the sharpen tool — which looks like a pointy cone of some sort. The sharpen tool increases the amount of contrast between colors and builds up edges.

✔ Together, the blur and sharpen tools are known as *focus tools*. The former downplays focus; the latter enhances it. Both tools are eloquently explained later in this chapter in the section, "Focusing from the hip."

✔ To lighten a dark area in the wallpaper, drag with the dodge tool, which looks like a circle on the end of a stick. This tool lightens up the area evenly.

✔ If an area on the wall has become faded over the years, you can darken it using the burn tool, which looks like a hand in the shape of an O.

✔ Are the colors just too darn garish? Or has the color been drained right out? I admit, these aren't common rec room problems, but if they do occur, you can take up the sponge tool to remedy them.

✔ The dodge, burn, and sponge tools are called *toning tools,* meaning that they change the colors in an image. The last two sections in this chapter are devoted to the toning tools.

See, don't you wish you had a crack at using these tools in real life? Seems to me that Bob Vila or that "Home Improvement" guy should get to work on them.

Uncovering hidden editing tools

When you first looked at Figure 9-4, you may have noticed that the toolbox in my figure doesn't look anything like the one on your screen. In order to show you all the tool icons, I enhanced the screen shot (using Photoshop, of course).

By default, the blur and dodge tools appear in the toolbox. As discussed in Chapter 2, the little arrow in the lower-right corner of the blur and dodge tools means that additional tools lurk behind the icons on a flyout menu. To get to the hidden tools on the flyout menu, press and hold on the icon and then drag across to the tool you want to use. Or just Option-click on the icon to cycle through the tools on the menu.

You can also cycle through the tools by using their shortcuts: Press R to select the tool that's currently showing in the blur/sharpen/smudge compartment of the toolbox; press Shift-R again to switch to the tool that's hidden. Likewise, you can press O (that's the letter O, not zero) and then Shift-O to cycle through the dodge, burn, and sponge tools.

Effects of the edit tools can be a little difficult to predict — especially for beginners. Remember, ⌘-Z will undo your last edit, and the History palette will allow you to go back to previous steps (described in detail in Chapter 11). You can use File⇨Revert to restore your image to the last-saved version.

Smudging Away Imperfections

The shark image shown in Figure 9-5 provides an ideal subject for demonstrating the powers of the proudest Photoshop editing tool, the smudge tool. Like so many rough-and-tumble sharks that occupy the inner cities of our oceans, this guy is no stranger to the occasional toothy brawl. Frankly, his face is a mess. If he were old enough to shave, I'd say that he had problems operating a razor. But because he's at that violent age where his friends think it's fun to rip an innocent tuna to shreds, I'm guessing that these marks are war wounds.

Figure 9-5:
This shark
is on the
road to ruin.

But whatever caused his scars, I can fix them with the help of the smudge tool. As you may recall from my earlier rec room analogy, the smudge tool pushes color from one portion of your image into another. When you drag with this tool, Photoshop "grabs" the color that's underneath your cursor at the start of your drag and smears it in the direction of your drag.

The smudge tool is a great contraption for smearing away scars, wrinkles, overly large noses, droopy ears, and all the other things that plastic surgeons keep their eyes out for. Figure 9-6 shows a magnified view of the smudge tool working its magic on the shark. The various sharkish defects are smoothed away to the point that the guy looks like he's made out of porcelain.

Smearing with style

Notice that in Figure 9-6, I rubbed with the grain of the detail. I traced along the shark's gills, rubbed along the length of its fins, and dragged up its snout, all in short, discreet strokes. I was planning on saying something

Figure 9-6:
As these before (top) and after (bottom) photos prove, the smudge tool can take years off a shark's face.

Smudge cursor

about how you don't want to rub a shark the wrong way, but my editor told me to lay off the puns. So, I'll just point out that you get more naturalistic results if you carefully trace along the details of your subject and don't simply drag haphazardly all over the place.

Retouching with the smudge tool requires a certain amount of discretion. If you really go nuts and drag over every single surface, you get an oil-painting effect, like the one shown in Figure 9-7. Don't get me wrong — you can create some cool stuff this way, but excessive smudging is not the same as retouching.

Figure 9-7:
You can
convert a
photo into
an oil
painting by
dragging all
over the
place with
the smudge
tool.

Smudge-specific controls

You can modify the performance of the smudge tool as follows:

✔ Click and Shift-click to smudge in a straight line. Or Shift-drag to smudge horizontally or vertically. These Shift-click and Shift-drag techniques work for all the edit tools, by the way.

✔ Select another brush size in the Brushes palette to enlarge or reduce the size of the smudge brush. You can likewise change the brush size for all the edit tools. To display the Brushes palette, press F5. (For more on changing brushes, see Chapter 8.)

✔ Double-click on the smudge tool icon in the toolbox to display the Smudge Options palette, shown in Figure 9-8. Or, if the smudge tool is selected, just press Return to display the palette.

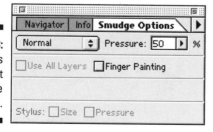

Figure 9-8:
The options
that affect
the smudge
tool.

✔ Adjust the Pressure slider by pressing on the black arrow to the right of the default setting of 50% to create more subtle retouching effects. Increase the Pressure setting to make the effect more pronounced.

✔ Remember that you can change the brush size from the keyboard by pressing the bracket keys and change the Pressure setting by pressing the number keys, as I explain in Chapter 8.

✔ The brush modes pop-up menu (in the upper-left corner of the Smudge Options palette) doesn't offer the Multiply, Screen, Overlay, or Difference options, which are discussed at the end of Chapter 8. Instead, you get two options, Darken and Lighten, which let you smear only those colors that are darker or lighter than the original colors in the image.

✔ You also have the Color brush mode, which lets you smear the colors in an RGB image without harming the detail. Pretty nifty.

✔ The other brush modes — Hue, Saturation, and Luminosity — range from nearly useless to completely useless. Don't worry about them.

✔ Change the brush mode back to Normal to make the smudge tool function, er, normally.

✔ Depending on your computer system, Photoshop may slow down dramatically when you increase the Pressure setting above 80% or 90%, select a large brush size, or change the brush mode. And if you do all three at once, the program may run so lethargically that you'll think you've crashed. Just go get a cup of coffee, and Photoshop should be finished when you get back.

✔ Select the Finger Painting check box to dip your brush into the foreground color before smudging. Photoshop applies a little dab of foreground color at the beginning of your drag and then begins to smear into the existing colors in the image as usual.

To temporarily turn on Finger Painting when the check box is deselected, press Option as you drag with the smudge tool. If the Finger Painting check box is selected, Option-Drag to smudge in the normal fashion.

✔ The Use All Layers check box doesn't make any difference unless you're editing an image with layers. It allows you to pierce through and pick up the colors from all of your layers.

Color Plate 9-1 shows before and after shots of a few effects mixed together. I created the second image by selecting the Finger Painting check box, setting the Pressure slider to 90%, and changing the brush mode to Color. I dragged several times with the smudge tool, about half the time with the foreground color set to red and the other half with it set to yellow.

All Them Other Edit Tools

The remaining edit tools fall into a group that experts call "the other guys." Whereas you may pick up the smudge tool every third day or so, you'll be lucky if you select one of the other guys once a week. Even so, they can prove fantastically helpful — well, moderately helpful, anyway — if used properly. The upcoming sections contain my choice bits of wisdom for using the other guys.

Focusing from the hip

It's true that the smudge tool is a wonderful little device. But it's not always the right tool for the job. For example, say that you have a harsh transition between two colors. Maybe one of the shark's teeth looks a little jagged, or you want to soften the edge of a fin. Which of the following methods would you use to fix this problem?

- ✔ Smear the colors a bit with the smudge tool.
- ✔ Soften the transition between the colors using the blur tool.

I prepared you for that question by saying that the smudge tool isn't always the right tool and using words like "soften," so naturally you chose the second answer. (You did choose the second answer, didn't you?) But believe me, there will come a time when you run into this exact situation and your first reflex will be to reach for the smudge tool.

So let me try to drive the point home a bit with the aid of Figure 9-9. The figure starts off with the harshest of all possible color transitions — that is, between white and its arch enemy, black. You want to smear the colors together so that they blend a little more harmoniously, so naturally you reach for the smudge tool. The problem with this method — as illustrated in the second example in the figure — is that you can't get a nice, smooth transition between the two colors no matter how hard you try. Even if you Shift-drag with the smudge tool, you get some inconsistent smudging. You also run the risk of smearing surrounding detail. All this happens because the smudge tool is designed as a free-form smearing device, not as an edge softener.

Meanwhile, an edge softener is sitting nearby waiting for you to snatch it up. If you drag the blur tool between the white and black shapes — whether you drag perfectly straight or wobble the cursor back and forth a bit — you get a softened edge like the one shown in the final example of Figure 9-9.

Harsh transition

Smeared with smudge tool

Figure 9-9:
The parable
of the harsh
transition,
the smudge
tool, and
the blur
tool.

Softened with blur tool

While I've got your attention, let me jot down a few other items about the focus tools:

- ✔ Just as the blur tool softens transitions, the sharpen tool firms the transitions back up.

- ✔ At least, that's what the sharpen tool is supposed to do. In practice, it tends to make an image overly grainy. Use this tool sparingly.

- ✔ You can adjust the impact of the blur and sharpen tools by changing the Pressure setting in the Blur or Sharpen Options palette — which you get to by pressing Return when the tool is selected or double-clicking on the tool icon in the toolbox. I like to set the Pressure to about 60% for the blur tool and 30% for the sharpen tool.

- ✔ When you work with the focus tools, you have access to the same brush modes as you do when using the smudge tool. The important ones are Darken, Lighten, and Color. Any of the three can help downplay the effects of the sharpen tool and make it more usable.

- ✔ If you want to adjust the focus of large areas of an image — or an entire image — use the commands under the Filter menu as described in Chapter 17. These commands work much more uniformly than the focus tools.

Dodge? Burn? Those are opposites?

Wondering why the dodge and burn tool icons look they way they do? It's because the dodge and burn tools have their roots in traditional stat camera techniques in which you shoot a photograph of another photograph to correct exposure problems. The dodge tool is supposed to look like a little paddle that you wave around to block off light, and the burn tool is a hand focusing the light. It may seem, therefore, that dodging would make the image darker and burning would make it lighter. But Photoshop is thinking in terms of negative film, where black is white, up is down, right is left, and Tweedle Dee is a Cornish game hen.

I must confess that, although I've been using Photoshop since I was in diapers, I still can't remember which tool lightens and which darkens without looking it up. To help both you and me remember, I offer the following:

✔ The dodge tool lightens images, just as a dodge ball lightens your body by about ten pounds when it tears off your head.

✔ The burn tool darkens images, just as a sunburn darkens your body and eventually turns it a kind of charbroiled color.

If those little insights don't help you remember how the dodge and burn tools work, nothing will.

Generally, you adjust the performance of the dodge and burn tools just like the other edit tools and the paint tools — by changing the brush size, alternating the brush mode, and so on. (You can read more about brush sizes and brush modes in Chapter 8.) To get to the Brush size options, press F5 to display the Brushes palette. To get to the other tool options, found in the Dodge or Burn Options palette, double-click on the dodge or burn tool icon in the toolbox, or — if you like to do things the easy way — just press Return.

A few of the options in the Toning Tools Options palette require some explanation:

✔ The Exposure slider bar, accessed by pressing the black arrow to the right of the default setting of 50%, indicates how much an area will be lightened or darkened. As always, lower the value to lessen the impact of the tool, and raise the value to increase the impact.

✔ The pop-up menu in the upper-left corner of the palette contains just three options: Highlights, Midtones, and Shadows. The default setting is Midtones, which lightens or darkens medium colors in an image and leaves the very light and dark colors alone. Figure 9-10 shows the result of dragging all over the shark with the dodge tool while Midtones was the active brush mode.

Figure 9-10:
By setting the brush mode to Midtones and dragging randomly with the dodge tool, I lightened the shark without eliminating contrast.

✔ The Shadows brush mode ensures that the darkest colors are affected, while Highlights impacts the lightest colors. In Figure 9-11, I set the brush mode to Shadows and scribbled with the dodge tool. The payoff is a shark that looks like it ate the world's supply of glowworms. Even the darkest shadows radiate, making the image uniformly light.

✔ To darken an image with similar uniformity, select the burn tool and set the brush mode to Highlights.

There is a variation of the dodge and burn tools in the form of the Color Dodge and Color Burn brush modes (explained in Chapter 8). When you use the regular dodge and burn tools, you simply lighten or darken your image. But when you use one of the painting tools with the Color Dodge or Color Burn brush modes, you can both lighten or darken and infuse the image with color. For example, if you want to lighten an image and give it a yellow-ish glow, paint with yellow and the Color Dodge brush mode.

Figure 9-11:
Using the
dodge
tool in
combination
with the
Shadows
brush mode
makes the
shark's
darkest
shadows
tingle with
light.

Playing with the Color knob

The sponge tool is designed to be used on full-color images. Don't try using it on grayscale images because it doesn't do you any good. It's not that it doesn't work — it does — it just doesn't work correctly. On a grayscale image, the sponge tool either lightens or darkens pixels like a shoddy version of the dodge or burn tool.

When you work on a color image, the sponge tool increases or decreases saturation. Ever used the Color knob on your television? Turn the knob up, and the color leaps off the screen; turn it down, and the colors look gray. What you are doing is adjusting the TV's saturation. Increasing saturation makes the colors more vibrant; decreasing saturation makes the colors more drab. The sponge tool works in much the same way.

Here's how you use the sponge tool:

1. **Select the tool.**

   Press the O key and Shift-O keys until the sponge icon appears in the toolbox.

2. **Press Return.**

   Photoshop displays the Sponge Options palette.

3. **Select the desired option from the pop-up menu in the upper-left corner of the palette.**

   Select Saturate to make the colors vibrant; select Desaturate to make the colors drab.

4. **Press a number key to change the Pressure value.**

   Or drag the slider bar in the palette, accessed by clicking on the black arrow next to the numeric setting. Either way, the setting affects the impact of the sponge tool.

5. **Drag with the tool inside a color image.**

   Watch those colors change.

The primary reason that the programmers provide the sponge tool is to desaturate colors that may get lost when you convert from RGB to CMYK. As I mention in Chapter 5, red, green, and blue can mix to form some very bright colors that cyan, magenta, yellow, and black can't express. So you can dab at the colors with the sponge tool to bring them more in line with the CMYK spectrum.

But I like to use the sponge tool for the exact opposite purpose — to make colors more saturated. Oh, sure, maybe you won't be able to print the colors correctly, but at least they'll be as bright as they can be. If dragging with the sponge tool set to Saturate doesn't affect the colors in an image, it's because the colors are already as bright as they can be.

Another good way to use the sponge tool is to provide a focal point for your image. Say that you have a color photo of a group of people and want to have one person stand out among the others. Select your person (see Chapter 12 for methods to select) and then choose Select⇨Inverse. Then carefully take the sponge, set the option to Desaturate in the Options palette, and drag over the other people. You will see their colors wash out while your chosen person remains bright and lively and stands out among the crowd. This technique works with any group of objects. You can also set the option to Saturate to make your chosen element brighter than the rest.

Chapter 10
Cleaning Up Goobers

$\bullet\ \bullet$

In This Chapter

▶ Using the Dust & Scratches command

▶ Previewing automated effects

▶ Setting the Radius and Threshold values

▶ Cleaning up an image with the rubber stamp

▶ Specifying a clone source

▶ Adjusting settings in the Rubber Stamp Options palette

$\bullet\ \bullet$

*I*f you've ever had an image scanned to disk or CD, you know the story. You send out a lovely photograph that you've cherished all your life, and the scan comes back looking like someone stuck it inside the lint trap of a dryer. Big, gnarly hairs wiggle across the image. Little dust flecks seem to have reproduced like rabbits. And if you really hit the jackpot, you may even spy a few fingerprints on your image. It's enough to make you call up the service bureau and ask them whether they recently employed a shedding malamute that hasn't been bathed in six weeks and has a penchant for jelly sandwiches.

Unfortunately, sarcasm doesn't get you anywhere. But the dust-busting tools discussed in this chapter can. With a keen eye and a little bit of elbow grease, you can scrub away those imperfections and make your image appear absolutely spotless.

Photoshop offers two methods for dusting away the specks:

✔ The Dust & Scratches command automates the removal of image imperfections, but it can do more harm than good by getting rid of important detail as well.

✔ The rubber stamp tool lets you *clone* (copy) portions of an image to cover up blotches. The rubber stamp takes more time to use than the Dust & Scratches command and requires a considerable amount of clicking and dragging, but it also results in a better-looking picture.

This chapter explains the pros and cons of each method and throws in a few other ideas for spit-shining your images as well.

Using the Dust & Scratches Command

Ever own a really nice sports car, like a Porsche or a Jaguar? Me neither, but I've known folks who have, and they can be amazingly protective of their automobiles. Most Porsche/Jaguar owners would sooner vote for a Socialist than take their cars through one of those drive-through wash joints where big floppy pieces of blue plastic flog your car and take little bits of your paint job along with them. Automobile aficionados know that the only way to clean a car is to tenderly rub its surface with specially treated pieces of felt dipped in no-tears baby shampoo.

Although I might think that those car buffers are off their rockers, I wholeheartedly endorse this policy when it comes to cleaning images. That's why I'm not so fond of the Dust & Scratches filter — it's akin to sending your image through a car wash.

I should mention that the Dust & Scratches command is a *filter,* meaning that it automatically corrects an image by mixing up the pixels in some predefined manner. It works much like filters that change the focus of an image (discussed in Chapter 17).

But just because I may not approve of the Dust & Scratches command, that's no reason not to give you a crack at it. You're an adult. I'm not your keeper. Who knows, maybe the command will even come in useful. Maybe you need to clean up an image in a hurry for that last-minute space in the company newsletter, and the car wash solution is the only one you have time to try.

With that enthusiastic endorsement out of the way, it's high time I show you how to use the Dust & Scratches filter. The lab rat for today's outing is Figure 10-1. This figure demonstrates another variety of splatter that can plague images — old photo gunk. The lines, scratches, and dots in this image weren't introduced in the scanning process; they were a part of the original photo. Shot near the beginning of this century, this picture of Halley's comet has held up amazingly well over the years. I hope to look half as good when I'm its age.

Incidentally, if you're a fellow lover of things extraterrestrial, you can't go wrong with Digital Stock's "Space & Spaceflight" CD, which includes about as many views of the sun, moon, planets, and outlying nebula as a person could hope for.

Figure 10-1:
Halley's
comet as it
appeared in
1910, replete
with old
photo gunk.

To tidy up an image that presents similar symptoms, choose
Filter⇨Noise⇨Dust & Scratches. Photoshop displays the strange and
mysterious Dust & Scratches dialog box, which is pictured in all its glory in
Figure 10-2 and explained in the next two sections.

If you select a portion of your image before you choose the Dust & Scratches
command, the command affects just the selected area.

┌Preview cursor ┌Preview box   Zoom buttons┐

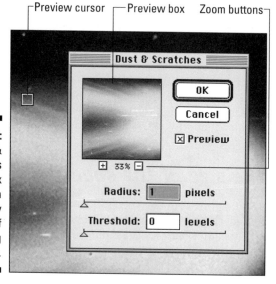

Figure 10-2:
The Dust &
Scratches
dialog box
provides a
hefty
supply of
previewing
options.

Previewing the filter effects

The makers of the Dust & Scratches dialog box know that it doesn't make a lick of sense, so they thoughtfully provide some preview options (all labeled in Figure 10-2) to enable you to see what happens when you make some otherwise meaningless adjustment. Here's how these preview options work:

- ✔ The preview box shows how your modifications look when applied to a tiny portion of the image.

- ✔ If you move the cursor outside the dialog box, it changes to a hollow square. Click on an area in the image to capture it inside the preview box.

- ✔ You can also scroll the contents of the preview box by dragging inside the box. Your cursor changes to a little hand.

- ✔ To magnify or reduce the contents of the preview box, click on the plus or minus zoom button.

- ✔ You can also access the standard magnifying glass cursor inside the preview box by pressing the ⌘ key (to zoom in) or the Option key (to zoom out).

- ✔ As long as the Preview check box is selected, Photoshop previews your settings in the image window as well as in the preview box.

- ✔ You can even use the standard hand and zoom cursors inside the image window while the Dust & Scratches dialog box is open. Just press the spacebar to get the hand cursor or ⌘ or Option to get the zoom cursors. This technique is a great way to preview an effect at two different zoom ratios, one inside the dialog box and one outside.

- ✔ If Photoshop seems to be slowing down too much as it tries to preview an effect in the image window, just click on the Preview check box to turn the function off.

I know, I know, you didn't want to know quite that much about previewing, but it will serve you well in the future. These same options are found in a few dialog boxes that I describe in Chapter 17 as well as a couple of others that you may decide to discover on your own (you Vasco da Gama, you).

Specifying the size of the speck

The Dust & Scratches dialog box (Filter⇨Noise⇨Dust & Scratches) offers just two options that affect the performance of the filter: the Radius and Threshold slider bars. The slider bars work as follows:

✔ Change the Radius value to indicate the size of the dust specks and the thickness of the hairs that you want to eliminate. In geometry, radius means half the width of a circle, so the Radius value is half the width of a dust speck. The minimum value is 1, meaning that the filter wipes out all specks and hairs up to 2 pixels thick.

✔ "Ah ha," you may think, "If I just crank up the Radius value as far as it goes (16 pixels), that should be enough to eliminate entire colonies of dust bunnies." Well, no. See, the Dust & Scratches filter doesn't really know a speck from a tiny bit of detail. So, if you have it rub out 16-pixel radius dust globs, it also rubs out 16-pixel details, such as Uncle Ralph's head. Figure 10-3 shows the effects of setting the Radius value to 1 on the left and 3 on the right. Notice how fuzzy the image became when I applied a 3-pixel radius? If you value my advice — I guess you value it to the tune of $19.99, anyway — you'll never set the radius value higher than 2.

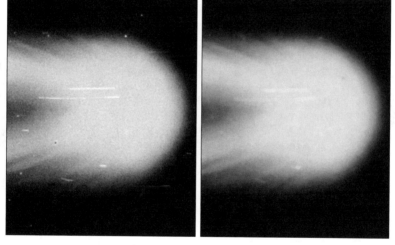

Figure 10-3: The results of applying the Dust & Scratches filter with the Radius slider set to 1 pixel (left) and 3 (right).

✔ The Threshold value tells Photoshop how different the color of a dust speck has to be from the color of the surrounding image to be considered a bad seed. The Threshold slider works just like the RGB sliders in the Color palette (discussed in Chapter 5) — that is, it varies from 0 to 255.

✔ The default Threshold value of 0 tells Photoshop that dust and image need only be 0 color levels different from each other. Because all colors are at least 0 levels different, Photoshop ignores the Threshold value and considers only the Radius value. Both images in Figure 10-3 were filtered with a Threshold value of 0.

✔ By raising the Threshold value, you tell Photoshop to be more selective. If you set the value to 10, speck and image colors must vary by at least 10 levels before Photoshop covers up the speck, as in the first example of Figure 10-4. If you raise the Threshold to 20 — as in the second example — Photoshop disregards still more potential impurities. Notice that the two horizontal streaks in the second image remain intact, having been ruled out by the Threshold setting. (By the way, I set the Radius value to 3 in Figure 10-4 — something I earlier warned you against doing — in order to make the effects of the Threshold setting more noticeable.)

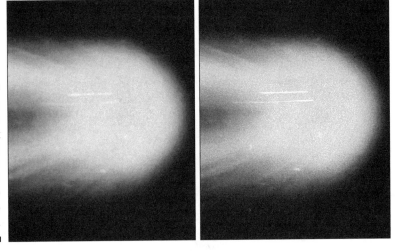

Figure 10-4: With the Radius set to 3 pixels, I set the Threshold to 10 (left) and then to 20 (right).

✔ If you set the Threshold value any higher than 100, the dust specks have to be white and the image black — or vice versa — to receive any attention. I don't recommend using values over 15.

In my long ramblings about the Radius and Threshold values, I neglected to mention one disconcerting fact. Even though the Dust & Scratches filter variously obliterated the detail in Figures 10-3 and 10-4, none of the images are completely free of spots and streaks. Admittedly, this old, moldy picture is a lot worse off than most of your images are likely to be, but the fact remains that the Dust & Scratches filter is an imperfect solution. Just like a cheap car wash, it gets rid of most of the dirt — but not all of it — and it takes away some of the paint and detailing along with it.

Spot Cleaning Your Image with TLC

If you're willing to expend a little extra energy and you can stand up to your friends when they call you compulsive, the tool of choice for cleaning up images is the rubber stamp. The fifth tool from the top on the left side of the toolbox, the rubber stamp lets you take a good portion of an image and paint it onto the bad portion. This miraculous process is called *cloning*.

You can also clone part of your image by copying and pasting it, as described near the end of Chapter 13. You should get familiar with both methods of cloning because both have their place in the retouching world.

Stamping out splatters

Want to see how the rubber stamp tool works? Try out these steps:

1. **Select the rubber stamp tool and press Return.**

   To select the rubber stamp from the keyboard, press the S key. Pressing the Return key — or double-clicking on the rubber stamp tool icon in the toolbox — displays the Rubber Stamp Options palette, shown on the right side of Figure 10-5.

2. **Make sure that the Aligned box is checked in the Rubber Stamp Options palette.**

   This option lets you clone from relative points in your image. You'll see what I mean in a sec.

3. **Start dragging randomly inside your image.**

   Whoops, I bet you got an error message, didn't you? If I'm right, the message says something about — I can almost see it; it's becoming clearer — Option-clicking to define a source! How do I know these things? Because I am psychic, that's how. Even from here in Boulder, Colorado, months before you'll read this, I can foresee the error messages in your future. Ah, really, it's nothing. Been able to do it since I was a kid.

   Okay, I'm lying, I just got that message myself, and I reckoned that you may get it, too. See, to use the rubber stamp, you have to tell Photoshop which portion of your image you want to clone before you begin cloning it. Photoshop isn't a mind reader, you know. I may be a mind reader, but Photoshop most certainly is not.

   Now that you've grasped this valuable lesson, grab a pen and put a big X through Step 3 so that you never make the same mistake again.

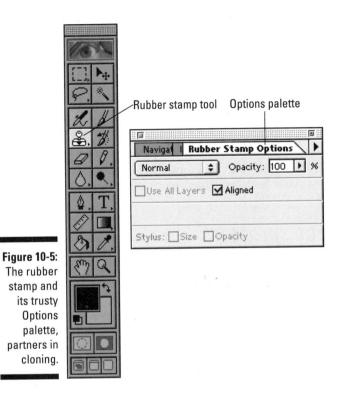

Rubber stamp tool   Options palette

Figure 10-5:
The rubber
stamp and
its trusty
Options
palette,
partners in
cloning.

4. **Option-click on the portion of the image that you want to clone.**

   For example, to fix that big goober near the beginning of the lower tail of Halley's comet, I Option-clicked at a location that appeared to contain similar gray values to the comet stuff that surrounds the goober, as demonstrated in Figure 10-6. The point is to pick a portion of your image that will blend in with areas around the blemish you want to eliminate.

   When you Option-click, the little upside-down triangle at the bottom of the rubber stamp cursor becomes white. Fascinating, huh?

   According to *Webster's,* the word *goober* is derived from the Kongo word *gnuba,* which means peanut. And peanut (wink) is exactly what I mean (nudge, nudge).

5. **Now click or drag on the offending blemish.**

   Actually, that mark on my comet looks more like a pimple than a peanut, doesn't it? To apply the digital zit cream, I clicked directly on the critter and purged it good. No muss, no fuss; the glitch is gone.

The dreaded cosmic goober

Option-click with rubber stamp

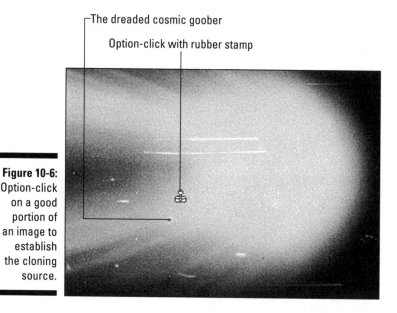

Figure 10-6:
Option-click
on a good
portion of
an image to
establish
the cloning
source.

When you click or drag with the rubber stamp, Photoshop displays a cross
cursor along with the stamp cursor, as shown in Figure 10-7. This cross
represents the clone source, or the area that you're cloning from. As you
move the mouse, the cross cursor also moves, providing a continual reference to the portion of your image that you're cloning. (Things work differently when you have the Aligned option unchecked in the Rubber Stamp
Options palette, however, as explained in the next section.)

Clone source   Rubber stamp cursor

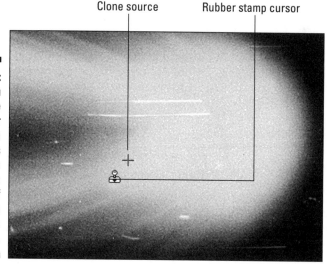

Figure 10-7:
When you
use the
rubber
stamp, a
small cross
follows you
to show you
what part of
the image
you're
cloning.

If the cloned area doesn't blend in well, just choose Edit⇨Undo (⌘-Z), Option-click in the image with the rubber stamp to specify a better source for your cloning, and click or drag with the tool to test out a different clone. You may have to do this several times to get it just right.

Just for the sheer heck of it, Figure 10-8 shows the comet after I finished using the rubber stamp. Now, isn't that way better than anything from Figures 10-3 and 10-4? And it took about 15 minutes. We can all afford 15 minutes, can't we?

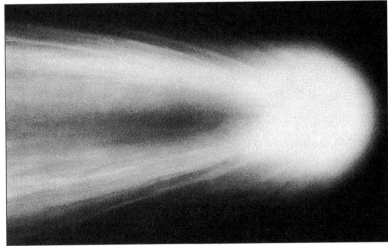

Figure 10-8: Halley's comet, all dressed up and nowhere to go for 76 years.

Performing more magic with the rubber stamp

If you never find out another thing about the rubber stamp tool, you'll be able to clean images quite easily after reading the preceding section. But the rubber stamp is an amazing tool with more facets and capabilities than any other Photoshop tool:

✔ To change the size or shape of the area that's cloned, change the brush size in the Brushes palette, just as you would for other painting or editing tools. (Press F5 to display the Brushes palette.) For more information about the Brushes palette, see Chapter 8.

✔ To make the clone more translucent or less translucent, use the Opacity slider in the Rubber Stamp Options palette. The slider can be accessed by pressing the black arrow to the right of the numeric setting. A setting of 100 makes your clone opaque. (To display the palette, press Return or double-click on the rubber stamp tool in the toolbox.)

✔ To clean up a straight hair or scratch, Option-click with the tool to specify the source for the cloning as you normally would. Then click at one end of the scratch and Shift-click at the other.

✔ If the first clone doesn't look exactly right but is pretty close, you may want to modify the clone slightly rather than redo it. Lower the Opacity setting in the Rubber Stamp Options palette by pressing a number key and then clone from a different position by again Option-clicking and dragging. This allows you to mix multiple portions of an image together to get a more seamless blend.

✔ The blocky rubber stamp cursor that appears by default makes predicting the outcome of your clone difficult. To get a better idea of the size of your clone before you click, press ⌘-K and then ⌘-3 to open up the Display & Cursors panel of the Preferences dialog box. (Or choose File⇨Preferences⇨Display & Cursors.) Select the Brush Size radio button from the Painting Cursors area of the dialog box. Now, your cursor reflects the size of your brush.

✔ Normally, the rubber stamp tool clones from a relative location. If you move your cursor to a different location, the clone source moves with you. But what if you want to clone multiple times from a single location? In this case, leave the Aligned box unchecked in the Rubber Stamp Options palette. Now, you can Option-click once to set the source and click and drag multiple times to duplicate that source.

✔ Photoshop 5 replaced the pattern option in the Rubber Stamp Options palette with the pattern stamp tool. The pattern stamp tool, which shares the same space as the rubber stamp tool, clones an area with a repeating pattern. To do this, you must first define a pattern by selecting a rectangular area and choosing Edit⇨Define Pattern. Drag with the pattern stamp tool, and you will see the pattern appear. Cool, but not really useful.

✔ You can clone between images. What am I talking about? If you have two images open, you can Option-click inside one image to specify the source and drag in the other image to clone. It's like painting one image onto another.

✔ Color Plate 10-1 shows an example of cloning between images. Starting with the two images on the left side of the figure (which I scaled to the same file size by using Image⇨Image Size, as discussed in Chapter 4), I Option-clicked inside the top image and then dragged with the rubber stamp inside the bottom image. I cloned the woman's face and blouse using a large fuzzy brush and then switched to a smaller brush for the touch-ups. To match the skin tones in the forehead and the base of the nose, I cloned from the woman's cheeks at an Opacity setting of 50%. Pretty gruesome, huh?

✔ If your image contains layers, as discussed in Chapter 15, remember that the rubber stamp tool normally clones only from the active layer. If you select the Use All Layers check box in the Rubber Stamp Options palette, the rubber stamp reads the pixels in all visible layers to create the clone. When you then click or drag with the rubber stamp, Photoshop paints the clone onto the active layer.

✔ All the brush modes that apply to the painting tools apply to the rubber stamp as well. This means that you can achieve interesting special effects by selecting the Multiply, Screen, Overlay, Difference, or Color option from the pop-up menu in the upper-left corner of the Rubber Stamp Options palette. For more on brush modes, see the end of Chapter 8.

✔ Try cloning between two different images with a special brush mode in effect. For example, if you clone with the Multiply brush mode, you emblazon the first image onto the second. If you have half an hour to waste, play with the different modes and see what you can do.

Chapter 11

Turning Back the Digital Clock

*H*ere's how you know that you're a consummate computer nerd: When you snag your favorite sweater, say something highly objectionable to your spouse, or spill a well-known staining agent on your newly installed carpeting, your first reaction is not one of panic or regret. You merely think, "Undo."

Unfortunately, the real world provides no Undo command. After a horrible deed is done, it takes an obscenely disproportionate amount of fussing, explaining, or scrubbing to fix the transgression.

Not so in the magical world of personal computing. Edit⇨Undo is standard equipment with just about every Macintosh (and Windows) program out there. With one press of ⌘-Z — the Undo command's keyboard equivalent — your previous operation disappears for good, leaving you one step backward in time.

But Photoshop 5 doesn't stop there. Finally, the number one wish-list item for Photoshop users everywhere comes true — *multiple undos*. This is undoubtedly the most important improvement that Version 5 brings to the table. Not only can you undo as many as 100 actions, but you can also actually *skip* previous steps. In other words, if you have performed five actions and want to return to the way your image looked after your second action, you are not required to first undo steps five, four, and three. You merely select step two in the digital undo command headquarters — the History palette. Now, not only can you turn back the digital clock, you can also truly travel back in time. Adobe definitely deserves an atta-boy for this powerful addition!

This chapter explains all the Photoshop methods for regaining the past so that you can edit worry-free, safe in the knowledge that everything you do can be undone. But before you explore the wide and wonderful world of the History palette, look at the Photoshop old and trusty ways of undoing what's been done.

Nuking the Last Operation

The more you work with Photoshop, the more reflexive your actions become. Certainly, this means that you can work more quickly, but it also means that you are likely to make more mistakes. Reflexive, after all, is a close cousin to thoughtless. And when you don't think, you can wander into some pretty nasty situations.

Doing the Undo

The Undo command ensures that you aren't punished for working reflexively. To get a sense of just how wonderful this command can be, try out these steps:

1. **Open an image.**

   If you already have an image open, good for you.

2. **Select the paintbrush tool and drag across the image.**

   Draw a mustache or something. Just make sure to draw a single brush stroke and no more.

3. **Take a break.**

   You've worked hard, you deserve it. Watch TV for your daily allowance of six hours. Take up macramé. Enlist in the armed forces. The point is, no matter how long you're away, Photoshop remembers the last operation you performed (as long as you don't have a power outage or some similar computing disaster).

4. **Choose Edit⇨Undo.**

   Actually, the name of the command should be Undo Paintbrush. The name of the Undo command changes to tell you what action you're about to undo.

   You can also choose the Undo command by pressing ⌘-Z. Either way, your brush stroke is gone.

After you choose the Undo command, the command changes to the Redo command. For example, if you choose Undo after completing Step 4, the command name is Redo Paintbrush. If you choose the Redo Paintbrush command, your brush stroke comes back, and the Redo Paintbrush command becomes the Undo Paintbrush command again. In other words, you can undo an action and redo it, then undo it and redo it, and so on, until you make up your mind or collapse from exhaustion, whichever comes first.

The Undo command works even after you choose File⇨Print. This means that you can adjust an image, print it to see how it looks, and undo the adjustment if you don't like it. Choosing File⇨Page Setup — or any other command except Print — wipes out your chance to undo that adjustment, though.

Undo limitations

Although the Undo command is certainly a good tool, bear in mind that it does have some limitations. So, here are a few guidelines to stash away in the back of your brain:

✔ You can't undo the Print command. Print involves marking up real pieces of paper, and the Undo command is powerless in the real world. Instead, Undo just ignores Print, as you saw in the preceding steps.

✔ File⇨Save and File⇨Save As are beyond the reach of the Undo command. After the Save command finishes, the image is saved, and the previous version of the image is gone. (The Save As command leaves the previous version of the image intact, so you need never worry when choosing it.)

✔ Not only can you *not* undo Save or Save As, these commands also render the Undo command null and void. After the Save operation completes, the Undo command appears dimmed, meaning that you can't choose it. The operation you performed before choosing Save is now permanent (doubly so, because the changes are saved to disk).

✔ You can't undo the Exit command. There's a surprise. Also, when you relaunch Photoshop, it has no idea what you did during the previous session, so you can't undo the last changes you made before quitting.

✔ You also can't undo changing a foreground or background color, adjusting a setting using one of the commands under the File⇨Preferences submenu, hiding or displaying palettes, changing a palette setting, or selecting a tool. Like the Print command, these operations are ignored by Undo, thus enabling you to undo the previous "significant" operation.

✔ You may think that Photoshop treats File⇨Page Setup like one of the File⇨Preferences commands because you're just adjusting printing preferences. But Photoshop remembers your changes inside the Page Setup dialog box and lets you undo them. So, if you want to undo a brush stroke or other operation after printing the image, don't choose Page Setup before Print.

The Powers of the Eraser

What artist's toolbox would be complete without an eraser? Immediately to the left of the pencil in the toolbox, the eraser tool lets you erase in a couple of ways:

✔ If you drag with the eraser in an image that contains only one layer, the tool paints in the background color, which is typically white. I suppose that you can call this process erasing, but it's really just painting in a different color. Who needs it?

✔ If your image contains more than one layer (layers are discussed in Chapter 15), the eraser works a little differently and becomes a lot more useful. If you drag the eraser on the background layer, the eraser paints in the background color, as usual. But on any other layer, the pixels you scrub with the eraser become transparent, revealing pixels on underlying layers. This assumes that the Preserve Transparency check box is turned off in the Layers palette. If this check box is turned on, the eraser paints in the background color.

✔ In Photoshop 4, if you Option-dragged with the tool, you revealed the image as it appeared when you last saved it to disk. In Photoshop 5, however, holding down the Option key with the eraser allows you to erase back to a chosen step in the History palette. This is explained further in the section on the History palette.

Adjusting your eraser

Though only one eraser tool is in the toolbox, Photoshop actually provides four kinds of erasers. To switch erasers, select an option from the pop-up menu in the upper-left corner of the Eraser Options palette, discussed later in this chapter.

You can also switch from one kind of eraser to the next from the keyboard by pressing Shift-E. The first press of E just selects whichever eraser you last used. Press Shift-E again to switch to the next eraser in the list. Press Shift-E a third time to get the next eraser, and so on.

Three erasers are named after painting tools — Paintbrush, Airbrush, and Pencil — and work exactly like these tools, down to the inclusion of the Wet Edges check box for the paintbrush option. This means that you can change the brush size in the Brushes panel and adjust the Opacity setting to partially reveal the image or, in a layered image, make pixels only partially transparent. (For a refresher on changing the brush size and opacity, review Chapter 8.)

The fourth option, Block, changes the eraser to the square, hard-edged, fixed-size eraser featured in Photoshop 2.5. The options in the Brush Size palette don't affect the block eraser, nor do the Opacity slider bar or any of the other settings in the Eraser Options palette except Erase to History. The block eraser can be useful when you want to completely erase general areas, but you probably won't take it up very often.

Abandoning Edits En Masse

Sometimes you make small mistakes, and sometimes you make big ones. If, after several minutes of messing about, you decide that you hate all your edits and want to return the entire image to its last saved appearance so that you can just start over again, you can do one of two things. First, you can select the top step, technically referred to as a *state,* in the History palette. This restores the image back to the way it appeared when you first opened it. Second, and only if all else fails, choose File⇨Revert. Photoshop displays an alert box to make sure that you didn't choose the wrong command; after all, you've been all thumbs today. If you click on the Revert button or press Return, the program reloads the image from disk and throws away all your changes. You have an advantage in using the History palette rather than the File⇨Revert command. The History palette restores the original image regardless of whether you saved along the way, whereas File⇨Revert reloads the last saved version, which may include some undesirable changes.

You can't undo File⇨Revert, so make sure that you really want to do it before you click on the Revert button.

The History Palette

Now that we opened the door to the History palette with the previous section, let's explore this new and powerful palette in detail.

Choose Window⇨Show History to display the History palette (see Figure 11-1). The History palette records all of your operations and creates a running list of the steps, which Adobe has dubbed *states.* Not state as in United States, but more like state as in State of the Union. In other words, the condition of your image in that point in history. Okay, so that analogy is a bit dramatic. As you perform each operation, Photoshop names each state and displays a corresponding icon according to the tool or command used. It ignores recording operations such as palette and tool settings and color and preferences changes.

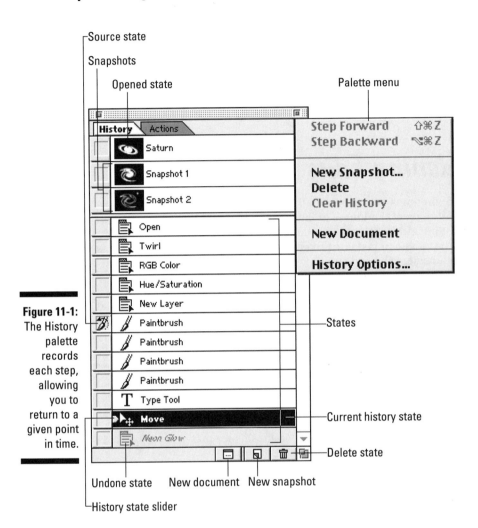

Figure 11-1:
The History palette records each step, allowing you to return to a given point in time.

Source state
Snapshots
Opened state
Palette menu

History   Actions

Step Forward   ⇧⌘Z
Step Backward   ⌥⌘Z

New Snapshot...
Delete
Clear History

New Document

History Options...

Saturn
Snapshot 1
Snapshot 2
Open
Twirl
RGB Color
Hue/Saturation
New Layer
Paintbrush —— States
Paintbrush
Paintbrush
Paintbrush
Type Tool
Move —— Current history state
Neon Glow
—— Delete state

Undone state   New document   New snapshot
History state slider

Here's a list of the History palette's features and functions and how to take advantage of them:

✔ To return to a previous state, click on it. Notice that Photoshop temporarily undoes all steps after that state and that they appear grayed out. Press ⌘-Z or choose Edit⇨Undo to return to your last state; you can also merely click on your last state.

✔ The grayed out states are referred to as *undone states.* You can redo an undone state by clicking on it. If you perform a new operation, the undone states disappear. Choose Edit⇨Undo (⌘-Z) immediately to get the undone states back. Once you move on to other commands, they are gone for good.

✔ To step backward through the palette one state at a time, press
⌘-Option-Z. To move forward, press ⌘-Shift-Z. These commands are
also accessible via the palette pop-up menu.

✔ Drag the history state slider (refer to Figure 11-1) forward and backward to scroll through and see each state rapidly disappear and
reappear in order.

✔ To set the source state — for painting with the history brush, erasing to
History, or filling with History — click in the column to the left of the
state list. The history brush icon appears.

✔ Select a source state (refer to Figure 11-1) in the palette and paint back
to it using the history brush (see details later in this chapter).

✔ Choose a source state in the palette, select Erase to History in the
Eraser Options palette, and erase back to that point in time. Alternatively, pressing the Option key while erasing will also Erase to History
(for more information read the next section).

✔ Make a selection in your image, and identify a source state in the palette.
Choose Edit⇨Fill, and in the Contents pop-up menu, select History. Press
Return. The selected area fills with what the image looked like at that
point in time while the unselected area remains unchanged. To quickly
fill an area with the source state, press ⌘-Option-Delete.

✔ You can save any state in the History palette as a snapshot — a freeze
frame, so to speak. Even after you've used up all your 100 steps, you
can revert to the way the image looked when you took the snapshot.
Choose New Snapshot from the palette pop-up menu or Option-click on
the page icon at the bottom of the palette (refer to Figure 11-1). Snapshots can be taken from the full document (all layers remain separately
intact), from merged layers (layers are flattened into a background), or
just the current layer (only the elements on the active layer are retained).
For more information on layers, see Chapter 15. You can also click on the
new snapshot icon. The dialog box is bypassed, and a snapshot is
created by using the default settings (full document). You can create and
store as many snapshots as your computer's RAM will allow.

✔ Unfortunately, snapshots are available only as long as your image is
open. They are not saved with the file. The only way to get a "permanent"
snapshot of your image is to create a new file from a chosen state. Select
a state in the History palette, and create a new file from that state by
choosing New Document from the palette pop-up menu or by clicking on
the new document icon at the bottom of the palette (refer to Figure 11-1).
You can also drag and drop the state onto the new document icon.

✔ The History Options command under the palette pop-up menu allows
you to set the number of maximum history states (from 1 through 100)
you want to retain. If your computer is low on RAM (32MB or less), you
may want to set this value to a lower number. Remember that once you
exceed your maximum, the oldest step disappears, then the next
oldest, and so on.

✔ Always have Automatically Create First Snapshot checked in the History Options dialog box. If this is unchecked, you don't get a snapshot of the opened state (refer to Figure 11-1). You can always go back to the first state; however, if you exceed your maximum number of history states, this first state disappears. Then, if you have saved any changes along the way, you cannot retrieve your original image.

✔ The Allow Non-Linear History option in the History Options dialog box permits undone states to remain when you perform a new operation. Note that you cannot undo a state without affecting later states. For example, you paint, airbrush, and pencil on an image. You can go back to the paint state and paint some more without losing your later airbrush and pencil states. However, you can't undo the airbrush state and retain the pencil state. Even if you delete the airbrush state, the strokes you applied remain on the image. Be aware that it can be somewhat confusing. Experiment with a test image until you get a good handle on it, or leave this option unchecked.

✔ If you are absolutely sure you are happy with your image and your computer is slowing down or running out of memory, you can delete the history states by choosing the Clear History command from the palette pop-up menu. If you change your mind, immediately press Edit➪Undo (⌘-Z). If you have multiple files open, you can clear all their histories at once by choosing Edit➪Purge➪Histories. You are prompted with a warning that this cannot be undone. Press Return. For either choice, you still retain your opened state — your original image — but all your other steps are deleted.

✔ You can delete a single state by selecting it and choosing Delete from the palette pop-up menu. You can also simply select the state and click on the trash can icon at the bottom of the palette (refer to Figure 11-1). Alternatively, you can drag and drop the state onto the trash can icon.

✔ Every file has its own history; therefore, you can work on multiple images simultaneously and independently of each other.

✔ Once your image is closed, its history disappears forever. The states and snapshots in the History palette are not saved with the file. Too bad. New wish list item, anyone? Remember what they say . . . be careful what you wish for. Imagine the gargantuan file sizes!

Erasing away the present

Although you will definitely make good use of the all-knowing, all-undoing History palette, the eraser tool provides a more flexible, fun way to blast to the past. You saw the capabilities of the regular eraser earlier in this chapter. Now, look at it after it has been further empowered as the magic eraser.

The following steps give you an opportunity to try out the magic eraser for yourself. In these steps, you paint a halo around the central subject of an image without harming the subject. First, you color outside the lines, and then you clean it up with the magic eraser:

1. **Open an image.**

   For these steps, open something with a strong central subject, such as a person or an animal. You can't go wrong with a fish like the one in Figure 11-2.

2. **Set the foreground color to white.**

   Just press D to get the default colors — black for the foreground and white for the background — and then press X to switch them.

Figure 11-2: This lingcod stands out proudly from his sur- roundings.

3. **Trace the central subject with the airbrush tool.**

   Don't worry about getting white all over the central subject. In Figure 11-3, for example, I've made a complete mess of things. There's no way to be careful with the airbrush — it sprays all over the place.

4. **Select the eraser tool.**

   To select the tool from the keyboard, press the E key.

5. **Press Return to display the Eraser Options palette.**

6. **Press Shift-E to cycle through the eraser styles and select the paint-brush style.**

Figure 11-3:
Using the
airbrush, I
traced
sloppily
around the
lingcod.

7. **Check on Erase to History in the Eraser Options palette.**

   Alternatively, you can leave it unchecked and press Option to access the magic eraser.

8. **Press F5 to display the Brushes palette and choose a medium-size, soft brush.**

9. **In the History palette, select the source state you want to erase back to.**

10. **Drag to erase inside the central subject (in my case, the lingcod).**

    As you drag, you reveal the way the image looked at that point in time.

Getting to the image shown in Figure 11-4 required that I perform Step 10 with some care and effort. I wanted to erase inside the subject only and leave the white airbrush paint intact in the background. Creating similar effects may take many strokes and many undos to get the image just right, but the practice is good for you. Just don't forget to either check on Erase to History in the Eraser Options palette or press the Option key every time you erase — teaches you patience and all that.

Here are some more things to know about erasing back to the history of your image:

   ✔ If you're erasing a multiple-layer image, the eraser tool erases changes to the active layer only.

✔ You can also select a portion of your image (explained in Chapter 12) and revert only that portion to a source state using the Edit➪Fill command. For details on filling, see Chapter 14.

Brushing back in time

Like the eraser tool, the History palette provides a more artistic, free-form way of revealing a previous state of an image.

Figure 11-4: The lingcod glows eagerly as he emerges from his nuclear chamber.

To brush back to a source state:

1. **Select the history brush tool.**

   To select the tool from the keyboard, press the Y key. There is no need to press the Option key.

2. **Press Return to display the History Brush Options palette.**

3. **Select a brush mode from the pop-up menu in the History Brush Options palette.**

   Being able to utilize the brush modes is an advantage the history brush has over the magic eraser. Different effects can be achieved by using various modes. See Chapter 8 for tips on these modes.

4. **Optional: You can check on the Impressionist box in the History Brush Options palette.**

   This paints back to the source state in a soft, smudgy, painterly *(a la Monet)* fashion. It's worth playing with. Remember, you can always undo.

5. **Press F5 to display the Brushes palette and select a brush size and style.**

6. **In the History palette, select the source state you want to brush back to.**

7. **Drag the history brush on the image.**

   As you drag, you reveal the way the image looked at that point in time.

Why won't the eraser or history brush work?

A few operations prevent the eraser tool and the history brush from reverting back to a source state. These same operations will also prevent filling a selection with History. Reverting to a source state by any of these methods works only if the image on-screen and the history states in the History palette share the same file size — that is, they each contain exactly the same number of pixels. Any operation that changes the size of the on-screen image throws a monkey wrench into the works. You will see the not-allowed cursor (a circle with a slash) when trying to use the history brush. An on-screen warning appears when you try to use the magic eraser, and the Erase to History check box is grayed out in the options palette. The History option in the Contents pop-up menu under Edit⇨Fill is grayed out as well.

The following operations prevent you from erasing or brushing to a source state:

- ✔ Trimming the image with the crop tool.

- ✔ Applying the Image Size command with the Resample Image check box selected. (As long as Resample Image is unchecked, you can change the dimension or resolution without causing problems.)

- ✔ Using the Canvas Size command.

- ✔ Applying any of the commands under the Image⇨Rotate Canvas submenu (except 180°) to the entire image.

You can still erase or brush to source states that appear *after* the operations, but not to any source states listed *prior* to that operation. Given all that the History palette, history brush, magic eraser, and fill with history operation can do, these limitations seem insignificant, minor — minuscule.

Part IV

Select Before
You Correct

The 5th Wave   By Rich Tennant

"I'VE GOT SOME IMAGE EDITING SOFTWARE, SO I TOOK THE LIBERTY OF
ERASING SOME OF THE SMUDGES THAT KEPT SHOWING UP AROUND THE CLOUDS.
NO NEED TO THANK ME."

In this part . . .

The first time children arm themselves with crayons and coloring books, they all do the same thing: They scribble. Few children have sufficient coordination to color tidily, and, frankly, I doubt that they see much point to it. But there's always one adult who says, "Darling, try to color inside the lines."

It's tough to unlearn a lesson that's ingrained into every one of us at such a trusting age, but the truth is, carefully coloring inside the lines is and always has been a counter-intuitive and nonartistic operation. It defeats expression-ism and prevents you from seeing the larger picture.

"This may be so," you might argue, "but what if I'm trying to perform a delicate adjustment to a complex image? I can't just start scribbling all over the place." Ah, but there's where you're wrong. That's exactly what you can do. See, any time you want to constrain an effect to a small area of your image, you should first select it. After you've done that, Photoshop automatically ensures that the larger image remains intact, no matter how sloppy your motor skills.

As you might expect, *selecting* is the topic of Chapters 12 through 14. Here, you find out how to select an element in your image, how to modify the selection if you don't get it exactly right the first time, and how to color selections.

So, the next time you see some kids coloring inside the lines, you'll know what to tell them. "Hey you kids, don't you know that tidy people never prosper? Break off the tips of those crayons and start scribbling!"

Chapter 12

The Great Pixel Roundup (Yee Ha)

- -

In This Chapter

▶ Picking the right selection tool

▶ Roping pixels with the lasso tools

▶ Drawing straight-sided selections

▶ Selecting with the new magnetic lasso

▶ Selecting rectangular and oval areas

▶ Using the magic wand

▶ Selecting with the Color Range command

▶ Creating paths with the pen tool

▶ Editing paths

▶ Using the new freeform and magnetic pen tools

▶ Exploring the Paths palette

▶ Creating clipping paths

- -

*I*f you're an old ranch hand, you may find it helpful to think of the pixels in your image as a bunch of cows. A pixel may not have any horns, and it rarely moos, but it's a cow all the same. Consider these amazing similarities: Both pixels and cows travel in herds. (Come on, when's the last time you saw one pixel out on its own?) They're both dumb as dirt. And obstinate to boot. And — here's the absolute clincher — you round them both up by using a lasso.

The only difference between pixels and cows is in the vernacular. When you lasso a cow or two on the lone prairie, it's called ropin'. When you lasso a mess of pixels, it's called selectin'. And after you select the desired pixels, you can do things to them. You can move them, duplicate them, and apply all kinds of alterations that I describe in future chapters. Selecting lets you grab hold of some detail or other and edit it independently of other portions of your image. It's a way of isolating pixels to manipulate them.

This chapter and Chapter 13 discuss methods for selecting portions of an image. With a little practice, you can rustle pixels better than most hands rope dogies, and that's no bull.

Learning the Ropes

Photoshop provides several selection tools, all labeled in Figure 12-1. These tools include the lasso, the polygon lasso, the new magnetic lasso, four so-called marquee tools, and an automatic color-selector known as the magic wand. Here's how they work:

- Drag inside the image with the lasso to select free-form areas. The shape of the selection conforms to the shape of your drag.

- Use the polygon lasso tool, which shares a flyout menu with the regular lasso, to draw polygon selections — that is, selections made up of straight sides. You can still use the old technique of holding down the Option key and clicking with the regular lasso, but you also have the option of using the dedicated polygon lasso tool.

- Photoshop 5 adds a new member to the lasso team — the magnetic lasso tool. Click the magnetic lasso tool on the edge of your object and then move the lasso around that edge. Keep reading this chapter for further details!

- The rectangular marquee tool lets you select a rectangular area. Just drag from one corner of the area you want to select to the other. The outline drawn with the tool looks like a border of moving dots — which is how marquee managed its way into the tool name.

- The elliptical marquee draws oval selections. The word *ellipse,* incidentally, is what mathematicians say when they're talking about ovals. In fact, I'd just call it the *ovoid marquee tool,* but I'm afraid that you'd think I was talking about a home pregnancy test.

- The single-column and single-row marquee tools select one solitary column or row of pixels in your image. Both these tools fall under the limited-use category.

- The magic wand selects areas of continuous color. For example, if you want to select the sky without selecting the clouds, you just click in the sky. At least, that's the way it's supposed to work, but you never know. The magic wand isn't always as magic as you may think.

Now that you know how the tools work, look at how to get to the tools. The arrow in the lower-right corner of the marquee and lasso tool icons in the toolbox indicates that a flyout menu of hidden tools lurks beneath each icon (see Chapter 2 for more information).

To switch between the tools on the flyout menus, you can Option-click on whichever tool icon happens to be visible in the toolbox at the time. You can also select tools using these keyboard shortcuts:

- Press the M key to access the active marquee tool. If the rectangular marquee is active, press Shift-M to toggle through the elliptical, single row, and single column marquee tools.

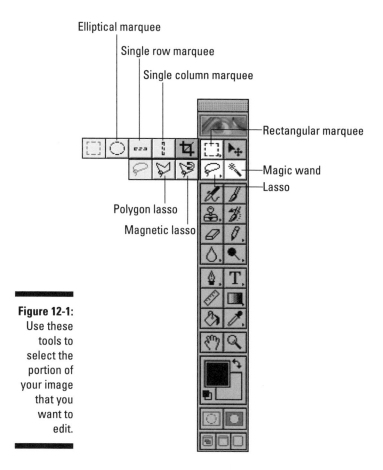

Elliptical marquee

Single row marquee

Single column marquee

Rectangular marquee

Magic wand

Lasso

Polygon lasso

Magnetic lasso

Figure 12-1:
Use these
tools to
select the
portion of
your image
that you
want to
edit.

✔ Press L to get the lasso tools. As with the marquee tools, the same
shortcut switches you between the three lasso tools: If the regular lasso
is active, pressing Shift-L brings up the polygon and the magnetic lassos.

✔ Press W to get the magic wand. The tool is more unpredictable than
magic, making W — for Wacky Wand — a logical keyboard equivalent.

Throwing Lassos

Both the regular and polygon lasso tools are so easy to use, your newborn
could master them. If you don't have a newborn, I guess you have to muddle
through on your own. The magnetic lasso is trickier, however, but nothing a
toddler couldn't pick up with a little guidance.

Using the regular lasso

I have only one instruction for using the lasso: Trace around the portion of the image that you want to select with the tool. That's it. In Figure 12-2, for example, I dragged around the mushroom to select it independently of its surroundings. As the figure shows, Photoshop displays a dotted outline around the selected area after you release the mouse button. This outline represents the exact path of your drag. (If you release before completing the shape — that is, before meeting up with the point at which you began dragging — Photoshop simply connects the beginning and ending points with a straight line. So you won't hurt anything if you release too early.)

I was careful to draw the outline just right in Figure 12-2. There's no trick to it; I've just had plenty of practice. If your outlines aren't quite so accurate, however, don't sweat it. There are plenty of ways to modify the outline after you draw it (see Chapter 13).

Lasso cursor ⌐   ⌐Selection outline

Figure 12-2:
I selected
the
mushroom
by dragging
around it
with the
lasso.

Drawing straight-sided selections

Suppose that you want to select that cube-with-a-ball thing in the center of the image. You can drag around it with the lasso tool, but a better option is to use the polygon lasso, which makes it easy to create selections with straight sides.

To select an object in this manner, click with the polygon lasso to set the beginning of the first line in the selection. Then move the mouse cursor to the point where you want the line to end and click again. Keep clicking to create new line segments. To complete the selection, you have two options. If you double-click, Photoshop draws a segment between the spot you double-click and the first point in your selection. You can also move the cursor over the first point in your selection until you see a little circle next to the polygon lasso cursor. Then click to close the selection.

The polygon lasso can also be used for images with both curved and straight segments. You can switch to the regular lasso in midselection to create a curved segment. Just press and hold down the Option key and drag to draw your curved line. When you release the Option key, the tool reverts back to the polygon lasso.

You can also press Option while drawing a selection with the regular lasso to access the polygon lasso. Press Option and click to set the endpoints of your straight-sided segments, as you normally do with the polygon lasso. To start another curved segment, just drag. You can keep the Option key down or not — it doesn't matter. But be sure that the mouse button is down any time you press or release the Option key, or Photoshop will complete the selection outline.

Selecting with the new magnetic lasso

This new lasso tool takes a little getting used to and may not produce a great selection in all cases. But it is easy to use, and if you take some time to understand the method behind its madness, it can be a quick remedy to your selection needs.

The magnetic lasso works best with high contrast images — that is, the element you want to select is a different color than the background. Using the settings in the Magnetic Lasso Options palette, the magnetic lasso analyzes the difference in the color of the pixels between the element you want to select and the background and snaps to your element's edge. Here's how to use this quirky tool:

1. **Select the magnetic lasso tool.**

   Press L and then Shift-L to use the keyboard shortcut.

2. **Click on the edge of the element you want to select.**

3. **Move the cursor around the edge of the element.**

   Don't press the mouse and drag — just *move* the mouse. Simple! The magnetic lasso creates an outline, with square anchor points, around the edge of the element. If the line is off the mark, back up your mouse and try again. If you need to delete an anchor point as you are moving around the edge, press the Delete key. To create your own anchor points, click with the mouse. Adding your own anchor points can be helpful if the magnetic lasso seems reluctant to stick to the edge you select.

4. **Continue around the element and click on your starting anchor point to close the outline.**

   You will see a small circle next to your cursor indicating closure of the outline.

5. **As soon as the outline is closed and you release the mouse, a selection marquee appears.**

6. **Press Esc or ⌘-period to cancel the magnetic lasso.**

To create a straight segment while using the magnetic lasso, press Option and click with the mouse. You will see the tool icon of your cursor change temporarily to the polygon lasso. Release the Option key and drag for a second to reset the tool back to the magnetic lasso. From then on, just move the cursor without clicking or dragging.

Exploring your lasso options

Whether you use the regular lasso, the polygon lasso, or the magnetic lasso, you can modify the performance of the tool via the two options common to all three tools in the Lasso Options palette (see the next section for options specific to the magnetic lasso). The palette is called the Polygon or Magnetic Lasso Options palette if you're using the polygon or magnetic lasso. To display the palette, double-click on the tool icon in the toolbox or press Return while the tool is selected.

Though small in number, the options for the lasso tools are some tough little hombres:

✔ First off, both options — Feather and Anti-aliased — affect future selection outlines drawn with the lasso tool. In short, Feather makes the outline fuzzy, and Anti-aliased slightly softens the edge of the outline. If you want to modify an outline that you've already drawn, you have to choose a command under the Select menu. Because these commands affect outlines drawn with any tool, I describe them in Chapter 13.

✔ Normally, selections drawn with the lasso tools have soft, natural-looking edges. This softening is called *anti-aliasing* (see Chapter 8). To turn the softening off, click on the Anti-aliased check box in the palette to get rid of the check mark. From now on, outlines drawn with the tool will have jagged edges.

✔ Figure 12-3 shows two lassoed selections moved to reveal the white background in the image. In the left example, the Anti-aliased check box was turned off; in the right example, the option was turned on. The edges of the left example are jagged; those of the right example are soft. (Chapter 13 explains all the ways to move selections. But if you want to try moving a selection now, just drag it with the move tool, which is the top-right tool in the toolbox. Or ⌘-drag with any other tool but the pen or hand tool.)

Anti-aliasing off   Anti-aliasing on

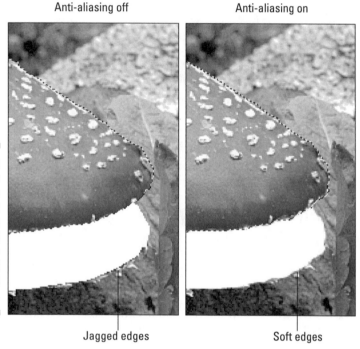

Figure 12-3: The difference between dragging a jagged (left) and anti-aliased (right) selection.

Jagged edges   Soft edges

✔ Most of the time, you want to leave the Anti-aliased check box turned on. Just turn it off when you want to select precise, hard-edged areas. (Which may be never. Who knows?)

✔ Enter a value into the Feather option box to make the outline fuzzy. The value determines the radius of the fuzziness in pixels. If you enter a value of 3, for example, Photoshop extends the fuzzy region 3 pixels up, 3 pixels to the left, 3 pixels down, and 3 pixels to the right. As demonstrated in the first example of Figure 12-4, that's a lot of fuzz. A higher value results in a more fuzzy selection outline, as witnessed in the right example, which sports a Feather value of 10.

Feather 3 pixels Feather 10 pixels

Figure 12-4:
A bigger
Feather
value
means
more fuzzy
fungus.

Looking at the unique magnetic lasso options

The magnetic lasso has unique options in the palette that are related to the sensitivity of the tool's operation. They are the following:

- ✔ **Lasso Width:** This option determines how close to an edge you have to move the mouse for Photoshop to "see" the element. You can set it to a higher number for smooth, high contrast elements, and it will still hug the edge of the element. Set it to a lower value if the image has a lot of nooks and crannies or the contrast isn't that high. The range of the lasso width option is 1 to 40 pixels. To change it while you are actually using the tool, press the [key to lower the number and the] key to raise the number.

- ✔ **Frequency:** The number in the Frequency option tells the magnetic lasso when to automatically insert anchor points. The range for frequency is from 0% to 100%. If you want more points, insert a higher number; for less points, use a lower value. High values are better for rough, jagged edges, and lower values are better for smooth edges. As you move around the edge of your element and create the outline, Photoshop pins it down with an anchor point.

✓ **Edge Contrast:** This option tells the magnetic lasso how much contrast is required between the element and the background before the lasso will be "attracted" or will hug that edge. The range for the edge contrast is 1% to 100%. If you find a good deal of contrast between the element and the background, use a higher value in order to get a cleaner selection. If the image is low contrast, lower the value for this option.

Start with default settings for the preceding magnetic lasso options, carefully make your selection, and see how it works. If your image is low contrast, you may want to lower the edge contrast to 5% or so. If edges are jagged or rough, try raising the frequency to around 70% and lowering lasso width to 5 pixels. If all else fails and the magnetic lasso just isn't behaving, you can always go back to the regular and polygon lassos. They may not be as high tech, but they are reliable.

Selecting Rectangles, Squares, Ellipses, and Circles

If you want to create a selection that's rectangular or elliptical, you use — guess what — the rectangular and elliptical marquee tools. The rectangular and elliptical marquee tools are so easy to use that they make the lasso look complicated. You just drag from one corner to the opposite corner, and release the mouse button. (Okay, ovals don't have corners, so you have to use your imagination a little bit.) The dotted marquee follows the movements of your cursor on-screen, keeping you apprised of the selection outline in progress.

But Photoshop has never been one to provide you with only one way to use a tool — or, in this case, two tools. For example, you can also use these tools to select perfect squares or circles. The program's cup of flexibility forever runneth over, and the marquee tools are no exception.

Grabbing a square or circle

Every so often, you may feel the urge to apply some puritanical constraints to your selection outlines. Enough of this random width and height business — you want perfect squares and circles. Lucky for you, Photoshop obliges these fussbudget impulses by letting you constrain shapes drawn with the marquee tool:

✓ To draw a perfect square, press the Shift key after you begin dragging with the rectangular marquee tool. To draw a perfect circle, press Shift after you begin dragging with the elliptical marquee tool.

✔ Drawing squares and circles is a little trickier than you might expect. For the best results, you should first begin dragging, then press and hold Shift, drag to the desired location and release the mouse button, and finally release Shift. In other words, press Shift after you start the drag and hold it until after you complete the drag.

✔ If you press Shift before dragging, you run the risk of adding to the previously selected area, as I describe in lucky Chapter 13. Here's the deal: If a portion of your image was selected before you started Shift-dragging, Photoshop sees to it that that area remains selected and selects the marqueed area as well. Meanwhile, the shape of the marquee is not constrained to a square or a circle. Befuddling, huh? If this happens to you, press ⌘-Z to undo the selection and try again, this time taking care to press Shift during — not before — your drag.

The marquee tools can come in handy not only for selecting part of your image, but for creating geometric shapes as well. For example, if you want to draw a rectangle, create a marquee with the rectangular marquee tool. Then choose Edit➪Stroke to *stroke* the marquee with the foreground color — in other words, to paint a line along the marquee. For more on the Stroke command, see Chapter 14.

Getting even more control over selections

Are you crazed for control? Do your tyrannical desires know no bounds? If so, you probably aren't appeased by drawing a square or a circle. What you want is to apply even more stringent constraints.

For example, say that you're the sort of pixel-oppressor who wants to select a rectangular or oval area that is exactly twice as wide as it is tall. With your marquee tool selected, press Return to display the Marquee Options palette. Then choose Constrained Aspect Ratio from the Style pop-up menu. The Width and Height option boxes then come to life, letting you specify an aspect ratio, which is a precise proportion between the width and height of a marquee. To make the marquee twice as wide as it is tall, enter **2** as the Width value. Then press Tab to highlight the Height value and enter **1**. The deed is done.

But that's not all. You can also set up the marquee to select a row or column of pixels that is a single pixel tall or wide. To do this, select the Single Row or Single Column icon from the marquee flyout menu in the toolbox. Then click to create the marquee. If you select Single Row, the marquee is 1 pixel tall and extends across the entire width of your image; if you select Single Column, the marquee is 1 pixel wide and as tall as your image. After you click to create the marquee, you can drag it to reposition it if necessary.

Finally, to constrain the marquee to an exact size, select Fixed Size from the Style pop-up menu. Then enter the exact dimensions of your desired marquee into the Width and Height option boxes. The values are always measured in pixels. It's very unlikely that you will ever want to do this — even if you live to be 103 — but I didn't want you to think that I neglected to explain one of these silly options for no good reason.

One last item submitted for your approval: Like the Lasso Options palette discussed earlier in this chapter, the Marquee Options palette sports Anti-aliased and Feather options, which respectively soften the selection outline and make it blurry. However, the Anti-aliased check box is dimmed when you use the rectangular, single column, and single row marquee tools. Perpendicular edges never need softening because perpendicular edges can't be jagged. Anti-aliasing, therefore, would be a waste of time.

Drawing from the center out

As I mentioned earlier, you draw a rectangle or oval from corner to opposite corner. But you can also draw a marquee from the center outward. To do this, begin dragging with either marquee tool and then press Option.

If you decide midway into your drag that you don't want to draw the shape from the center outward, just release the Option key and continue dragging. What was once the center of the marquee now becomes a corner.

To draw a square or circle from the center outward, press both Shift and Option after you begin dragging with the appropriate marquee tool. (If you press Shift and Option before you begin dragging, you select the intersection of two selections, as explained in Chapter 13.)

Wielding the Wand

The magic wand is even easier to use than the marquee tools. (Pretty soon, things will get so easy that you won't need me at all.) But it's also the most difficult selection tool to understand and predict. To use the tool, you just click inside an image. Photoshop then selects the area of continuous color that surrounds the cursor.

'Scuze me while I click the sky

Figure 12-5 provides an example of how the magic wand works. In the first image, I clicked with the magic wand tool in the sky above the fake dinosaur. Photoshop automatically selected the entire continuous area of sky. In the second example, I made the selection more apparent by pressing ⌘-Delete, which filled the selection with the white background color. I also got rid of the selection outline by deselecting the area. (Don't worry, I explain deleting and deselecting in full, rich detail in future chapters.)

Figure 12-5:
Look what
happens
when I click
in the sky
above the
T-Rex with
the magic
wand (top)
and fill the
selection
with white.

Notice that the wand selects only uninterrupted areas of color. The patch of
sky below the creature's tail, for example, remains intact. Also, the selection
bit slightly into the edges of the dinosaur. Very small pieces along the top of
the plastic behemoth were removed when I pressed ⌘-Delete.

Teaching the wand tolerance

You can modify the performance of the magic wand by double-clicking on the wand icon in the toolbox or pressing Return with the tool selected. Either way, the Magic Wand Options palette appears, offering three options — Anti-aliased, Use All Layers, and Tolerance.

I covered Anti-aliased earlier in this chapter, in the section "Exploring your lasso options," so I'm not going to beat that poor horse anymore. The Use All Layers option comes into play only when your image contains more than one layer (see Chapter 15). When Use All Layers is turned off, the magic wand selects colors only on the active layer. If you want the magic wand to select colors from all visible layers, turn the option on.

That leaves the Tolerance value, which has the most sway over the performance of the magic wand. It tells Photoshop which colors to select and which not to select. A lower Tolerance value instructs the wand to select fewer colors; a higher value instructs it to select more colors.

Color Plate 12-1 shows what I mean. Each row of images demonstrates the effect of a different Tolerance value, starting with the default value of 32 at the top and working up to 180 at the bottom. In each case, I clicked at the same location, just to the right of the big giraffe's schnoz. The left image in each row shows the selection outline created when I clicked; the right image shows what happened when I filled the selection with white and then deselected the selection.

In the color plate, a Tolerance value of 32 selected too little sky; a value of 180 selected all the sky but also got some huge chunks of giraffe face and rolling foothill. A value of 90 appears to be just right.

The problem is that finding the best Tolerance setting is a completely random exercise in the futile art of trial and error. Like changes to any tool setting, changes to the Tolerance value have no effect on the current selection. You have to click with the magic wand to try out each and every new value. In fact, here's the typical approach:

1. **Click with the magic wand tool.**

   The point at which you click marks the base color — the one Photoshop uses to judge which other colors it should select.

2. **Express displeasure with the results.**

   Gnash your teeth for good measure.

3. **Press Return.**

   Pressing Return while the magic wand is active displays the Magic Wand Options palette — if it's not already visible — and highlights the Tolerance value.

4. **Enter a new Tolerance value and press Return.**

   Enter a higher value to select more colors next time around; enter a lower value to select fewer colors.

5. **Choose Select⇨Deselect or press ⌘-D.**

   Photoshop deselects the previous selection.

6. **Repeat Steps 1 through 5 until you get it right.**

Believe me, even longtime Photoshop hacks like me who've been using the software since Copernicus discovered that the Earth orbits the sun go through this ritual every time they use the magic wand tool. What can I say? It's a useful little tool, but it requires some experimenting.

Selecting with the Better Magic Wand

Photoshop provides an even better magic wand in the form of the Color Range command, which is found under the Select menu. This command lets you select multiple areas of color at a time, even if they aren't continuous. Also, you can adjust the equivalent of the Tolerance setting and see its effect on the selection before you apply the command. The Color Range command is a little complex, but it makes the magic wand look like dog meat.

If you were to investigate the Color Range command and its accompanying dialog box on your own, you might mistake it for one of the most complicated Photoshop functions. But deep down inside, it's a pussycat. You just have to know which options to use and which to ignore.

Strolling through the Color Range

Because we're venturing into some pretty unfriendly territory, I'm going to step you through the Color Range command. Just look where I tell you to look and avert your eyes from the scary stuff, and you won't go wrong.

1. **Select the eyedropper tool.**

   You select the eyedropper by pressing the I key.

2. **Click on a spot inside the area you want to select.**

   Use the eyedropper as though it were the magic wand tool. Nothing becomes selected, of course, but you change the foreground color. The Color Range command uses the foreground color as the base color, just as the magic wand uses the color on which you click as the base color.

3. **Choose Select⇨Color Range.**

   The Color Range dialog box shown in Figure 12-6 appears. I've taken the liberty of dimming all the options that aren't important.

Selection preview

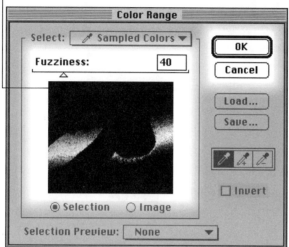

Figure 12-6:
The slider bar, the selection preview, and the OK and Cancel buttons are the only important elements of this dialog box.

The Selection Preview box shows your selection in black and white. The white areas are selected, the black areas are not selected, and the gray areas are blurred selection edges (just as though you had feathered them).

In case you're wondering what that big black blob is in the middle of Figure 12-6, it represents the giraffe image shown in Color Plate 12-2. Before choosing the Color Range command, I clicked to the right of the big giraffe's snout.

4. **Change the Fuzziness value from 1 to 200 to adjust the tolerance.**

   As with the magic wand's Tolerance setting, higher Fuzziness values select more colors, and lower values select fewer colors. As you change the value, the Selection Preview box shows you how the new Fuzziness setting affects the selection. In Figure 12-7, you can see how the selected area — in white — grows as I increase the Fuzziness value.

5. **Click on OK when you finish.**

   Or press Return. Photoshop selects the area displayed as white in the selection preview.

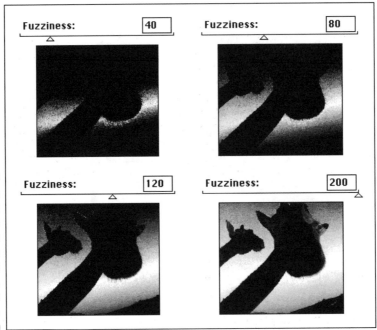

Fuzziness: 40

Fuzziness: 80

Fuzziness: 120

Fuzziness: 200

Figure 12-7:
Increasing
the
Fuzziness
value
spreads the
selection,
shown in
white.

The left example in Color Plate 12-2 shows the result of applying the Color Range command with a maximum Fuzziness value of 200 to the giraffe image. I then pressed ⌘-Delete to fill the selection with white, and deselected the image to arrive at the right example. The Color Range command selected colors on both sides of the giraffe, even though I lifted the base color from the right half of the sky.

The Color Range dialog box offers an Invert check box, which does the same thing as the Select⇨Inverse command. Invert selects everything that's currently not selected and deselects everything that's selected. In other words, it selects the exact opposite of what's currently selected. For more on the Select⇨Inverse command, see Chapter 13.

If you choose the Color Range command when a portion of your image is selected, the command selects colors only if they fall inside the current selection. Colors outside the selection are ignored. Therefore, unless you specifically want to isolate part of your image to create a precise selection, be sure to press ⌘-D to deselect the image before choosing Select⇨Color Range. Doing so makes the entire image accessible to the command.

Broadening your color base

Despite the Color Range command's prowess, I wouldn't call Color Plate 12-2 an unqualified success. A lot of blue remains in the second example that the magic wand managed to pick up in Color Plate 12-1.

The fact is, the magic wand and Color Range commands evaluate colors differently (which is why their color-sensing options — Tolerance and Fuzziness — have different names). The wand uses the Tolerance value to decide whether colors are similar to the base color and then selects them. The Color Range command selects all occurrences of the base color in an image and then feathers the selection according to the Fuzziness value. So the magic wand creates definite selection outlines with anti-aliased edges; the Color Range command creates more nebulous ones with blurry edges.

But there's more to the Color Range command, Horatio, than is dreamt of in your philosophy. Unlike the magic wand, the Color Range command lets you specify more than one base color. After choosing Select⇨Color Range, move the cursor outside the Color Range dialog box and over the image. The cursor changes to the eyedropper, allowing you to change the base color if you want to. Press and hold the Shift key, and you see a small plus sign appear next to the eyedropper. Click with this cursor to add a second base color. Continue to Shift-click to add a third base color, fourth, fifth, and so on. Add as many as you like.

In Color Plate 12-3, I specified three base colors. I set the first one before choosing Select⇨Color Range by clicking to the right of the giraffe's nose with the eyedropper tool, just as in Color Plate 12-2. I set the other two by Shift-clicking in the image while inside the Color Range dialog box, once above the giraffe's ear and once below its neck (as the cursors in the color plate indicate).

Adding base colors increased the size of the selected area. To make the selection outline less blurry, I lowered the Fuzziness value to 60. The first image in Color Plate 12-3 shows the resulting selection outline; the second image shows what happened when I filled the selection with white and then deselected the selection. Even though the background is now completely white, the giraffes still blend in naturally, an effect that you can't easily achieve with the magic wand.

It is possible to add too many base colors. As a result, you may select portions of your image that you don't want to select. If this happens, you can delete base colors from inside the Color Range dialog box by Option-clicking on the image. When the Option key is pressed, a little minus sign appears next to the eyedropper cursor.

If adding and deleting base colors starts to get confusing, you can reset the selection in the Color Range dialog box by clicking on the image without pressing Shift or Option. This returns you to a single base color.

The Best Tool for the Job

The variety of selection tools and methods we've just explored have an advantage and a disadvantage — the advantage is that they are easy to use, the disadvantage is that sometimes they aren't that precise and require some additional cleanup. Fortunately, you have another option. The last remaining selection tool is the pen tool. Of course, as you know, there's a catch. Although the pen tool yields the most precise selection, it is also a difficult tool for novices to master. Many new Photoshop users try it, can't get it to do what they want, and vow never to touch it again, while reaching for the friendly magic wand or lasso.

Before you're totally dissuaded from using the pen tool, let me mention that Photoshop 5 is trying to make your relationship with the pen tool an amicable one. This new version adds two additional pen tools — the freeform pen tool and the magnetic pen tool. This section tells you what you need to know about pens and paths.

The path to a better selection

Before you move on to how to use the pen tools, consider the product they make — paths. Unlike the other selection tools, using the pen tool does not produce a selection marquee right away. As you click and drag around your chosen element, you create the three components of a path — anchor points (like those you saw with the magnetic lasso), straight segments or lines, and curve segments or curves. These paths are referred to as *Bezier paths,* which means that the paths are based on a mathematical model where a path is controlled by direction lines and handles (explained in detail soon).

After the path is drawn, you can then fine-tune the appearance by moving, adding, deleting, or converting anchor points. The path hovers over the image in its own unique space. You won't see a separate layer in the layer palette (for more on layers, see Chapter 15), but you will see the path "layer," for lack of a better word, in the Paths palette. After you create the path, you can fine-tune the path through editing and then turn the path into a selection. The pen tools and Paths palette, as shown in Figure 12-8, work together to handle the world of paths and their selections.

Creating paths with the pen tool

Now that you know what a path is, look at how to create a path with the pen tool. You can start with straight lines and then graduate to curves. Remember that this isn't easy the first few times, so hang in there:

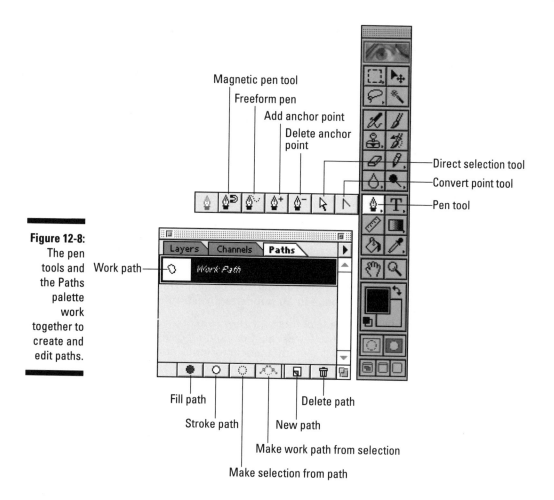

Figure 12-8:
The pen tools and the Paths palette work together to create and edit paths.

Magnetic pen tool
Freeform pen
Add anchor point
Delete anchor point
Direct selection tool
Convert point tool
Pen tool
Work path
Fill path
Stroke path
New path
Delete path
Make work path from selection
Make selection from path

1. **Select the pen tool.**

   The keyboard equivalent is the P key.

2. **To draw a straight line, click the mouse where you want the line to begin and then to end, leaving anchor points at those positions.**

   A straight segment, or line, connects the two anchor points. Drawing straight lines requires just a click and release of the mouse, no dragging. To draw a constrained line — horizontal, vertical, or a 45° angle — hold the Shift key down as you click. To create connecting straight lines, repeat the process. To end the path, click on the pen tool. Better yet, hold down the ⌘ key, which will give you the direct selection tool (white arrow), and click away from the curve. Release the ⌘ key, and the pen tool reappears.

3. **To draw a curve, you position the cursor where the curve is to begin, press the mouse, drag toward the bump of the curve, and release the mouse.**

   You create an anchor point, along with two direction lines, and at the end of those, direction points. These direction lines and points control the appearance of the curve — in other words — its angle and how steep or flat it is.

4. **Move the cursor to the end of the curve, press the mouse, and drag in the opposite direction, away from the bump.**

   You now see another anchor point, a set of direction lines and points, and the actual curve. See finished curve in Figure 12-9.

   In your Pen Options palette, check on the Rubber Band option. Photoshop will then draw a segment between the last anchor point you create and wherever your cursor is located, thereby giving you a kind of preview of how the path will appear.

5. **To create multiple, alternating curves, just continue Steps 4 and 5, dragging your mouse in an opposite direction each time.**

   Try and keep anchor points on either side of the bump, not on top. Also, try and use the fewest anchor points possible to create your path. Remember, a path is a mathematical formula, and the less complex it is, the fewer problems you'll have.

   How far should you drag? Imagine that your curve is a piece of string and you stretch it into a straight line. Divide that line into thirds. The distance you drag your mouse is one-third the length of that line.

   At what angle should you drag? You should drag straight from the anchor point for a steeper curve and at an angle from the anchor point for a flatter curve.

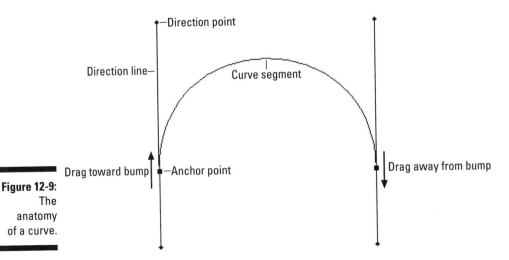

Figure 12-9:
The anatomy of a curve.

6. **Creating curves that all go in the same direction is a little more involved. After you create your first curve, position your cursor over the second anchor point.**

   You see a *caret* (a fancy name for an upside down V symbol) next to your cursor. This caret tells you that you are converting this anchor point, which is smooth (curvy), to a corner (pointy).

7. **Hold down the Option key, press the mouse, and drag toward the bump of the next curve.**

   You now see another direction line appear.

8. **Release the mouse and release the Option key.**

9. **Move your cursor to where you want the curve to end and drag away from the bump to create your second curve.**

10. **Repeat Steps 6 through 9 to create similar, connecting curves.**

11. **To create a straight line from a curve or vice versa, you need to also convert points where the path changes from one to the other.**

    After drawing your curve, position your cursor over the second anchor point, and click your mouse. This creates the corner point by deleting one of the direction lines. Move your cursor to where your line will end and then click. You then see your straight line segment. To return to a curve, position your cursor on the last anchor point you drew and drag your mouse toward the bump of your next curve, adding a direction line in the process. Finish the curve by positioning your cursor where you want your curve to end and drag away from the bump.

12. **Return to your first anchor point and click if you want to close the path.**

    You see a small circle next to your cursor, which indicates that the path will be closed upon clicking.

13. **If you choose to leave the path open, end the path by clicking on the pen tool.**

    Alternatively, you can hold down the ⌘ key, which gives you the direct selection tool (white arrow), and click away from the curve.

Editing paths to perfection

When first working with the pen tool, you'll probably find it difficult to draw a perfect path. Fortunately, you can easily fine-tune your path by using the melange of edit tools (refer to Figure 12-8) that share space with the pen tool. The following are tips to getting your path exactly the way you want them.

✔ To move an anchor point, select the direct selection tool. The tool looks like a white arrow, shares a space on the flyout menu with the pen tool, and its keyboard shortcut is the A key. With the direct selection tool, click on the anchor point you want to move. (Notice that the point becomes solid, whereas the unselected anchor points are hollow.) Press the mouse and drag to move the anchor point. You can also click on the curve or straight line to move those.

✔ To change the shape of the curve, you can move the direction points. Click on the anchor point of the curve you wish to alter. Move the cursor to the upper direction point (the one going the same direction as the bump), press the mouse, and lengthen or shorten the direction line. Notice how the curve steepens or flattens, respectively. By rotating the direction line (moving left or right), the slope of the curve will change.

✔ Two tools allow you to delete or add an anchor point in your path. The add anchor point tool looks like the pen tool with a small plus sign next to it. The delete anchor point tool looks like the pen tool with a small minus sign next to it. To add an anchor point, simply click the tool in the path where you need an anchor point. Note that it always adds a smooth point. To delete an anchor point, position the cursor over the anchor point you no longer need and click. It disappears while keeping your path intact.

✔ To convert an anchor point from smooth to corner or vice versa, you need to select the convert point tool. This is the last tool in the flyout menu of the pen tool and looks like a caret (the same symbol you saw when holding down the Option key with the pen). Position your cursor on the anchor point you want to convert. If the anchor point is a corner point, press the mouse and drag away from the anchor point to create the direction line that will create a smooth point. If the point is a smooth point, simply click (don't drag) over the anchor point, and the point becomes a corner.

✔ To copy a path, select it, hold down the Option key, and drag the path away from the original.

✔ If the path is open and you want to continue the path, click or drag on the endpoint with the pen tool and continue drawing. Your addition to the path will then be connected.

✔ If the path is open and you want to close the path, click or drag on the endpoint with the pen tool and go back to the first anchor point in your path. You will see a circle appear next to your cursor to assure you the path is closing.

✔ And finally, to delete a path, select the entire path and press the Delete key, or select a point on the path and press Delete twice.

✔ Photoshop 5 gives you another option in editing your paths by letting you apply transformations to a path, such as scale, rotate, and skew, without affecting the underlying image. See the section on transforming selections and paths in Chapter 13.

The new freeform and magnetic pen tools

Hopefully you survived the tedious and technical explanation of paths and the various pen tools, because now I want to introduce you to two kinder and gentler versions of the pen — the freeform pen and the magnetic pen tools (refer to Figure 12-8).

The freeform pen acts much like the lasso tool. Simply drag around the element you want to select, and the tool creates an outline that follows your cursor. After you release your mouse, Photoshop provides the anchor points, lines, and curves for that path. None of that Bezier curve drawing business! To create straight lines with this tool, press the Option key while the mouse button is pressed and click to create the anchor point. When you want to return to drawing curves, release the Option key, keeping the mouse button pressed. If you release the Option key while the mouse button is not pressed, Photoshop ends your path.

You find an option called Curve Fit in the Freeform Pen Options palette. The Curve Fit option is the amount of error Photoshop allows when trying to fit your cursor movement to a path. You can enter a value from .5 to 10 pixels, the default setting being 2 pixels. This means that Photoshop does not register any movement of your cursor that is 2 pixels or less. Setting the value to .5 pixel makes the freeform pen very sensitive to your movement; setting it to 10 pixels, makes it less sensitive. To get a better idea of the Curve Fit setting, try using the freeform pen at each of these settings and compare the path it makes. Remember that once your path is created, it can always be cleaned up by using the editing methods just described.

The magnetic pen acts much like the magnetic lasso. Begin by clicking on the edge of the element you want to select. Move, don't drag, the cursor around the edge. Notice how it hugs the edge of your element, creating anchor points and segments. To create an anchor point yourself, click your mouse. To create straight segments, you can press the Option key and click. To return to the regular magnetic pen, release the Option key, click again and continue moving the cursor.

You also find the Curve Fit option in the Magnetic Pen Options palette. The lower the value, the more sensitive the tool behaves, and the closer it follows the edge. The disadvantage is that this lower value creates an overabundance of anchor points. The other options — Pen Width, Frequency, Edge Contrast — operate exactly like the magnetic lasso options. For details, see the section, "Looking at the unique magnetic lasso options," earlier in this chapter.

The Paths palette

As stated earlier in this section, the pen tools work in concert with the Paths palette. Here are some tips on how to understand and use this palette. Refer to Figure 12-8 to see the Paths palette.

- ✔ When you create a path, it automatically appears in the Paths palette as a Work Path in its own space, a kind of path layer. You can create a new space for a path prior to drawing it by selecting the page icon at the bottom of the Paths palette.

- ✔ You can delete a path by dragging it to the trash can icon at the bottom of the palette.

- ✔ Paths can be filled. To fill a path, select the path in the Paths palette, choose the Fill Path command from the pop-up menu, or press the Option key and click on the fill path icon (a solid circle) at the bottom of the palette. The dialog box gives options for contents, opacity, and feathering. For details on contents and opacity options, see the section on fills in Chapter 14. The feathering option gradually dissolves the edges of the fill into the background. The Anti-aliased option just slightly softens or blurs the edge of the fill so that the edge doesn't appear as jagged. If you select one or more paths with the direct selection tool, the Fill Path command changes to Fill Subpath, allowing you to fill only the selected paths.

- ✔ Paths can also be stroked with color. To stroke a path, select the path in the Paths palette, choose the Stroke Path command from the pop-up menu, or press the Option key and click on the stroke path icon (an outlined circle) at the bottom of the palette. In the dialog box, choose the paint or edit tool you want to use to apply color to the stroke. If you select one or more paths with the direct selection tool, the Stroke Path command changes to Stroke Subpath, allowing you to stroke only the selected paths.

- ✔ Photoshop uses the current tool options and the brush size when it strokes your path. Be sure and check the particular tool's options palette and the active brush size in the Brushes palette prior to stroking the path.

- ✔ If your end goal in all this pen and paths business is to simply make a nice, clean selection, now is the time. Choose Make Selection from the Paths palette menu. You can choose to feather your selection by adding pixels to the radius or leave the feather radius at 0 for a harder-edged selection. You can also anti-alias the selection to slightly blur the edges so it doesn't appear as jagged. If you have another selection active at the time you go to make your path into a selection, you can have Photoshop add, subtract, or intersect with that other selection. The dialog box can also be reached by pressing the Option key and clicking on the make selection icon in the Paths palette. After the path is made into a selection, it acts like any other selection, as described in the beginning of this chapter and also in Chapter 13.

✔ To make your selection quickly, press Enter on the numeric keypad while your path is selected in the Paths palette and a path or selection tool is active. You can also ⌘-click on the path in the Paths palette.

✔ Photoshop can also work in reverse and take a selection and create a path. With your selection active, choose Make Work Path from the Paths palette pop-up menu. A dialog box appears asking you for a tolerance value. This number controls how sensitive Photoshop is to the nooks and crannies in the selection marquee when it creates the path. The lower the value, the more sensitive it is, and the better it approximates your selection. But the lower value may create too many anchor points. The default of 2.0 is a good starting point. Remember, the path can always be edited and cleaned up. To quickly create a path from a selection, click on the "make work path from selection icon" in the Paths palette.

✔ To hide the path once the selection is made, choose Turn Off Path from the Paths palette pop-up menu or simply click your mouse in the gray area below the path names in the Paths palette.

✔ And last, but not least, you will want to save your paths. After going to all that trouble to make the path, be sure and save it so that it can be used again with your image. Unlike layers, paths are mathematical formulas and take up very little storage space. To save a path, choose the Save Path command from the Paths palette pop-up menu, or simply double-click on the Work Path in the Paths palette. Name the path and click on OK.

Cutting away with clipping paths

One of the more common uses for creating a path, outside making a nice clean selection, is to make a clipping path. A clipping path allows areas that fall outside your path to be transparent, while displaying the area inside the clipping path. Say that you want to import a flower into PageMaker, or another page layout, or illustration program and place it against a colored background. Without a clipping path, the flower will appear against a rectangular white background, regardless of whether the background was transparent in Photoshop (as shown in Figure 12-10). Read on to find out how to create these unique paths.

1. **Using one of the selection tools, make your path around the part of the image you want to display.**

   A Work Path appears in the Paths palette.

2. **Save the path by double-clicking on the Work Path in the Paths palette. Enter a name and click on OK.**

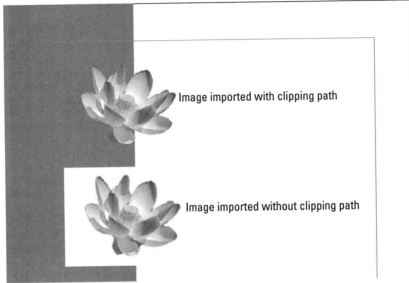

Image imported with clipping path

Image imported without clipping path

Figure 12-10:
Note the difference between importing an image with and without a clipping path.

3. **Choose Clipping Path from the Paths palette pop-up menu.**

   In the dialog box, choose your path name from the Path pop-up menu. Choose a flatness of 3. Simply put, *flatness* represents how closely your curves approximate a true mathematical curve. A higher number leads to more of a polygon shape, but easier printing.

4. **Choose File➪Save As and choose Photoshop EPS from the Format pop-up menu.**

5. **Leave Preview at Macintosh (8 bits per pixel) and encoding as Binary and click on OK.**

   The file is now ready to be imported into your page layout or drawing program.

Clipping paths are notorious for causing printing problems, especially if too many are used or if the paths are too complex (many anchor points). Use clipping paths only when you have no other option. For example, if you want to silhouette an element against a background, composite the element and background in Photoshop and then import the composited image into your page layout or drawing program. Not only does this process ensure that the file will print, but it also ensures that the file prints much faster.

Version 5 helps you create images with transparency via the Export Transparency Image Assistant, located under the Help menu. The Assistant steps you through exporting an image with transparency. It helps you prepare the image for print or the Web. To use the Export Transparency Image Assistant, you must have an active selection marquee or your element must be on a transparent layer (see Chapter 15). With either of these two scenarios, go to Help➪Export Transparency Image Assistant, and answer the questions.

Chapter 13
More Fun with Selections

*I*n the old days, image-editing programs expected perfection from their users. If you didn't get a selection outline right the first time, too bad. You had to start over and try again.

Photoshop broke this heartless trend by expanding its range of selection options. In other words, it got smarter so that you and I can be dumber. Like all the world's best computer programs, Photoshop knows that human beings are a pretty fallible lot and need all the help they can get.

So Photoshop lets you modify a selection outline after you draw it. You can select additional pixels or trim the selection down to a smaller area. You can even smooth out sharp corners, expand a selection to include all similar colors, or swap the selected and deselected portions of the image. All things considered, Photoshop is about the most flexible selector there ever was.

This chapter explains how to modify an existing selection and also touches on more techniques that you can use with the selection tools discussed in Chapter 12. It also tells you how to move and clone selections and explores a wealth of commands under the Select menu that you probably haven't even looked at yet. By the end of this chapter, you'll have a clearer understanding of selection outlines than any other kid on the playground (unless he or she reads this chapter, too).

The Wonders of Deselection

Before I plow into all that whiz-bang, awesome stuff that Photoshop lets you do to a selection outline, I need to touch on selection's exact opposite, deselection. Though this may seem at face value to be a ridiculously boneheaded topic — one that hardly merits space in a scholarly tome like *Photoshop 5 For Macs For Dummies* — deselecting is actually an integral step in the selection process.

Suppose, for example, that you select one part of your image. Then you change your mind and decide to select a different portion instead. Before you can select that new area, you have to deselect the old one. You can deselect an existing selection outline in several ways:

- ✔ Click anywhere in the image with one of the lasso or marquee tools.

- ✔ To get rid of an existing selection and create a new one at the same time, just drag or click to create the new selection as you normally would. Photoshop automatically deselects the old selection when you create a new one.

- ✔ Click inside the selection with the magic wand. (If you click outside the selection, you not only deselect the selection, you also create a new selection.)

- ✔ Choose Select⇨Deselect or press ⌘-D.

Version 5 has provided a great new feature called Reselect. In previous versions, once you deselected your selection, you could regain the selection only if you immediately pressed ⌘-Z, the Undo command. Once you performed another action, it was irretrievable and you had to create your selection again. You can now deselect, perform numerous actions, and regain you most recent selection by choosing Select⇨Reselect or pressing ⌘-Shift-D.

Selecting Everything

When no part of an image is selected, the entire image is up for grabs. You can edit any part of it by using the paint or edit tools or any of about a billion commands. But you can also make the entire image available for edits by choosing Select⇨All (⌘-A) to select everything.

Beginning to see the mystery here? If you can edit any part of the image by deselecting it, why choose Select⇨All, which also lets you edit everything? Because some operations require a selection, that's why. In fact, if you want to apply any of the following operations to your image in its entirety, you must first press ⌘-A:

  ✔ Clone an image by Option-dragging it with the move tool, as discussed later in this chapter.

  ✔ Cut, copy, or paste an image using any of the commands under the Edit menu (discussed in Chapter 15).

  ✔ Apply Edit⇨Stroke (explored in Chapter 14) on the Background layer of an image (as explained in Chapter 15).

  ✔ Apply the Edit⇨Free Transform command or any of the commands under the Edit⇨Transform submenu on the Background layer of an image. (The Transform commands are explored later in this chapter and in Chapter 20.)

Unless you're doing one of these things, you need never worry about Select⇨All. A deselected image usually serves just as well.

Selective Arithmetic

I almost never like the first selection outline I create. Whether I draw it with a lasso or marquee tool, the magic wand, the Color Range command, or sometimes even with the pen, I usually have some problem with the selection. I didn't quite get the hair selected right, or that finger is still clipped off. Whatever the problem, I can remedy it by adding to the selection outline or subtracting from it. And so can you.

Chapter 12 explains how you can Shift-click on an image while inside the Color Range dialog box to add base colors and Option-click to delete base colors. These two keys — Shift and Option — are the universal add and subtract selection modifiers throughout Photoshop.

Adding and subtracting from a selection

To add an area to the current selection, Shift-drag with a lasso or marquee tool. Or Shift-click with the magic wand. It doesn't matter which tool you used to select the image previously, nor does it matter whether you Shift-click inside or outside the selection.

For example, in the obligatory person-holding-up-the-Tower-of-Pisa photo in Figure 13-1, I first selected the tower by dragging around it with the lasso tool, as shown in the left example. To add the woman to the selection, I pressed Shift and dragged around her perimeter, creating the selection outline shown in the right example.

Figure 13-1:
First, I
selected
the tower
(left), and
then I
pressed
Shift and
dragged
around the
woman to
select her,
too (right).

To remove an area from a selection, Option-drag with a lasso or marquee tool or Option-click with the magic wand. To deselect the gap between the woman's legs in Figure 13-1, for example, I could Option-drag with the lasso tool. To deselect the area under the right arm (her left arm), I could Option-click with the magic wand.

Here are a few more addition and subtraction items to keep in mind:

✔ When you're adding to a selection, a little plus sign appears next to your cursor. When you're subtracting from the selection, a little minus sign appears. And when you're selecting the intersection of two existing selections (as explained next), a little multiply sign appears. See, your math teacher was right — knowing arithmetic comes in handy in all kinds of situations.

✔ You can also use the Shift and Option keys in conjunction with the Color Range command. Press Shift and choose Select➪Color Range to add to the selected area; press Option and choose the command to subtract from the selection.

Intersecting a selection with a selection

If you press the Shift and Option keys together while clicking with the magic wand or dragging with a lasso or marquee tool, you select the intersection of the previous selection and the newest one. (Like that made any sense, right?) Take a look at Figure 13-2. I first dragged around the black rectangle. Then I Shift-Option-dragged around the gray rectangle. Photoshop then selected all portions of the second marquee that fell inside the first marquee and deselected everything else, leaving me with the selection shown in the right half of the figure. That's an *intersection*.

Figure 13-2:
I marqueed the black rectangle and then Shift-Option-marqueed the gray rectangle (left). Photoshop then selected the intersection of the two marquees (right).

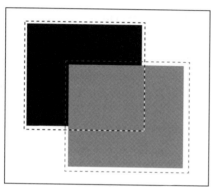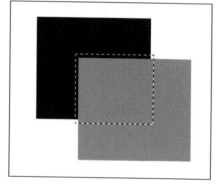

 Try selecting an area with the lasso or one of the marquee tools and then Shift-Option-clicking inside the selection with the magic wand. Or click with the magic wand and then Shift-Option-drag with one of the other selection tools. Either technique lets you limit the area of colors selected with the magic wand tool.

As I discussed earlier in this chapter, if a portion of your image was selected using the Color Range command, you can Shift-choose or Option-choose the command again to add to or subtract from the selection. If you don't press a key when choosing Select⇔Color Range, Photoshop selects an area inside the current selection. In other words, Photoshop already creates an intersection, so you don't gain anything by pressing both Option and Shift when choosing this command.

Avoiding keyboard collisions

In Chapter 12, I discuss a variety of ways to use the lasso and marquee tools while pressing keys. Pressing Option while using one of the lasso tools, you may recall, temporarily accesses one of the other lasso tools. Pressing Shift while using a marquee tool results in perfect squares and circles.

But what happens when you start combining all these add, subtract, and intersect shortcut keys with the ones discussed in Chapter 12? The following list answers your most burning questions:

✔ To add a square or circular area to an existing selection, start by Shift-dragging with the appropriate marquee tool. You get an unconstrained rectangle or oval, just as though the Shift key weren't down. Then midway into the drag — here's the catch — release the Shift key and then press it again, all the while keeping the mouse button down. The shape snaps to a square or circle with the second press of Shift. Keep the Shift key down until after you release the mouse button. Bet you didn't see that one coming.

✔ Pressing Option to temporarily access the polygon lasso when the regular lasso is active causes trouble when you have an existing selection because pressing Option in that scenario sets you up to subtract from the selection. So if you want to add or subtract a straight-sided selection, use the polygon lasso — don't try to Option-click with the regular lasso.

✔ The same advice goes if you want to find the intersection of a selection and a straight-sided shape.

Automatic Selection Discombobulators

Shift-dragging, Option-dragging, and all those other wondrous techniques that I just finished describing — and, possibly, you just finished reading about — are wildly helpful when it comes to selecting complex details. But they aren't the only selection modifications you can make. Photoshop offers a handful of automatic functions that reshape selection outlines, blur them, and otherwise mess them up.

All the commands discussed in the next few sections — Grow, Similar, Inverse, Feather, and so on — reside under the Select menu. I don't discuss every command under the Select menu, just the ones you need to know. But you can take it from me, the commands I don't mention are just so much wasted space.

Extending the magic wand

Two commands, Grow and Similar, are extensions of the magic wand tool. The Grow command expands the size of the selection to include still more continuous colors. For example, if clicking with the magic wand doesn't select all the colors you want it to, you can either increase the Tolerance value inside the Magic Wand Options palette and reclick with the tool or just choose Select⇨Grow to incorporate even more colors. It's kind of a clunky method, especially because the Grow command doesn't have a keyboard shortcut. I prefer to Shift-click with the wand tool, but every once in a while, the Grow command works like you'd expect. (You can use the Grow command with selections made with tools other than the magic wand, by the way.)

The Similar command selects all colors that are similar to the selected colors regardless of whether they're interrupted by other colors. In other words, Similar selects all the continuous colors that Grow selects, as well as all similarly colored pixels throughout the image.

Both Grow and Similar judge color similarity exactly like the magic wand tool does — that is, according to the Tolerance value in the Magic Wand Options palette. So, if you increase the Tolerance value, the commands select more colors; if you decrease the value, the commands select fewer colors. For example, if you want to select all colors throughout the image that are exactly identical to the ones you've selected so far, enter **0** into the Tolerance option box, and choose Select⇨Similar.

Swapping what's selected for what's not

Sometimes it's easier to select the stuff you don't want to select and then tell Photoshop to select the deselected stuff and deselect what's selected. This technique is called *inversing a selection,* and you do it by choosing Select⇨Inverse or pressing ⌘-Shift-I.

For example, suppose that you want to select the clock tower shown on the left side of Figure 13-3. A typical work of baroque madness, this building has more spikes and little twisty bits than a porcupine. Therefore, selecting it would prove a nightmare.

Selecting the sky, on the other hand, is quite easy. By clicking and Shift-clicking a couple of times with the magic wand tool (set to the default Tolerance of 32), I was able to select the entire sky in a matter of two or three seconds. Then, when I chose Select⇨Inverse, I "inversed" the selection so that the building was selected and the sky was deselected. To better show off the selection, I filled it with white, as shown in the example on the right.

Figure 13-3:
This building (left) is too darn ornate to select easily, but it's a snap to select the sky and then inverse the selection. Filling the selection with white shows how accurate the selection is (right).

Making the selection fuzzy around the edges

Chapter 12 explains how you can blur the edges of a selection created with the lasso or marquee tools by increasing the Feather value in the corresponding Options palette. But more often than not, you want to leave the Feather value set to 0 and apply your feathering after you finish drawing the outline.

To feather an existing selection, choose Select⇨Feather or press ⌘-Option-D. A dinky dialog box with a single option box appears on-screen. Enter the amount of fuzziness, in pixels, that you want to apply to the selection, and press Return. The selection outline probably won't change very much, but you see a distinct blurring effect when you edit the selection.

You can use feathering to make an image appear to fade into view. For example, take a look at the kid-in-a-basket image shown on the left side of Figure 13-4. I selected the elliptical marquee tool and encircled the little duffer. Then I chose Select⇨Inverse to select the background instead. Next, I chose Select⇨Feather, entered a value of 8 pixels, and pressed Return. Finally, I pressed ⌘-delete to fill the selection with white. The result is the locket with fuzzy edges, as shown on the right side of Figure 13-4. Isn't he just adorable?

Figure 13-4:
A tiny tot trapped in a basket (left) receives a classic feathering treatment (right).

Using Border, Smooth, and the rest

The remaining selection outline modifiers, found in the Select⇨Modify submenu, aren't quite as useful, but they come in handy every now and then:

- The Border command selects an area around the edge of the selection. You tell Photoshop the width, in pixels, of the border you want to select. This command is probably the least useful command of the bunch. If you want to color the outline of a selection, it's easier to use Edit⇨Stroke, as described in Chapter 14.

- Select⇨Modify⇨Smooth rounds off the corners of a selection outline. If the selection is very irregular and you want to straighten the twists and turns, use this command. Photoshop asks you to enter a value from 1 to 16 to tell it how far it can move any point in the outline. Enter 2 or 3 to be safe.

- If you want to increase the size of a selection a few pixels outward, choose Select⇨Modify⇨Expand and enter the number of pixels. The maximum value is 16 pixels; if you want to expand the outline farther, you have to choose Expand a second time.

- Select⇨Modify⇨Contract is the opposite of the Expand command. This command shrinks the selected area by 1 to 16 pixels all the way around.

Transforming Selections and Paths

Photoshop 5 has added flexibility in the arena of selections and paths by giving you the ability to transform both without affecting the underlying pixels. In Version 4, selections could be transformed only in Quick Mask mode, and paths couldn't be transformed at all.

Transforming selections

To transform a selection marquee or outline, choose Select⇨Transform Selection. You see a box with handles and a *centerpoint* (also referred to as an *origin point*) framing your selection marquee, as shown in Figure 13-5. Using this box you can apply the following transformations:

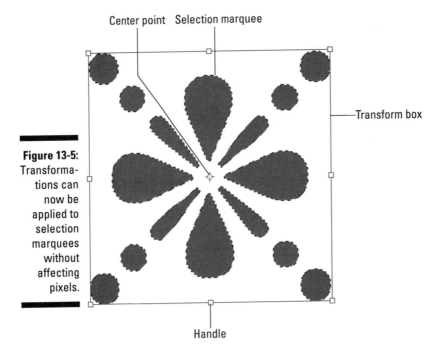

Figure 13-5:
Transformations can now be applied to selection marquees without affecting pixels.

Scale: Drag any handle to scale your selection. Press Shift-drag to maintain proportions. Press Option-drag to scale from the center point outward. Note that the centerpoint can be moved by dragging.

Rotate: Position the centerpoint where you want the axis for the rotation to be. Drag outside the transform box to rotate the selection. Your cursor appears as a double-headed curved arrow.

- ✔ **Skew:** To skew a selection marquee, ⌘-Option-drag a side or a top or bottom handle. Skew permits distortion on a given axis.

- ✔ **Distort:** ⌘-drag a corner handle. Distort allows handles to move independently with no axis restrictions.

- ✔ **Perspective:** ⌘-Shift-Option-drag a corner handle. The opposite corner handle on the same side will move as well.

- ✔ **Flip Horizontal or Vertical:** Press the Control key and click on your image to access the context-sensitive pop-up menu (described and shown in Chapter 2) and choose Flip Horizontal or Flip Vertical.

- ✔ **Numeric:** If you want to make a transformation by entering a numeric value, press the Control key and click on your image, which enables you to access the context-sensitive pop-up menu and choose Numeric. You can move, scale, skew, or rotate via this dialog box. Enter values and click on OK.

- ✔ **Rotate 180°, 90° CW, and 90° CCW:** To rotate in these predetermined amounts, press the Control key and click on your image, which enables you to access the context-sensitive pop-up menu and choose the rotation value.

After you finish transforming, press Return or double-click inside the transform box. To cancel, press Esc or ⌘-period.

Transforming paths

After the transform box is around the path, the transformation methods for paths are exactly the same as for selection marquees, except that distort and perspective can be applied only to whole paths. The big difference between transforming paths and selections is in how you first select the path.

To transform all paths:

1. **Choose the direct selection tool.**

   Press A for the keyboard shortcut for this tool.

2. **Click on the image (anywhere except on the paths) with the direct selection tool.**

3. **Choose Edit⇨Free Transform Path.**

   The keyboard shortcut is ⌘-T.

To transform a single path:

1. **Choose the direct selection tool.**

2. **Option-click on the path with the direct selection tool.**

3. **Choose Edit⇨Free Transform Points.**

   The keyboard shortcut is ⌘-T.

To transform a part of a path:

1. **Choose the direct selection tool.**

2. **Select the points you want with the direct selection tool.**

3. **Choose Edit⇨Free Transform Points.**

Version 5 lets you repeat your last transformation on another path by pressing ⌘-Shift-T or choosing Edit⇨Transform⇨Again. This repeat transformation command also works with selections and layers (see Chapter 15), but not with selection marquees (outlines) alone.

Moving and Cloning Selections

Before bidding a fond farewell to Chapter 13, I want to quickly touch on the two most common things you can do with a selection: Move it and clone it.

Here's the lowdown:

✔ To move a selection, grab the move tool, the four-headed arrow, (press V to select the tool from the keyboard), and drag the selection. A little pair of scissors appears by your cursor to show that you're about to remove the selection from its current home. When you move the selection, the area where the selection used to be is filled with the background color, as illustrated in Figure 13-6.

✔ You can temporarily access the move tool by pressing ⌘ when any tool but the hand or pen tool is selected.

✔ To nudge a selection 1 pixel, press one of the arrow keys while the move tool is selected. Or press ⌘ and an arrow key when any tool but the pen or hand tool is selected. The up arrow nudges the selection 1 pixel up; the right pixel nudges it to the right, and so on, just like you'd think. To nudge a selection 10 pixels, press Shift along with an arrow key while the move tool is selected.

✔ To clone and move a selection, Option-drag with the move tool or ⌘-Option-drag with any other tool but the hand or pen tool. Your cursor changes into two arrowheads — your reminder that you're creating a clone of your selection.

Figure 13-6:
After selecting the Washington Monument (top), I dragged it to a more convenient location (bottom), leaving a gaping hole in the Capitol skyline.

✔ To clone and nudge, select the move tool and then press Option and one of the arrow keys. Or, when any other tool but the hand or pen tool is selected, press ⌘ and Option as you press the arrow keys. Press Shift and Option with an arrow key to clone the selection and move it 10 pixels.

✔ To move a selection outline without moving the image inside it, select a lasso, marquee, or magic wand tool. Then just drag the selection outline or nudge it with the arrow keys. This is a great way to reposition a selection outline without disturbing so much as a single pixel in the image.

✔ You can move and clone selections and selection outlines between images just as you would within a single image. Just drag the selection or selection outline from its current window into the other image window. For more on this topic, see Chapter 15.

✔ Yet another way to move a selection is to use the Edit⇨Free Transform command, discussed in Chapter 20. Free Transform enables you to move, resize, rotate, and distort your image by manipulating a special selection marquee. To move the selection, just drag inside the marquee. To discover how to perform other Free Transform tricks, also see Chapter 20.

✔ When you're moving or cloning a selection, those animated dots that parade around the outline — called *marching ants* in some quarters — can be downright distracting. Sure, the ants permit you to see the boundaries of your selection, but sometimes you need to see how the edges of the selection blend in with their new surroundings. To do this, choose View⇨Hide Edges or press ⌘-H.

✔ To bring back the marching ants, press ⌘-H.

Chapter 14
Coloring inside the Lines

• •

In This Chapter

▶ Painting and editing inside a selection outline

▶ Using the paint bucket tool

▶ Filling from the keyboard

▶ Using the Fill command

▶ Reverting a selection

▶ Creating gradients

▶ Applying different types of gradients

▶ Stroking a selection

• •

*E*ver spray-painted with a stencil? In case you've never engaged in this riveting pastime, let me explain how it works:

1. **Hold the stencil up to the surface you want to paint.**

2. **Spray recklessly.**

When you take the stencil away, you discover a painted image that matches the shape of the stencil. It's the epitome of a no-brainer.

In Photoshop, a selection outline works the same way. Just as a stencil isolates the area affected by the spray paint, a selection outline isolates the area affected by a paint or edit tool. You can also fill a selection outline with color or trace around the selection outline.

Sounds easy, doesn't it? Like an unremarkable bit of information that virtually flings itself at the attention of the most casual observer. Like something you could have figured out on your own, for example, and saved $19.99. Well, whatever it sounds like, I intend to walk you through every nuance of painting, filling, and tracing selections. Chapters 12 and 13 explain how to create and manipulate selection outlines. This chapter shows you what to do with them. (The selection outlines, that is, not the chapters. You already know what to do with the chapters — tear them out and use them to line the parrot cage.)

Put Down Newspaper Before You Paint

If some portion of an image is selected, Photoshop treats all deselected areas as protected. You can use any paint or edit tool inside the selection without worrying about harming areas outside the selection.

In this chapter, I took a jar-in-a-nook, which has a certain austere beauty about it — it's just the sort of prop that would feel right at home in a hoity-toity kitchen of the idle rich — and, overcome with desire, I mucked it up. Specifically, I painted inside the jar without harming the background. And you can, too. To this end, do the following:

1. **Select the jar.**

   This is the only step that takes any work. You might start out by selecting the body of the jar with the elliptical marquee tool. If you have problems getting the marquee exactly on the jar — it's hard to know where to start dragging so that it comes out right — just make sure that the marquee is approximately the right size, select one of the marquee or lasso tools, and then use the arrow keys to nudge the outline into position. After you select the body to your satisfaction, you can Shift-drag with the lasso tool to incorporate the neck of the jar into the selection as well.

2. **Make any modifications you deem necessary.**

   In this case, you may want to blur the selection outline a tad using Select⇨Feather, as explained in Chapter 13. If your selection outline isn't dead on, the Feather command helps to fudge the difference a little.

3. **Choose View⇨Hide Edges or press ⌘-H.**

   This step is extremely important. By hiding the selection outline, you can see how your edits affect the image without those distracting animated dots, referred to as *marching ants,* getting in your way.

4. **Paint and edit away.**

   Feel free to use any tool you want. You can paint with the paintbrush, airbrush, or pencil; edit with the smudge, focus, or toning tools; clone with the rubber stamp; use the magic eraser and erase to a previous version of the image — all with the assurance that the area outside the selection will remain as safeguarded from your changes as the driven snow (or whatever the saying is).

While editing away, try not to press ⌘-D or click with one of the selection tools. Because the selection outline is hidden, you won't notice any difference when you deselect the image. If you do inadvertently deselect, press ⌘-Z right away. If you wait until after you apply a brush stroke, ⌘-Z undoes the stroke but not the selection outline.

All is not lost, however! A great new feature in Version 5 is the Reselect command under the Select menu. Even after performing several actions, you can retrieve your last selection by choosing Select⇨Reselect or pressing ⌘-Shift-D.

In Figure 14-1, I painted inside my selected jar using a single tool — the air-brush — with a single brush size and only two colors, black and white. As a result, I was able to transform the jar into a kind of marble. Looks mighty keen, and there's not so much as a drop of paint outside the lines.

Figure 14-1:
Using the airbrush, I painted inside the selected jar. (You can't see the selection outline because it's hidden.)

This stenciling feature is so all-fired handy that I almost always select an area before applying a paint or edit tool. The fact is, the selection tools are easier to control than the painting or editing tools, so you may as well take advantage of them.

Dribbling Paint from a Bucket

Photoshop enables you to fill a selection with the foreground color, the background color, a pattern, or a gradual blend of colors called a *gradient*. You can even fill a selection with a previous version of the image — referred to as the *history source state* in Version 5 (see Chapter 11 for details).

But before I explain any of these eye-popping options, I want to cover the paint bucket tool, which is part selection tool and part fill tool. The second tool from the bottom on the right side of the toolbox, the paint bucket tool (looks like a tilted bucket of paint) lets you fill an area of continuous color by clicking on the area.

In Figure 14-2, for example, I set the foreground to white and clicked with the paint bucket tool on the row of broccoli in the jar. Photoshop filled the broccoli with white, turning it into the rough facsimile of cauliflower.

To adjust the performance of the paint bucket, press Return to open the Paint Bucket Options palette, also shown in Figure 14-2. As with the magic wand tool, the Tolerance value determines how many pixels in your image are affected by the paint bucket. The only difference is that the paint bucket applies color instead of selecting pixels. You can also select the Anti-aliased check box to soften the edges of the filled area. (In Figure 14-2, the Tolerance value was 32, and Anti-aliased was turned on, as it is by default.)

Paint bucket tool

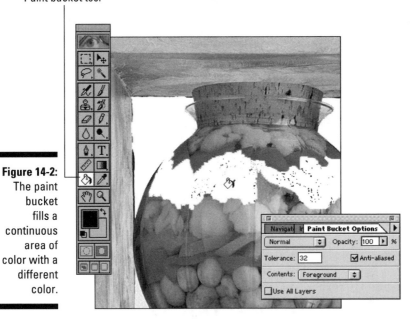

Figure 14-2:
The paint bucket fills a continuous area of color with a different color.

The problem with the paint bucket tool is that it's hard to get the Tolerance value just right. You usually end up choosing Undo several times and resetting the Tolerance value until you find the value that colors only the pixels that you want to color. Overall, I consider the paint bucket a poor tool for filling areas in Photoshop. If you select an area in your image by using the magic wand tool, which chooses pixels of continuous color surrounding the cursor (discussed in Chapter 12) and then fills the area with a color (described in the next sections), you produce the same effect as with the paint bucket, *and* you have more alternatives at your disposal.

If you decide to ignore my advice and take up the paint bucket at your earliest opportunity, you can select the tool quickly by pressing the K key. You know, for bucKet.

Applying Color to Selection Innards

Now that I've expressed my opinion regarding the paint bucket — ick, yuk, stay away — it's time to move on to the essential methods for filling a selection outline in Photoshop:

- ✔ To fill a selection with the foreground color, press Option-Delete.

- ✔ To fill a selection with the background color, press ⌘-Delete.

- ✔ When you're working on a layer and want to fill the opaque part of a selection with the foreground color while leaving the rest of the selection transparent, press Shift-Option-Delete. Press ⌘-Shift-Delete to fill the opaque area with the background color. (And if all this makes no sense at all, you may want to turn to Chapter 15, which explains layers and transparency.)

- ✔ Choose Edit⇨Fill to display the Fill dialog box, which lets you fill the selection with translucent color, a pattern, or history (*history* is what Version 5 calls a previous saved step; see Chapter 11).

- ✔ Drag with the gradient tool to create a gradient (a gradual blend) between two or more colors.

Two of these options — Edit⇨Fill and the gradient tool — require more discussion than I have devoted to them so far, which is why the rest of this chapter is so filled to the gills with text.

Fill, I Command You!

Choose Edit⇨Fill to display the Fill dialog box, shown in Figure 14-3. The Use pop-up menu lets you specify the color or stored image with which you want to fill the selection; the Blending options let you mix the filled colors with the colors already inside the selection. All these options are discussed in more detail in this section.

Figure 14-3:
Specify
how you
want to fill a
selection by
using the
options in
the Fill
dialog box.

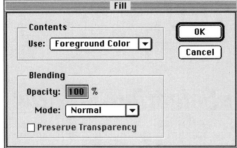

You can also display the Fill dialog box by pressing Shift-Delete.

Select your stuffing

The most important part of the Fill dialog box is the Use pop-up menu. Here you select the stuff you want to use to fill the selection. The options are as follows:

✔ The Foreground Color option fills the selection with the foreground color, and the Background Color option fills the selection with the background color. I can see by your expression that you're not surprised by this news.

✔ The next option, Pattern, fills a selection with a repeating pattern. To use this option, you must first define the pattern by selecting a rectangular area and choosing Edit⇨Define Pattern. If no pattern has been defined, the Pattern option is dimmed. The Pattern option doesn't serve much of a practical purpose (which I reiterate in Chapter 10 when discussing the pattern stamp tool).

✔ Choose the History option to fill the selection with a previously saved step of that portion of the image. In short, the History palette remembers all your previous steps, which are called *source states*. You select a previous source state in the palette, and the selection fills with the image as it appeared at that point in time. If this is totally confusing, be sure and check out Chapter 11.

✔ The last three options — Black, 50% Gray, and White — fill the selection with black, medium gray, and white, respectively. What's the point? Not much. If the foreground and background colors are set to blue and orange and you don't want to change them, I suppose that you might find these options useful. And pigs might fly. You just never know.

How not to mix colors

You can enter a value into the Opacity option box of the Fill dialog box to mix the fill color or history source state with the present colors in the selection. You can also mix the fill and the selected color using the options in the Mode pop-up menu, which include Multiply, Screen, Difference, and other wacky brush modes (see Chapter 8 and Color Plate 8-2).

Notice that I said you can do these things, not that you should. The truth is, you don't want to use the Fill dialog box's Blending options to mix fills with selections. Why? Because the Fill dialog box doesn't let you preview the effects of the Blending options. Even seasoned professionals have trouble predicting the exact repercussions of Opacity settings and brush modes, and it's likely that you will, too. And, if you don't like what you get, you have to undo the operation and choose Edit➪Fill all over again.

The better way to mix fills with selections is to copy the selection to a new layer, fill it, and experiment with the Opacity slider and mode options in the Layers palette. Naturally, you have no idea what I'm talking about if you haven't read the supremely insightful Chapter 15. Until then, take my valuable advice and be content to ignore the Opacity and Mode options in the Blending area at the bottom of the Fill dialog box.

The Preserve Transparency check box comes into play when you're working on a layer other than the background layer, as discussed in Chapter 15. If the check box is turned on, only the opaque pixels in a selection are filled when you apply the Fill command — the transparent areas remain transparent. If the check box is turned off, the entire selection is filled. The option is dimmed if the Preserve Transparency option in the Layers palette is turned on.

The Ever-Changing Color Sea

The third tool from the bottom on the right side of the toolbox, the gradient tool, lets you fill a selection with a fountain of colors that starts with one color and ends with another. By default, the two colors are the foreground color and background color.

But Photoshop can do more than create simple two-color blends. You can create custom gradients that blend a multitude of colors and vary from opaque to transparent throughout the blend.

Version 5 further improves the gradient tool, which got a major makeover in Photoshop 4. Photoshop now has five gradient types — linear, radial, angle, reflected, and diamond. Foreground and background colors can also be reversed from within the Gradient Options palette. And less visible banding occurs with the gradients created. (*Banding* is a problem in which you can see distinct bands of color in a printed gradient — that's a bad thing in 9 out of 10 households.)

Checking out the gradient tool

The following steps provide one of those in-depth introductions to the gradient tool that folks find so helpful nowadays:

1. **Select some portion of your image.**

    In Figure 14-4, I selected the jar again. I love that jar. It's so pristine; it just begs for me to mess it up.

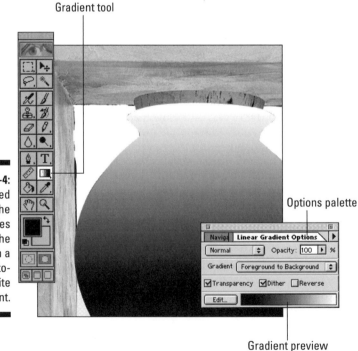

Gradient tool

Figure 14-4: I replaced the vegetables inside the jar with a black-to-white gradient.

Options palette

Gradient preview

If you don't select a portion of your image before using the gradient tool, Photoshop fills the entire image with the gradient. (Or, if you're working on a layer, as discussed in Chapter 15, the gradient fills the entire layer.)

2. **Select the gradient tool.**

   To do it quickly, just press the G key.

3. **To toggle through the various gradient tools, press Shift-G.**

4. **Select the Foreground to Background option from the Gradient pop-up menu in your chosen gradient's Options palette.**

   To display the palette, press Return. The Foreground to Background option is the default setting. It creates a gradient that begins with the foreground color and ends with the background color.

5. **Set the foreground and background colors the way you want them.**

   This step is up to you. You can stick with black and white or select new colors with the eyedropper tool or Color palette. For the purposes of Figure 14-4, I just set my colors to the defaults, black and white.

6. **Begin dragging at the point where you want to set the foreground color.**

   In Figure 14-4, I began my drag at the bottom of the jar.

7. **Release where you want to position the background color.**

   I released at the top of the jar. The result is a black-to-white gradation.

If you Shift-drag with the gradient tool, Photoshop constrains the direction of your drag to a horizontal, vertical, or 45° diagonal angle.

Changing the way of the gradient

You can muck around with the performance of the gradient tool by double-clicking on its toolbox icon or pressing Return to display the Options palette for the chosen gradient tool (refer to Figure 14-4).

Like the Opacity settings and brush modes available inside the Fill dialog box, the Opacity and brush mode options inside the Options palette for each of the gradients are best ignored. If you want to mix a gradation with the existing colors in a selection, create the gradation on a layer and select options inside the Layers palette, as discussed in Chapter 15.

Choosing between the five gradient tools

Photoshop 5 gives you five gradient tools, which are described below and illustrated in Figure 14-5.

- ✔ **Linear:** Creates a gradient in which colors blend in a straight line.
- ✔ **Radial:** The colors blend in concentric circles, from the center outward.

  Note: In every example in Figure 14-5, the foreground color is black and the background color is white. You almost always want to set the lighter color to the foreground color when using the radial option because doing that creates a glowing effect. If the foreground color is darker than its background compatriot, the gradation looks like a bottomless pit as you can see from the radial gradient shown in Figure 14-5.

- ✔ **Angle:** Creates a conical gradation with the colors appearing counterclockwise.
- ✔ **Reflected:** If dragged from edge to edge of your selection, a reflected gradient acts like a linear gradient. However, if dragged from the interior to an edge of the selection, the gradient reflects back on itself.
- ✔ **Diamond:** Like the radial gradient, this tool creates concentric shapes — in this case, diamonds or squares, depending on the angle you drag.

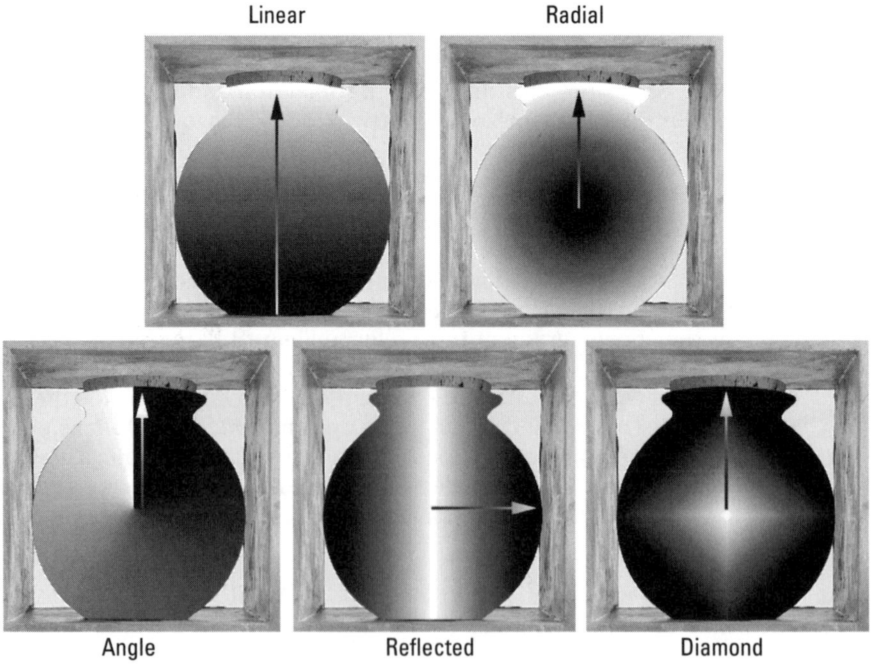

Linear   Radial

Figure 14-5:
Jar filled
with five
different
gradient
types —
Linear,
Radial,
Angle,
Reflected,
and
Diamond.

Angle   Reflected   Diamond

Choosing gradient options

You find three check boxes in the Gradient Options palette: Transparency, Dither, and Reverse.

- ✔ The Dither check box is easy. When turned on, it helps eliminate banding. Leave the check box turned on unless you're feeling especially contrary and want to create a banding effect.

- ✔ The Transparency check box is a little more complicated. Here's the scoop: Gradients can include areas that are partially or fully transparent. In other words, they fade from a solid color to a more transparent color. When the Transparency check box is turned off, Photoshop creates the gradient by using all opaque colors, ignoring the transparency information.

  The best way to get a grip on what the Transparency check box does is to try a little experiment. First, turn on the check box and press D to get the default foreground and background colors. Then, choose the Transparent Rainbow option from the Gradient pop-up menu and draw a gradient. You get a fill pattern that consists of a multicolored rainbow with your background peeking out at the beginning and end of the gradient. Next, draw the gradient with the Transparency check box turned off. You now get a fill of a multicolored rainbow with no background peeking out because Photoshop is ignoring the transparency at either end of the gradient. In most cases, you don't need to bother with the check box — just leave it turned on.

- ✔ When the Reverse check box is checked, the gradient will start with the background color and end with the foreground color. This option is useful for creating radial gradients while keeping the default colors intact.

Selecting your colors

The Gradient pop-up menu lets you change the way colors blend inside the gradation and select from a variety of prefab gradients. Here's a description of those gradients:

- ✔ Normally, Foreground to Background is selected. This option does just what it sounds like it does: It blends between the foreground and background colors, as in the examples in Figure 14-5.

- ✔ If you select one of the Transparent options, the gradient tool blends the foreground color into the original colors in the selection. The examples in Figure 14-6 were created with the Foreground to Transparent option selected.

- ✔ The remaining options in the Gradient pop-up menu create a variety of factory-made gradients, some involving just a few colors and others blending a whole rainbow of colors.

Figure 14-6:
Here's the
jar filled
with a
linear and a
radial
gradient
with the
Foreground
to
Transparent
option
selected.

Linear

Radial

Foreground to Transparent

When you select a gradient from the pop-up menu, Photoshop displays the gradient in the gradient preview at the bottom of the Options palette, as labeled earlier in Figure 14-4.

If none of the existing gradients suits your taste, you can create your own custom gradient, as I did in Color Plate 14-1. The next section explains the ins and outs of building your own gradients.

Becoming a gradient wizard

You can design your own custom gradient by editing an existing gradient or starting an entirely new gradient from scratch. To do either, display the Options palette for your chosen gradient tool by double-clicking on the gradient tool icon in the toolbox or pressing Return with the tool selected. Then click on the Edit button at the bottom of that gradient tool's Options palette. The Gradient Editor dialog box, shown in Figure 14-7, appears. Uh-oh. Looks like you've ventured too far into geek space, doesn't it?

The Gradient Editor dialog box is a bit complex, and chances are you won't use it much. But I don't want you to feel as though you didn't get the full value for your $19.99, so the following list gives you a brief introduction to the dialog box:

  ✔ The scrolling list at the top of the dialog box lists all the prefab gradients — the same ones in the Gradient pop-up menu in the Options palette of your chosen gradient tool. Select the gradient you want to edit from this list. Then click on Duplicate to create a copy of the gradient and give it a new name. Now, you can edit that gradient without worrying about wrecking the original.

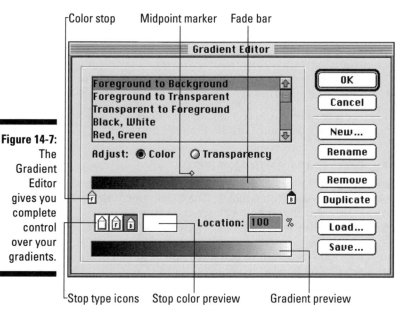

Color stop   Midpoint marker   Fade bar

Figure 14-7:
The
Gradient
Editor
gives you
complete
control
over your
gradients.

Stop type icons   Stop color preview   Gradient preview

✔ To create a new gradient that isn't based on an existing gradient, click on New.

✔ The two radio buttons, Color and Transparency, let you adjust, uh, the color and transparency of the gradient. When the Color button is selected, the fade bar (labeled in Figure 14-7) shows the gradient colors. You can then add, change, or delete colors from the gradient, as explained in the next section.

✔ When the Transparency button is turned on, you can change the transparency of your gradient, as explained in the section (appropriately named), "Changing the transparency," later in this chapter. The fade bar displays the opaque colors in the gradient in black and the transparent areas in white. Gray areas represent colors that are partially transparent.

✔ The little house-shaped boxes beneath the fade bar are called *color stops* when the Color button is selected and *transparency stops* when the Transparency button is selected. You use these stops to change the colors and transparency of the gradient, as explained in the upcoming two sections.

✔ The preview bar at the bottom of the dialog box displays both the colors and transparent areas of your gradient. Transparent areas are represented by a gray-and-white checkerboard pattern.

✔ The Save button saves your gradient to a different location on disk. You don't need to save the gradient using this button unless you want to store your gradient in some spot other than where the rest of the gradients are located, however. After you edit a gradient and click on OK, the gradient is automatically added to the Gradient pop-up list in the Options palette for the gradient tools.

✔ To remove a gradient from the list, select the gradient in the Gradient Editor dialog box, and click on the Remove button.

Changing, adding, and deleting colors

To change one of the colors in the gradient, first check to see whether the roof on that color's color stop is black. The black *roof* indicates the active color stop — the color that is to be affected by your changes. If the roof isn't black, click on the color stop to make it active.

After you activate the color stop, you have one of three choices. Click on the far-left stop type icon (labeled in Figure 14-7) to change the color to the one showing in the stop color preview box (also labeled in Figure 14-7). To change the color in the color preview box, you can click on a color in your image, a color in the Color palette, or a color in the fade bar.

If you click on the F or B stop type icons, you change the color marked by the color stop to the foreground or background color, respectively. Keep in mind that if you change the foreground or background color, the color in the gradient changes automatically. The change doesn't affect gradients that you've already drawn, but it does affect any future gradients you create.

Here's some more stuff you need to know about playing with the colors in your gradient:

✔ To add a color to the gradient, select a stop type icon and then click just below the fade bar at the point where you want the color to appear. You get a new color stop icon representing the color.

✔ To remove a color from the gradient, drag its color stop down and away from the fade bar.

✔ If you drag a color stop to the right or left, you can change the position of the color in the gradient. Suppose that you have a gradient that fades from black to white. If you want more black and less white, drag the black color stop toward the white stop.

✔ The little diamonds on the top of the fade bar represent the midpoint between two colors. Using the example of a black-to-white gradient again, the midpoint marks the spot at which the gradient contains equal amounts of black and white. To move a midpoint, just drag the diamond.

✔ The Location option box shows the placement of the active color stop or midpoint marker. If you want to be terribly precise, you can enter a value into the Location box to position a color stop or midpoint marker instead of dragging the icons.

✔ When a color stop is active, a value of 0% (zero) represents the very beginning of the gradient; 100% represents the very end. Midpoint values are always relative to the two color stops on either side of the midpoint. A value of 50% places the midpoint an equal distance from both color stops. For reasons unknown, the minimum and maximum Midpoint values are 5% and 95%. Just thought you might like to store that useless bit of information in your memory banks.

Changing the transparency

Hold on to your stomach — now we're really veering into the land of the propeller heads. Photoshop lets you adjust the amount of transparency in a gradient. You can make a portion of the gradient fully opaque, completely transparent, or somewhere in between the two.

Suppose that you want to create a gradient that starts out white, gradually fades to completely transparent, and then becomes completely white again. In other words, you want to create a variation of the effect shown back in Figure 14-6. Here's how to create such a gradient:

1. **Make the foreground color white.**

2. **Inside the Gradient Editor dialog box, choose the Foreground to Transparent gradient from the scrolling list.**

   The gradient you want to create is similar to one that already exists, so you may as well save yourself the trouble of starting from scratch.

3. **Click on Duplicate and give your new gradient a name.**

   Photoshop creates a copy of the Foreground to Transparent gradient for you to muck up.

4. **Click on the Transparency radio button.**

   The fade bar now shows your gradient in terms of transparent and opaque areas. Black represents opaque areas; white represents transparent areas; gray areas represent everything in between. The preview bar at the bottom of the dialog box shows you the opaque areas in their actual colors and transparent areas in a gray and white checkerboard pattern.

When you have the Transparency button selected, the color stops become transparency stops, enabling you to change the opacity of different portions of your gradient. The midpoint marker represents the spot at which the gradient is 50% white and 50% transparent.

5. **Click on the far-right transparency stop.**

   In this example, the far-right stop represents the completely transparent end of the gradient.

6. **Change the value in the Opacity option box to 100.**

   (The Opacity option box replaces the stop type icons and the stop color preview box when you have the Transparency radio button selected.) You now have a gradient that fades from fully opaque white to . . . fully opaque white. Wow, that's exciting, huh?

   It's tempting to press Return after you change the option box value, but don't — pressing Return closes the dialog box. The value you enter into the option box takes effect without a press of the Return key. To switch to another option box, press Tab.

7. **Click in the middle of the fade bar to create a new transparency stop.**

   By default, each new stop you create is 100% opaque.

8. **Change the value in the Opacity option box to 0 (zero).**

   You now have a gradient that starts out fully opaque, becomes transparent in the middle, and becomes opaque again at the end. Apply the gradient to an image to get a better idea of what you just created. Heady stuff, eh?

You can also add as many transparency stops as you want and set different Opacity values for each. To move a transparency stop, just drag it right or left; to delete a stop, drag it off the bar. To move a midpoint, drag it right or left.

The Transparency check box in the Options palette for the gradient tools determines whether transparency settings are ignored when you apply a gradient. If the check box is turned off, your gradient is completely opaque. For example, if you turn off the check box when applying the gradient created by the preceding steps, you get a completely white gradient instead of one that fades from white to transparent and back again.

Your Image Needs Strokes, Too

The last item on today's agenda is Edit⇨Stroke, a command that traces borders around a selection. When you choose this command, Photoshop displays the Stroke dialog box shown in Figure 14-8. Enter the thickness of the border you want into the Width option box. This value is measured in pixels.

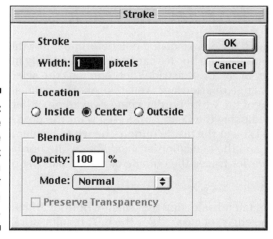

Figure 14-8:
Use the
Stroke
dialog box
to draw a
border
around a
selection.

In Figure 14-9, for example, I traced a 16-pixel-wide black border around the jar (which is the maximum Width value, incidentally). Then I swapped the foreground and background colors, chose Edit⇨Stroke again, and entered 8 into the Width option box. The result is a white border inside a black border. Slick, huh? (Oh, come on, say it is, even if it's just to make me feel better.)

Figure 14-9:
The classic
double-
border
effect, so in
demand at
today's
finer jar
emporiums.

How the border rides the track

The Location options in the Stroke dialog box determine how the border rides the selection outline. The border can cruise around fully inside or fully outside the selection, or it can sit astride (centered on) the selection. Why might you want to change this setting? Well, take another look at Figure 14-9. Suppose that instead of the white border being flanked on either side by black (which I created using the Center option), I want the borders to sit beside each other. If I select the Inside option, the white border appears inside the selection, and the black border inside the white border. If I select Outside, the white border traces the outside of the jar, and the black border extends even farther.

Actually, I don't recommend selecting the Outside option. It has a nasty habit of flattening the edges of curves. For the best results, stick with Inside or Center.

Mix your stroke after you press Return

Like the Blending and Opacity options in other dialog boxes, the ones in the Stroke dialog box don't provide you with a preview of how the effect will look when applied to your image. So, if you want to play with the blend modes or opacity of your stroke, ignore the options in the dialog box. Instead, create a new layer (as explained in Chapter 15), and do your selecting and stroking on that layer. You can then adjust the blend mode and opacity via the Layers option palette (also discussed in Chapter 15).

On the off chance that you're curious about the Preserve Transparency check box, it affects only images with layers. If you don't have any layers going, don't worry about it. (Again, layers are explained in Chapter 15.) Even if your image does contain layers, don't worry about this option. It just ensures that the transparent portions of layers remain transparent.

Part V
So, You Say You're Serious about Image Editing

The 5th Wave   By Rich Tennant

"...AND THROUGH IMAGE EDITING TECHNOLOGY, WE'RE ABLE TO RE-CREATE THE AWESOME SPECTACLE KNOWN AS TYRANNOSAURUS GWEN."

In this part . . .

One of the great legacies of Walt Disney — the man, not the company — was his insistence that animation take full advantage of its unreal medium. He and his staff perfected techniques, camera angles, and character movements that would have proven impossible had the studio been working with live actors and sets. Ironically, these very unreal techniques produced the effect of heightened realism, in which backgrounds shifted on multiple planes, cameras swooped and glided without regard for terrain, and characters moved more gracefully and far more expressively than their human counterparts.

Simply put, Walt figured that there was no point in creating cartoons if all you intended to do was slavishly adhere to the dictates of real life. The same argument can be made for digital image editing. What's the point of going to all the trouble of scanning an image to disk and opening it up in Photoshop if you're not going to take it beyond the boundaries of real life in the process? In a word, none. In a few more words, if you're going to use Photoshop, there's no reason not to make every image you create more real than reality.

Chapters 15 through 18 show you how. Here, you discover how to mix images to create breathtaking visual collages, add type to your images, automatically correct the focus of images, stamp images in metal and create other special effects, and bring out brilliant colors that you never knew were there. In other words, you discover how to turn your images into something much better than they were.

Chapter 15

Layers upon Layers upon Layers

. . . .

In This Chapter

▶ Working with layers

▶ Combining images

▶ Pasting an image inside a selection outline

▶ Dragging and dropping selections

▶ Scaling an image to fit the composition

▶ Moving and merging layers

▶ Aligning and distributing layers

▶ Adjusting the Opacity setting

▶ Applying blend modes

▶ Erasing holes in layers

▶ Using the Layer Effects feature

. . . .

Insofar as "high art" is concerned, the heyday for surrealism was 60 to 70 years ago. But the problem with guys like Max Ernst, René Magritte, and even Salvador Dalí was that they never got around to learning how to use Photoshop. Oh, sure, Ernst and Magritte were long dead by the time Photoshop debuted, and Dalí may have had better things to do in his final days than learn a new piece of software. But still, think of what they could have done. A paintbrush is great, but it pales when compared to Photoshop as a means for merging photo-realistic images to create flat-out impossible visual scenarios.

Color Plate 15-1 shows what I mean. No matter how hard you work at it, you can never assemble these elements in a photo shoot. It's just so darn difficult to squeeze a giant fish, the Reims Cathedral in France, and the planet Neptune into the same room. If you had talent streaming like fire-hydrant jets out your ears, you might be able to paint the image, but most of us would have thrown in the towel at the prospect of re-creating a High Gothic cathedral facade that took a team of thirteenth century masters 65 years to carve.

But we live in a sparkling modern age, filled with more dazzling masterworks of automation than we know what to do with. Thanks to one such masterwork — I speak here of Photoshop, naturally — I was able to throw together Color Plate 15-1 in a couple of hours. Altogether, the composition comprises eight separate images; however, it required not so much as a single stroke of a painting or editing tool. I simply selected the images, combined them, blended them together, and erased a few stray pixels that weren't doing the final study in surrealism a lick of good.

Because it can be difficult to distinguish every one of the eight images, Color Plate 15-2 shows each one on its own. The arrows indicate the order in which the images are stacked on top of each other. For example, the underwater kelp jungle in the lower-right corner of Color Plate 15-2 lies at the bottom of the composition in Color Plate 15-1; the photo of Neptune in the upper-left corner of the second color plate rests at the top of the composition. The image appears as if I cut out a picture of the kelp and pasted it onto a page, cut out the fish and pasted it on the kelp, cut out the astronaut and pasted him in front of the fish, and so on.

Some images are blended together using the same brush modes I discuss in Chapter 8 — for example:

✔ The Multiply mode darkens colors as though they were painted on top of each other with watercolors (see Chapter 8 for more details). I used Multiply to blend the nebula — the image just below the flower in Color Plate 15-2 — with the fish to create the black eye effect in Color Plate 15-1.

✔ The spray coming out of the fish's mouth is the comet from the upper-right corner of Color Plate 15-2. I blended the two using the Screen mode.

✔ I blended the Reims Cathedral and Neptune with the images behind them using modes I haven't discussed yet. Respectively, these modes are Luminosity and Hard Light. I explain more about them in the section "Playing around with blend modes," near the end of this chapter.

This is the point at which you ask, "Yeah, yeah, yeah, but how in the world do I pull off something like this?" Well, wouldn't you know it, that's what this chapter is all about. I tell you how to get different images into the same document, how to assign them to separate layers, and how to mix them together using modes and the eraser tool. And, remarkably, it's all a lot easier than you may think.

Pasting Images Together

Suppose that you want to paste the fish image from the bottom of Color Plate 15-2 into the neighboring kelp image. How do you go about it? Here's one approach:

1. **Open the fish image and select the fish.**

2. **Press ⌘-C.**

   ⌘-C is the time-honored keyboard shortcut for the Edit⇨Copy command, which places a copy of your selection onto the Clipboard. The Clipboard is a temporary storage area for image data. Any previous occupant of the Clipboard — sent there via Edit⇨Copy or its close cousin, Edit⇨Cut — is displaced by the fish.

3. **Open the kelp image.**

4. **Press ⌘-V.**

   That's the shortcut for the Edit⇨Paste command, which dumps the current contents of the Clipboard into your image. Consider fish and kelp combined into one. The original fish image remains intact because the fish you pasted into the kelp was merely a copy.

But these steps aren't the only way to combine images. You also have these options at your disposal:

   ✔ To cut a selection from one image and paste it into another, choose Edit⇨Cut and then Edit⇨Paste. The selection is removed entirely from the first image and planted in the second.

   ✔ You can clone a selection between images by dragging it with the move tool or ⌘-dragging it with any tool except the hand or pen tool.

   This method of cloning between images is known in the computer world as *dragging and dropping,* by the way.

   ✔ To transfer an entire image to another image window, choose Select⇨All (⌘-A) before dragging or using the Cut or Copy commands.

   ✔ For a weird but occasionally useful trick, use Edit⇨Paste Into to paste an image inside an existing selection, as described in the upcoming section "Filling a selection with a selection."

When you use the Paste command, Photoshop places the pasted image on a new layer. When you drag and drop a selection from one image to another, Photoshop places the selection on a new layer as well. For more on working with layers, start reading at the section "Excuse Me, but What's a Layer?" and keep going to the end of the chapter.

If you've dabbled in previous versions of Photoshop, you've probably encountered a floating selection at one time or another. For those who are uninitiated, a *floating selection* is created when you use the move tool to move or clone an image. The floating selection hovers over the surface of an image in a temporary layer labeled "floating selection." It doesn't much matter whether you're familiar with floating selections because Photoshop 5 has virtually eliminated them. When you move or clone a selection with the move tool, you technically still get a floating selection; however, it won't be labeled, it won't appear in the Layers palette, and you can't even do much with it. You can move it without affecting underlying pixels; deselect it, in which case it pastes onto the image; or delete it. The near obliteration of floating selections is a Photoshop 5 feature that falls into the "Bad Move, Adobe!" category.

Filling a selection with a selection

The Edit⇨Paste Into command lets you insert an image into an existing selection outline. For example, I wanted to paste the fish behind some of the vegetation in the neighboring kelp image so that the fish would appear to be intertwined with his environment. In the first example of Figure 15-1, I selected an area inside the kelp stalks and feathered the selection by choosing Select⇨Feather, as discussed in Chapter 13. Then I chose Paste Into (⌘-Shift-V) to create the fish-inside-the-kelp shown in the second example. (Note that I've hidden the selection outlines in the second example so that you can better see the transitions between fish and stalks.)

Figure 15-1: After selecting an area of kelp (left), I chose the Paste Into command to introduce the fish to his new kelpy home (right).

Photoshop pastes the selection to a new layer. You can then move and blend the pasted image just as though it were a floating selection. It's just that the pasted image is invisible outside the boundaries of the previous selection outline.

You can also paste into the unselected area of an image by pressing the Option key as you choose Edit⇨Paste Into. If I had done this with the image in Figure 15-1, for example, the fish would show through the exact opposite areas of the kelp bed that he does now.

Resizing an image to match its new home

When you bring two images together, you always have to deal with the issue of relative size. For example, the fish that I've been having so much fun with is too large for its surroundings. Here's how to ensure that the two images you want to combine are sized correctly:

1. **Magnify the two images to exactly the same zoom factor.**

   To see them side by side, a zoom ratio of 50% or smaller is necessary.

2. **If either of the two images appears disproportionately large, scale it down by using Image⇨Image Size.**

   In this case, you don't care at all about the dimensions or resolution of the image; all you care about is the file size — that is, the number of pixels comprising the image. If the image you want to copy or drag (fish) is too large, scale it down just enough to fit inside the destination image. If the destination image (kelp) is too large, reduce it as desired. Keep ⌘-Z ready in case you accidentally go too far. (See Chapter 4 for more information about the Image Size command.)

   Be careful not to over-reduce! Remember that you're throwing away pixels and, therefore, sacrificing detail. If you go too far, you can always restore the original by choosing File⇨Revert, or undoing your steps using the History palette, as discussed in Chapter 11.

3. **Combine the two images.**

   Copy and paste, drag and drop, or punt on fourth down.

4. **Position the image more or less where you want it.**

   For my part, I stuck the fish in the upper-right corner.

5. **Choose Edit⇨Transform⇨Scale.**

   This command lets you fine-tune the relative size of the imported image with respect to its new home. A marquee with four corner handles surrounds the image.

6. Drag a corner handle to scale the image.

Shift-drag a handle to scale the image proportionally. The first example in Figure 15-2 catches me in the act. After you release the handle, Photoshop previews how the resized image will look. Don't worry that the preview is a little choppy; the scaled image will be smooth.

Figure 15-2:
Use the
Scale
command
to refine the
image size.

Don't scale the image up; only scale it down. Otherwise, Photoshop has to make up pixels, which is most assuredly not one of the program's better capabilities.

7. Move your cursor inside the transform box and double-click.

After you resize the image as desired — you can drag the corner handles all you want — move your cursor inside the box. Double-click or press Return to accept the image's new size and tell Photoshop to work its magic. The resized image will appear perfectly smooth.

If the scaled image looks choppy after you double-click, you probably have a preference set wrong. Choose File⇨Preferences⇨General or press ⌘-K and select the Bicubic option from the Interpolation pop-up menu.

If you decide that you don't want to scale the image before you double-click or press Return, press Esc or ⌘-.(period) to get rid of the box. If you've already double-clicked or pressed Return, you can restore the image to its original size by pressing ⌘-Z.

Excuse Me, but What's a Layer?

Here's a little analogy to get things rolling. Imagine that you have three sheets of acetate — you know, like folks used to slide into overhead projectors to bore audiences before the days of multimedia presentations. Anyway, on one sheet you draw a picture of a fish. On a second sheet, you draw a fishbowl. And on a third sheet, you draw the table on which the fishbowl sits. When you stack all the sheets on top of each other, the images blend together to create a seamless view of a fish in his happy home.

Layers in Photoshop work just like that. You can keep different elements of your image on separate layers and then combine the layers to create a composite image. You can rearrange layers, add and delete layers, blend them together using different opacity values and blend modes, and do all sorts of other impressive things.

Another advantage of using layers is that you can edit or paint on one layer without affecting the other layers. That means you can safely apply commands or painting tools to one portion of your image without worrying about messing up the rest of the image — and without bothering to select the element you want to edit.

Layers debuted in Photoshop 3. They played a much bigger role in Version 4. Now, in Version 5 with the near death of floating selections, layers are even bigger stars.

You aren't restricted to the layers that Photoshop creates automatically, however. You can create as many new layers as your computer's memory allows. In the case of the image shown in Color Plate 15-1, I kept kelp, fish, astronaut, nebula, cathedral, flower, comet, and Neptune on separate layers. Though they may appear to blend together along the edges, they are, in fact, as distinct as peas in a pod.

Photoshop also lets you create a special kind of layer called an adjustment layer. An *adjustment layer* allows you to play with the color-correction commands without permanently affecting any of your image layers. For more on that juicy topic, see Chapter 18.

Finding your way around the Layers palette

The Layers palette, shown in Figure 15-3, is the Grand Central Station for managing layers. To display the palette, choose Window⇨Show Layers or just press F7.

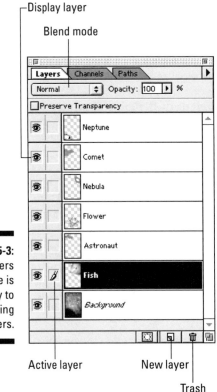

Display layer

Blend mode

Figure 15-3:
The Layers
palette is
key to
managing
your layers.

Active layer

New layer

Trash

Here's what you need to know to navigate the Layers palette:

✔ The Background is the bottom layer in the image. Every image has a
Background (unless the Background has been turned into a layer —
read on to see how).

✔ The order of the layers in the Layers palette represents their order in
the image. The top layer in the palette is the top layer in your image,
and so on.

✔ You can edit only one layer at a time — the *active layer*. The active layer
is the one that's highlighted in the Layers palette and that has a little
paintbrush icon to the left of its layer name. To make another layer
active, just click on its name.

✔ Press Option-] (right bracket) to move up one layer; press Option-[(left
bracket) to activate the next layer down. Press Shift-Option-] to move
to the top layer; press Shift-Option-[to move to the Background or
bottom layer.

✔ An eyeball icon next to a layer name means that the layer is visible. To hide the layer, click on the eyeball. To display the layer, click on the eyeball column to bring the eyeball back.

✔ To hide all layers but one, Option-click on the eyeball in front of the name of the layer you want to see. Option-click again to redisplay all the layers.

✔ If you hide the Background layer, you see a checkerboard pattern surrounding your images. The checkerboard represents the transparent areas of the visible layers.

✔ To find out how to use the blend mode pop-up menu and the Opacity setting at the top of the palette, read the upcoming section, "Tending Your Many Splendid Blends."

✔ To create a new, blank layer, click on the new layer icon at the bottom of the palette (refer to Figure 15-3). To create a duplicate of an existing layer, drag the layer to the new layer icon.

When you create a layer in the manner mentioned in the preceding paragraph, Photoshop gives the layer a name like Layer 1 or Layer 2, and so on. If you want to name the layer, double-click on the layer name in the Layers palette and enter a name in the Layer Options dialog box that appears.

✔ Alternatively, you can create the layer by choosing the New Layer or Duplicate Layer command from the Layers palette menu (click on the right-pointing arrow at the top of the palette), or choose Layer⇨New Layer or Layer⇨Duplicate Layer. If you use this method to create a layer, Photoshop prompts you to give the layer a name.

✔ To delete a layer, drag it to the Trash icon. Keep in mind that you're throwing away the layer along with the image on it. Layers can also be deleted via Layer⇨Delete Layer or by choosing Delete Layer from the Layers palette pop-up menu.

✔ In Chapter 14, I mention that you can paint inside a selection outline to paint just the selection and leave the surrounding areas untouched. But when you send a selection to a layer, the selection outline disappears. So how do you paint only inside the image on a layer? For example, maybe I want to paint stripes on my fish without going outside the lines. The solution is to select the Preserve Transparency check box near the top of the Layers palette. The transparent areas around the fish stay transparent, allowing you to paint only inside the opaque and translucent fishy bits.

✔ For a quick way to turn the Preserve Transparency check box on and off, press the forward slash key (/).

✔ Just in case you ever want to re-create that selection outline around the elements on a layer, though, Photoshop gives you an easy way to do it. Just ⌘-click on the layer name in the Layers palette.

Moving and manipulating layers

Layers are flexible things — you can move them, group them together, shuffle their order, and otherwise rearrange them as though they were a deck of playing cards. Here's a look at some of the more common layer-manipulation moves you may need to make:

✔ To move an image on a layer, drag it with the move tool or ⌘-drag with any other tool except the hand or pen tool. To move the layer in 1-pixel increments, press an arrow key with the move tool selected or press ⌘ plus an arrow key with any tool but the hand or pen. To move the layer in 10-pixel increments, press Shift as you press the arrow key.

✔ Turn on the Pixel Doubling check box in the Move Options palette (press Return with the move tool selected to display the palette). This option speeds up on-screen previews when you drag layers. The drawback is that Photoshop displays only every other pixel, making the preview a little blotchy.

✔ To link an active layer to another layer, click on the second column of the layers palette — just to the left of the layer name — next to the layer that's not active. A little link icon appears in the column. Now, you can move, scale, and rotate both layers at once. To remove the link, click on the link icon.

✔ Can't figure out what layer holds the element you want to edit? With the move tool selected, press Control-Option-click on the element. Or ⌘-Control-Option-click with any tool but the hand or pen tool. Photoshop automatically activates the appropriate layer.

✔ After you get a few layers going, you can move one in front of or behind another by dragging it up or down in the list of layers in the Layers palette. A heavy black line shows where the layer will be inserted. You can't "reorder" the Background or move any layer below the Background until you convert it to a layer. To convert, double-click on the Background in the Layers palette, enter a name for the layer, and press Return. Or you can leave the default name of Layer 0 and press Return.

✔ To add a new Background, choose Layer➪New➪Background.

✔ Another way to rearrange layers is to use the commands in the Layer➪Arrange submenu. Click on the layer that you want to move in the Layers palette. Then choose Layer➪Arrange➪Bring to Front (⌘-Shift-]) to make the layer the topmost layer. Select Bring Forward (⌘-]) to move the layer one level up. Select Send Backward (⌘-[) to move the layer one level down. Select Send to Back (⌘-Shift-[) to move the layer to just above the Background layer.

✔ You can copy an entire layer to a new image by selecting the layer in the Layers palette and dragging and dropping the layer to the new image. The layer is dropped at the spot where you release the mouse button and resides one layer above the active layer in the new image.

Flattening and merging layers

Sadly, layers aren't all fun and games. To put it bluntly, they come at a steep price and require some concerted management skills. First, if an image contains layers, saving it in any format other than the Photoshop format (refer to Chapter 6) merges all the layers into one. The Photoshop format is the only format that preserves layers. Second, every layer you add, also makes your file size grow. And third, layers can really slow down Photoshop. To keep running at peak efficiency, it's best to juggle as few layers as possible at a time.

If you want to save your image for use in a different program but you're not willing to sacrifice your layers just yet, you can save the composition to a different file and flatten it — that is, smush all the layers together. To do this, choose File⇨Save a Copy. The familiar Save dialog box appears on-screen, but it includes an additional Flatten Image check box. No need to turn on Flatten Image; just select TIFF, JPEG, or some other option from the Save As pop-up menu, and Photoshop selects Flatten Image for you.

In addition, you can choose to check on Exclude Non-Image Data. Doing so eliminates paths, guides, color profiles, thumbnail previews, and a few other non-image data items, thereby creating the smallest file size possible. Then name the image and press Return. Photoshop saves the flattened image to a different file; the layers in the on-screen image remain intact. Even the name on the title bar remains unaffected, meaning that the next time you press ⌘-S, Photoshop saves to the original file in the Photoshop format, not the Save a Copy file in the new format.

But useful as that is, you're still going to want to merge layers every so often to keep your image manageable. Otherwise, operations slow to a snail's pace, and that's an insult to the snail. Slow is hardly the word. So here are your merging options:

- ✔ To merge several layers into one, hide all layers except the ones you want to merge. In other words, eyeball icons should appear in front of the layers you want to merge. Hide the eyeball if you don't want to merge the layer. Then choose Merge Visible from the Layers palette menu (by dragging from that right-pointing arrowhead in the upper-right corner of the palette) or from the regular Layer menu at the top of the Photoshop window. Or, even simpler, press ⌘-Shift-E.

- ✔ You can merge one layer into the layer below it by choosing Layer⇨Merge Down or pressing ⌘-E. You can also choose the Merge Down command from the Layers palette menu.

- ✔ If you want to flatten the entire image and get rid of all the layers, choose the Flatten Image command from the palette menu or from the Layer menu. You can undo the command right after you choose it by pressing ⌘-Z. If you performed other operations after flattening, you can undo by using the History palette (see Chapter 11 for details).

Aligning layers

Photoshop 5 gives you a nifty new feature — aligning and distributing layers. Here are the steps to make sure your layers are neat and orderly:

To align:

1. **In the Layers palette, select the anchor layer that all of the other layers will align to.**

   The selected anchor layer remains stationary, and the other layers align to the anchor.

2. **Link the layers you want to align. Click in the second column next to the layer thumbnail to display the link icon.**

3. **Choose Layer⇨Align Linked and then select one of the alignment commands.**

To distribute:

1. **In the Layers palette, link three or more layers that you want to distribute.**

   The distribute feature evenly spaces the layers between the first and last elements.

2. **Choose Layer⇨Distribute Linked and select one of the distribute commands.**

Tending Your Many Splendid Blends

Being able to segregate different portions of your image onto separate layers is a great help for editing one part of your image without harming another. But as image editing goes, this aspect of layers isn't terribly exciting. The real fun begins when you start playing around with different options that Photoshop gives you for blending all your various image layers together.

Fooling with layer opacity

One neat trick to try with a layer is to make it partially translucent by using the Opacity slider in the Layers palette. In Figure 15-4, for example, I made the fish partially translucent by setting the Opacity to 70%. In the second example, I made him even more ghostly by lowering the Opacity to 30%. Whether the image is on its own layer or temporarily floating, you can use the Opacity slider bar in the Layers palette to achieve this effect. To access the slider bar, click on the right-pointing arrow to the right of the Opacity numeric setting.

Opacity: 70%   Opacity: 30%

Figure 15-4: Hey, kids, it's Phantom Phish, the exciting translucent character whose merchandising will clutter markdown shelves any day now.

To change the Opacity setting for a layer from the keyboard, make sure that a selection tool — marquee, lasso, wand, move, crop, or type — is selected, and press a number key. Press 9 for 90%, 8 for 80%, and so on, down to 1 for 10%. To return to 100%, press 0. You can also enter more specific Opacity values — such as 72 — from the keyboard.

To see Phantom Phish in color, turn to Color Plate 15-3. In the upper-left image, both the fish and the cathedral are positioned on their own layers, and both layers are fully opaque. In the upper-right image, I changed the Opacity for both layers to 50%. Sends a chill down your spine, doesn't it?

Keep in mind that the Opacity setting applies only to layers. You can't change the Opacity of the Background layer, kelp, because nothing lies behind it. You'd be looking through the kelp into the empty void of digital space, a truly scary prospect. The same is true for the blend modes discussed in the next section.

Playing around with blend modes

The options in the blend mode pop-up menu in the upper-left corner of the Layers palette correspond exactly to the brush modes in the Options palette (see Chapter 8). You have Multiply, Screen, Overlay, and the rest of the gang. These options aren't called brush modes when they're applied to layers because no brush is involved. You can call them overlay modes or blend modes; some folks call them *calculations*. But just plain modes is fine, too.

✔ Multiply burns the floating image into the images behind it, darkening all colors where they mix. Screen does just the opposite, lightening the colors where they mix.

I love descriptions like that — because they make no sense. Pure wonderful computer gibberish. If you want sense, take a look at the lower-left example in Color Plate 15-3. I applied Multiply to the fish and Screen to the cathedral. Imagine this: The kelp background is a poster on a wall. The fish is printed on a piece of transparent film and tacked in front of the kelp. The cathedral is a slide loaded in a projector and shined onto the poster. This is precisely how Multiply and Screen work.

✔ The Difference mode has no real-world analogy. It creates a photo negative — or inversion — of the blended images according to their colors. Where one of the images is black, no inversion takes place. Where the images are light, you find lots of inversion. In the lower-right example of Color Plate 15-3, for example, the cathedral looks normal at its base because the kelp beneath it is black. The center of the kelp is white, however; so the fish's face changes from yellow to its opposite — that is, blue — and the top of the cathedral changes from light brown to deep violet.

✔ Overlay, Soft Light, and Hard Light are similar options. Overlay multiplies the dark colors and screens the light ones, as witnessed by the fish and cathedral in the upper-left example of Color Plate 15-4. Soft Light — applied to the fish in the upper-right example in the color plate — produces a more subtle effect. Hard Light is more dramatic than Soft Light or Overlay. You can still see the base of the cathedral in the upper-right image in Color Plate 15-4, even though it overlaps the black area of the kelp. Meanwhile, the base of the Overlay cathedral is swallowed up in the murk.

✔ Like Multiply and Screen, the Color and Luminosity modes produce exactly opposite effects. The Color mode blends the color of the layer with the detail from the underlying images. Luminosity keeps the detail from the layer and mixes it with the colors of the underlying images.

In the lower-left image in Color Plate 15-4, for example, Color is applied to both fish and cathedral. The colors from the fish are bright; those of the cathedral are muted. But you can see each stalk of kelp clearly because Color doesn't obscure detail.

In the lower-right image, I applied the Luminosity mode to fish and facade. Now, you can clearly see the fish pores and the cathedral carvings, but the color comes from the kelp.

✔ For some other interesting effects, experiment with the Color Dodge, Color Burn, and Exclusion modes. Suppose that you have two layers, a Background layer and Layer 1. Color Dodge lightens the pixels in the Background layer and infuses them with colors from Layer 1. Color Burn darkens the pixels and infuses them with color. Exclusion works similarly to Difference; it turns all black pixels white, all white pixels black, and all medium colors gray.

✔ Darken is another mode that can be useful. Say that you want to composite something like a scanned handwritten letter or sheet of music over an image. Obviously, you want only the handwriting or music notes to appear and not the white paper, which would obscure the underlying pixels. By choosing Darken, only the dark pixels appear, the light area appears transparent. Lighten does just the opposite — displays the light pixels and makes the dark pixels transparent.

✔ You can skip the other blend modes — Dissolve, Hue, and Saturation. They range from boring to duller than dull, and they rarely come in handy.

Just so you know, you can mix a translucent Opacity setting with a blend mode. But you can't select more than one blend mode at a time. It would be fun to combine Luminosity with Multiply, for example — you know, to apply detail that only darkens — but you just can't do it. Oh well.

Erasing holes in layers

If a layer has a lot of weird little flecks in it or some other distracting gook, you can erase it away with the eraser tool. When you work on a layer, the eraser tool erases transparent holes in the layer, assuming the Erase to History check box in the Eraser Options palette is not turned on (see Chapter 11 for more on Erase to History). If Erase to History is turned on, you can Option-drag with the eraser to make holes in the layer. Also, the Preserve Transparency check box must be deselected in the Layers palette. If the check box is turned on, the eraser paints over pixels in the background color.

Figure 15-5 shows examples of erasing parts of the fish layer. In the first example, I erased around the outside of the fish; in the second example, I erased inside the fish. In both cases, the eraser was set to the Airbrush mode, ensuring soft, subtle transitions between the opaque pixels in the layer and the transparent ones.

Figure 15-5:
Two ways
to erase a
fish layer,
around the
outside
(left) and
inside
(right).

Using Layer Effects to Shine and Shadow

Photoshop 5 has made the application of drop shadows, glows, and bevels mere child's play with the addition of the new automated Layer Effects feature. Layer Effects can be applied to regular layers and type layers (see Chapter 16), but not to a Background.

Here is a step-by-step guide to applying a layer effect:

1. **Make a selection using one of the selection methods described in Chapter 12.**

2. **Press ⌘-J.**

   This command quickly copies and pastes the selection to a new layer. Alternatively, you can take the long road and choose Edit⇨Copy, click on the new layer icon at the bottom of the Layers, and choose Edit⇨Paste.

3. **Choose Layer⇨Effects.**

4. **Select one of the five effects (described later in this section) from the Effects submenu.**

   A dialog box with various settings appears. For all of the effects, make sure and have the Apply and Preview boxes checked on. Play with the settings while viewing the effect on your image. Note that numeric settings can be entered or you can access the pop-up sliders for each setting by clicking on the right-pointing arrow adjacent to the numeric setting.

5. With the Apply box checked on, press Return.

The various effects and their settings are described in the following list, yet a picture is worth a thousand words. See Figures 15-6 and 15-7 for examples.

✔ **Drop Shadow:** Applies a soft shadow behind the element. In the dialog box, you specify settings for blend modes and opacity. Color can be specified by clicking on the color swatch, which takes you to the Color Picker (see Chapter 5 for more on color). The Angle value sets the angle of the light source. Distance determines how far the shadow is offset from the object. The Blur and Intensity settings determine the softness and size and prominence of the shadow.

Drop Shadow

Inner Shadow

Figure 15-6:
The new Layer Effects feature makes it easy to apply shadows and glows to images and type.

Outer Glow

Inner Glow

✔ **Inner Shadow:** Applies a shadow on the element itself. The effect is one of a shadow being cast onto the image. The settings are the same as for drop shadow.

✔ **Outer Glow:** Creates a glow or halo effect. You can control the Blend Mode, Color, Opacity, Blur, and Intensity settings.

✔ **Inner Glow:** Makes a glow on the element itself. The settings are the same as outer glow, with the addition of Center and Edge. Center applies the glow over the whole image except the edge, whereas Edge applies only to the element's edge.

Outer Bevel   Inner Bevel

Emboss   Pillow Emboss

Figure 15-7:
The Bevel
and Emboss
Effects
provide four
styles to
choose
from.

✔ **Bevel and Emboss:** There are four Bevel and Emboss styles. Outer Bevel creates a 3D raised edge around the outside of the element. Inner Bevel makes an edge on the element itself. Emboss combines inner and outer bevels to give the effect that the element is raised off the page. Pillow Emboss reverses an inner bevel to give the impression that the element is punched in along the edges and raised in the center. The Bevel and Emboss effect has some unique settings. Because this effect is more 3D in nature, there are settings for Highlight and Shadow (each with separate Blend modes and Opacity options) and Depth. Depth affects how raised or sunken the edge appears. The Up radio button positions the highlight along the edge, closest to the light source and the shadow on the opposite edge. The Down radio button does the opposite and positions the shadow near the light source.

Now that you have an understanding of what Layer Effects are and what they look like, here are some things to remember when working with Layer Effects:

✔ Effects can be combined on a single layer and applied all at once. When you are in an effect's dialog box, click on the Next or Prev buttons to toggle through all of the effects available. Alternatively, you can press ⌘-1 through ⌘-5 to access each effect.

✔ You have the choice of having the effect combined with the image on the same layer (great for moving and transforming the layer as a unit) or putting the effect on a separate layer. To put the effect on a separate layer, apply the effect first, then select the "effected" layer, and choose Layer⇨Effects⇨Create Layer. You will notice a new layer in the Layers palette with a name such as "Layer 1's Drop Shadow."

Putting the effect on a separate layer allows you greater manual editing capability; however, you will not be able to edit the effects via the Layers⇨Effects menu described in the next bullet. Notice that the Effects icon (a cursive f symbol) disappears from the layer in the Layers palette

✔ Effects can be edited. If you decide you want to change the effect, double-click on the Effects icon on the layer in the Layers palette. The Effects dialog box appears, allowing you make adjustments. Uncheck the Apply box to remove the effect entirely. To apply a new effect, click on the Next or Prev button until you reach your desired effect, adjust your settings, check on the Apply box, and click on Return.

✔ For shortcut access to the Effects submenu, Control-click on the Effects icon in the Layers palette to bring up the context-sensitive Effects submenu. (See Chapter 2 for more on context-sensitive menus.)

✔ Effects can be copied and pasted onto other layers. Select the layer containing the effect. Choose Layer⇨Effects⇨Copy Effects and select the layer on which you want to apply the effect. Then choose Layer⇨Effects⇨Paste Effects. To copy an effect onto multiple layers in one fell swoop, link the layers together (described earlier in this chapter) and choose Layers⇨Effects⇨Paste Effects to Linked.

✔ Effects can be hidden. Choose Layer⇨Effects⇨Hide All Effects. To have them reappear, choose Layer⇨Effects⇨Show All Effects.

✔ A Global angle can be specified, thereby ensuring that all the shadows and highlights of all your elements look consistent. In other words, all your effects have the same light source. You wouldn't want one of the elements in your image to look like it was photographed at 9 a.m. and the other to look like it was shot at 2 a.m. — would you? To set a global angle, choose Layer⇨Effects⇨Global Angle and enter the angle you want. Then, just make sure that the Use Global Angle check box is on in the Effects dialog box. The great thing is that if you change the angle on a single Effect, *all* the effects that have been applied to your layers adjust to that new angle automatically. No fuss, no muss.

✔ To remove an effect on a layer, choose Layer⇨Effects⇨Clear Effects. You can also Option-double-click on the Effects icon in the Layers palette. If multiple effects have been applied, repeat the process until all effects are removed. To remove only one multiple effect on a layer, press Option and choose Layer⇨Effects. From the submenu, select the effect you want to remove.

Chapter 16
Digital Graffiti

. . . .

In This Chapter

▶ Using the new and improved type tools

▶ Working with a type layer

▶ Entering and editing text in the Type Tool dialog box

▶ Cutting and pasting text

▶ Assigning formatting attributes

▶ Creating outline type

▶ Adding drop shadows

▶ Making your text translucent

. . . .

Chapters 12, 13, and 14 — known collectively as Part IV — lead you on a merry tour of the various tools and commands for selecting a part of your image. But those chapters skip one other type of selection outline you can create in Photoshop, and you'll never guess what it is. Not in a million years. Give up? The answer is *text*. That's right, Photoshop lets you build a selection outline out of numbers, vowels, consonants, and any other character you can tap in from your keyboard.

The Photoshop approach to text makes it an ideal program for subjecting large letters to special effects. The bigger your text, the better it looks. On the other hand, you shouldn't mistake Photoshop for a word processor. Don't attempt to use Photoshop to create large chunks of text or even medium-sized chunks of text; instead, use a desktop publishing program like PageMaker.

The New and Improved Type Tools

One of the weakest tools in Photoshop went out and pumped up for its role in Version 5. Tired of getting sand kicked in its face, the lonely type tool took charge, demanded its own layer, insisted on editability and requested two new type tools be thrown in for good measure. Lucky for you, Adobe obliged.

One of the most important new features of Photoshop 5 is editable type. When you create type, it is placed on its very own layer called, amazingly enough, a *type layer*. You can then edit the contents, attributes, and orientation at any time by double-clicking on the type layer in the Layers palette. Previous versions of Photoshop forced you to re-create the type from scratch for even the most minor of changes.

Photoshop 5 provides four tools for creating type — two old and two new — and they all share the same flyout menu in the toolbox. The regular type tool's icon looks like a big letter T. The type mask tool looks like a dotted outline of the letter T. The new vertical type tool and vertical type mask tools look like their cousins, with the addition of a vertical arrow next to the letter T. To select the type tool that is visible in the toolbox, press T on your keyboard. Press Shift-T to select any of the other type tools. Isn't it great when icons and keyboard shortcuts make so much sense?

Here's a briefing on the type tools:

✔ The regular type tool creates text on a new type layer (layers, in general, are explained in excruciating detail in Chapter 15), which allows you to work with the text without worrying about touching the underlying image. The text contents and attributes can be edited by double-clicking on the layer in the Layers palette. Although you cannot use painting or editing tools on a type layer, you can make the text more or less translucent by adjusting the Opacity percentage in the Layers palette, and you can blend the text with the underlying layers using the blend modes pop-up menu.

✔ The vertical type tool performs exactly like the regular type tool except that type is entered and appears along a vertical axis. Great for Asian fonts, not quite as useful for Roman letters.

✔ The regular type mask tool creates your text as a selection outline. You can manipulate, edit, paint, and otherwise play with the selection outline as you would any other selection outline. And because the type mask tool works like any other selection tool, you can use it to add to or subtract from an existing selection outline (see Chapter 13). Note that the type created with the type mask tool *cannot* be edited like type created with the type tool.

✔ The vertical type mask tool operates like the regular type mask tool. The only difference is that the selection outline runs along a vertical axis.

So, which tool do you use when? If you want to retain true editability, obviously, use the regular type tool. Otherwise, it depends on what sort of effect you're trying to create. If you want opaque type, use the regular type tool. If, on the other hand, you want to create character outlines such as those shown in the top example in Color Plate 16-1, use the type mask tool and then stroke the selection outline using Edit⇨Stroke. If you want to soften the edges of your letters — for example, to create a fuzzy shadow behind your letters, as in the middle example in the color plate — you can use the type tool in combination with the new Layer Effects feature. (I give the how-tos for creating both these examples later in this chapter.) The type mask tool can also be used to create the shadow effect. It just involves more steps and a different approach.

Just remember that the basic difference between the two tools is that one creates editable type on a new type layer, and the other gives you a selection outline in the shape of your characters. Pick the tool that gives you the quickest route to the effect you're trying to achieve.

The biggest disadvantage of the type mask tool is that when you deselect the text selection, the text becomes permanently fused to the underlying image. But you can get around this problem by creating a new layer in the Layers palette before you click with the type mask tool. Now, any text you create exists on its own layer and can easily be moved, rotated, painted, and so on. Remember, however, that a regular layer is not the same as a *type* layer. A type layer provides for editability of contents and attributes. Read on!

Putting Your Words On-Screen

To type a few letters in Photoshop, select any of the type tools and click inside the image. It doesn't really matter where you click, by the way. Photoshop positions your text at the spot you click, but you can always move the text after you create it. (However, if a selection outline is active and you click inside it with the type mask tool, Photoshop deselects the current selection. You need to click again to create your text.)

Instead of responding with a little blinking cursor or some other subtle doohickey that you may have come to expect from working in other programs, Photoshop goes all out and displays the Type Tool dialog box shown in Figure 16-1. This dialog box is where you enter, format, and otherwise get text ready for its debut inside the image window.

Actually, when you first click with the type tool, Photoshop may display a message telling you that it's reading fonts. This means that Photoshop is trying to load all the typefaces available to your system into memory. Just wait out the message. It goes away soon enough, and the dialog box appears in all its glory.

Alignment icons

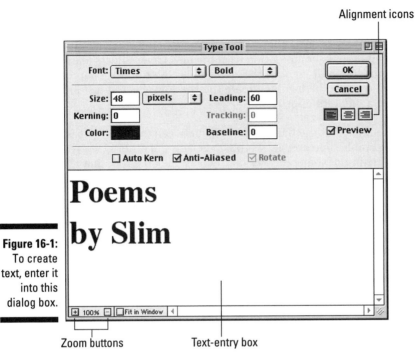

Figure 16-1:
To create
text, enter it
into this
dialog box.

Zoom buttons   Text-entry box

Typing what must be typed

When you first enter the Type Tool dialog box, the text-entry box (refer to
Figure 16-1) is active. Here's where you enter the text that you want to add
to your image. If this is the first time you've entered text in Photoshop, a
little vertical line called an *insertion marker* blinks away next to the left side
of the box. If you've entered text before, the previous text appears highlighted, thus allowing you to edit the text or enter new text. You can do a
number of things inside the text-entry box:

- ✔ Start typing away to create the text you want to add to your image. If
  existing text in the box was highlighted, Photoshop replaces it with the
  new text.

- ✔ After entering your text, you may find that you've made a mistake or
  two. To delete a letter, click in front of it and press the Delete key. To
  add text, click at the point where you want to insert it and enter the
  new text from the keyboard.

- ✔ When you move the cursor inside the text-entry box, it changes to an
  I-beam. To replace text, drag over it with the cursor to highlight it and
  then start whacking those keys. To delete more than one letter, highlight the letters and press Delete.

✔ Photoshop places all words on a single line in the image unless you insert a paragraph by pressing the Return key. In Figure 16-1, for example, I typed Poems, pressed Return, and then typed by Slim.

✔ To control the way your type is displayed in the text-entry box, you can do the following: Resize the box by dragging the lower-right corner. Click on the zoom buttons (+ or –) in the lower-left corner to zoom in or out. Click on the percentage value to return to a 100% view. Set the magnification so that all of your text is always visible by checking on the Fit in Window box (note that this disables the zoom buttons).

When inside the text-entry box, you can access the Cut, Copy, Paste, and Undo commands under the Edit menu. These commands enable you to move text around and undo mistakes. For example, to move some letters from one place to another, follow these steps:

1. **Highlight the text you want to move.**

   Drag over the text with the I-beam cursor.

2. **Press ⌘-X.**

   Photoshop removes the text and puts it in a special location in your computer's memory called the *Clipboard*. ⌘-X, by the way, is the shortcut for the Edit⇨Cut command.

3. **Click at the point where you want to move the text.**

   Your click repositions the insertion marker.

4. **Press ⌘-V.**

   ⌘-V is the shortcut for the Edit⇨Paste command. Photoshop retrieves the text from the Clipboard and inserts it at the desired spot.

Changing how the type looks

The remaining options inside the Type Tool dialog box determine how your text looks. These options control the typeface, the type size, the type color, the amount of space between lines and letters, and all that other rigmarole. When all these characteristics get together in the same room, they're usually called *formatting attributes.* You can, of course, make additional enhancements to the appearance of your text after you return to the image window, but the formatting options let you set up the fundamental stuff.

In previous versions of Photoshop, all text in the text-entry box was formatted the same. For example, you couldn't highlight a single word and assign it a different typeface than you assign to its neighbors. Version 5, however, allows you to mix most formatting attributes within the text entry box. Color and alignment are the only two attributes that cannot be mixed. Here's how to assign various attributes to your text:

✔ Select a typeface and type style from the Font pop-up menu. Assuming that you installed Photoshop correctly, type styles such as bold and italic appear in their own submenus.

✔ In order to successfully use PostScript fonts in Photoshop, you must be using ATM (that's Adobe Type Manager, not Automatic Teller Machine or Arbitrary Toaster Molester). If your text comes up smooth and beautiful, not to worry. If your text is so jagged that it looks like you drew it on an Etch a Sketch — as in the case of Bad type in Figure 16-2 — something's wrong. Either use a different font or consult with your local computer know-it-all to figure out the problem.

Figure 16-2:
If your text looks smooth (top), super. If not (bottom), try a different font or ask your local computer guru for help.

Good type
Bad type

✔ Enter the size of the text into the Size option box. The Size value is measured in either points (one point equals $1/72$ inch) or pixels, depending on the setting in the pop-up menu to the right of the option box.

✔ The Leading value controls the amount of space between lines of type. Of course, Photoshop doesn't do anything like that, but old terms die hard. If you don't enter a Leading value, Photoshop assigns spacing equal to 120% of the Size value. If you do enter a value, I recommend that it be equal to at least 90% of the Size value to keep the lines from overlapping. In Figure 16-3, for example, the Size value was 144 pixels and the Leading value was 130 pixels.

✔ Kerning controls the spacing between two letters. Positive values move letters apart, negative values move letters closer together. Kerning values are measured in units that are $1/1000$ of an em space. The width of an em space depends on your font size. For example, in a 10-point font, 1 em equals 10 points; in a 100 point font, 1 em equals 100 points. To manually kern, first deselect the Auto Kern box. Click your I-beam to set an insertion point between two letters and then enter a kerning value. Leaving Auto Kern checked turns on the kerning built into the font by its manufacturer.

Figure 16-3:
Here's how
the Size
(dark gray)
and Leading
(light gray)
values are
measured.

Leading

Size

✔ The tracking value controls the spacing between more than two letters. If you want to adjust the spacing of a word or sentence, enter a positive or negative value to move letters apart or together, respectively. Tracking is also measured in units of $^1/_{1000}$ of an em space. To use tracking, highlight your word or words and enter a tracking value.

✔ Baseline shift refers to the distance the type sits from its baseline. Type can be raised or lowered to create superscripts and subscripts for items such as fractions and trademark and copyright symbols. To adjust the baseline shift, highlight the character and enter a baseline value. Positive values move horizontal type above and vertical type to the right of the baseline. Negative values move type below or to the left of the baseline.

✔ Like the Size value, Leading, Kerning, Tracking, and Baseline Shift values are all measured in points or pixels, depending on the pop-up menu setting.

✔ By default, the color that appears in the type tool dialog box is the current foreground color. It is probably better to define your type color using the Color palette before you type, but if you are feeling fickle, you can change the color while in the type dialog box. Simply click on the color swatch, which takes you to the Color Picker. Click in the color spectrum bar to get the basic color you want and then select the exact color by clicking in the big square on the left. You can also specify a color by entering values in the RGB or CMYK boxes. For more on defining color see Chapter 5.

✔ Select an Alignment option to determine whether multiple lines of text are aligned by their left edges, right edges, or centers.

✔ Color and alignment are formatting attributes that affect each and every character in the text entry box equally and without prejudice.

✔ The Rotate check box is available only when you create vertical type. Checking on this box rotates the type 90°.

- ✔ Always select the Anti-aliased check box. If you turn it off, your text has tiny jagged edges, and you don't want that. (This check box doesn't cure big, huge jags created by the font problems I mentioned earlier.)

- ✔ Always have the Preview check box on. This lets you see the text on your image as you type and allows you to actually go onto your image area and move the text to fine-tune its placement while the type tool dialog box is still open. Very convenient!

Bringing text and image together

To instruct Photoshop to create your text, click on the OK button or press the Enter key on the numeric keypad. If you press the other Enter key, you run the risk of wiping out the letters in the text-entry box because that Enter key adds a paragraph return. (Okay, a few of you may have noticed that the Enter key does activate the OK button when you're editing the Size, Leading, Kerning, Tracking, or Baseline values, but it's best to get in the habit of pressing Enter on the numeric keyboard just to be safe.)

Photoshop then creates your text in the image window. In the Layers palette (Windows⇨Show Layers), notice that the type appears on its own layer annotated with a capital letter T icon indicating that it's a type layer. The name of the type layer corresponds to the text you typed.

If the bottoms of some of your characters that dip down low — such as g, p, and y — are getting cut off, you need to change a setting inside ATM. To open the ATM control panel, choose the Control Panels command from the Apple menu and then double-click on the ~ATM filename. (Or choose Apple⇨ Control Panels⇨ATM if you use System 7.5. or later.) Next, select the Character shapes radio button. Click in the close box to close the control panel and restart your computer by choosing Special⇨Restart at the Finder. (Be sure to save any open images in Photoshop before you restart your machine.)

Editing the Type Layer

If you notice a misspelled word or some other typographical gaffe, don't attempt to drag over the text with a type tool to edit it. Instead, double-click on the type layer in the Layers palette. The type tool dialog box reappears, and you can edit the contents or any of the attributes. Press Return or click on OK, and the revised text appears in the image window. Type layers save with the image, so you can revise the text at any time, as long as you don't flatten the layers, that is (see Chapter 15 for more on layers).

Here are some things you can do to a type layer and still edit the text:

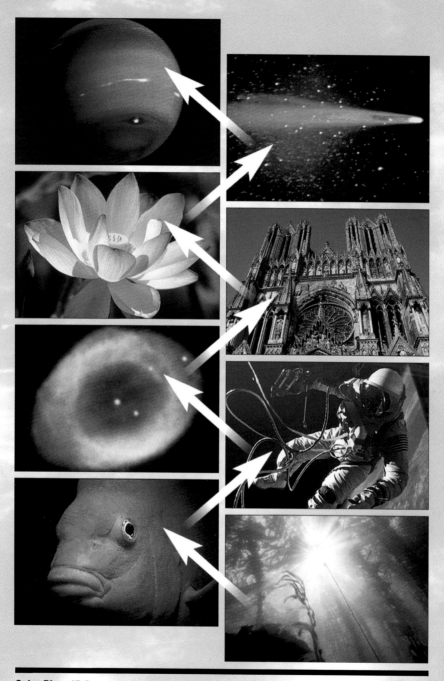

Color Plate 15-2:
The eight images I used to create Color Plate 15-1. The arrows show the layering order of the images, from the kelp (lower right) at the bottom of the heap to the planet Neptune (upper left) at the top.

Normal, 100% Opacity

50% Opacity

Fish: Multiply; Cathedral: Screen

Difference

Color Plate 15-3:
After positioning the cathedral on one layer, the fish on a layer beneath it, and the kelp in the Background layer (top left), I experimented with various Opacity settings and modes. First, I changed the Opacity of both layers to 50% (top right). Then I returned the Opacity to 100% and applied the Multiply mode to the fish and the Screen mode to the cathedral (bottom left). Finally, I applied the Difference mode to both layers (bottom right).

Overlay

Fish: Soft Light; Cathedral: Hard Light

Color

Luminosity

Color Plate 15-4:
Continuing from Color Plate 15-3, I applied the Overlay mode to both fish and cathedral
(top left). Then I applied Soft Light to the fish and Hard Light to the cathedral (top right).
Finally, I tried out the Color (bottom left) and Luminosity (bottom right) modes on both
layers.

Color Plate 16-1:
Photoshop lets you create some wild type effects that are either difficult or impossible to produce in other programs. Some examples include double outline type (top), text with soft drop shadows (middle), and translucent text (bottom).

Color Plate 17-1:
Starting with the original inset image, I selected the dark portions of the image with Select⇨Color Range, applied the Add Noise filter with an Amount value of 100 and the Gaussian option selected, and then followed things up with the Motion Blur filter. The only difference between the top and bottom images was the setting of the Monochromatic check box in the Add Noise dialog box. In the top image, it was turned off; in the bottom image, it was on.

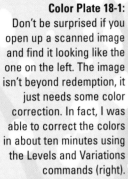

Color Plate 18-1:
Don't be surprised if you open up a scanned image and find it looking like the one on the left. The image isn't beyond redemption, it just needs some color correction. In fact, I was able to correct the colors in about ten minutes using the Levels and Variations commands (right).

Color Plate 18-2:
The results of adding blue (left) and yellow (right) to the image by using Image➪Adjust➪Variations. Colors that have little or no blue or yellow in them — such as the reds in the bows and the greens in the packages and apples — remain virtually unaffected.

Color Plate 18-3:
Here, I used the Levels command to correct the colors in a muted image. For reference, the histogram and Input Levels options from the Levels dialog box are inset with each step. Starting with the uncorrected Photo CD scan (top left), I adjusted the black slider triangle (top right), the white triangle (bottom left), and the gamma point (bottom right) to create a sound image with excellent color depth.

Color Plate 18-4:
The colors of paradise lost (left) and found again (right) by selecting the Saturation radio button inside the Variations dialog box and increasing the saturation.

Original   More Blue   More Blue

More Magenta   More Magenta   More Blue

Color Plate 18-5:
I fixed an image that had a preponderance of yellow and green (top left) by clicking on the labeled previews in the Variations dialog box. For example, to produce the top middle image, I clicked on the More Blue preview; to get the top right image, I clicked on the same preview again.

✔ You can reorder or duplicate the type layer, just as you can with a regular layer. To move the layer in front of or behind another one, drag it up or down in the list of layers in the Layers palette. A heavy black line shows where the layer will be inserted. To duplicate, drag the layer onto the new layer icon at the bottom of the Layers palette.

✔ Move or clone the text. Drag with the move tool to position the text. Option-drag to clone the text.

✔ Change the orientation of a layer. Choose Layer⇨Type⇨Horizontal or Vertical to change the orientation.

✔ You are able to apply any of the blend modes and adjust the opacity of the type layer.

✔ Perform transformation commands, such as rotate, skew, and scale. Perspective and Distort transformation are not available to type layers.

✔ Apply Layer Effects (see more later in this chapter) to the type layer. Even after the effect is applied, if the type changes in any way, such as a different font or even a different word, the effect dynamically updates to the changes. Miraculous!

✔ Fill the type with the foreground or background color by using the fill command keyboard shortcuts. Press Option-Delete to fill with the foreground color. Press ⌘-Delete to fill with the background color. Note that the Edit⇨Fill menu command is grayed out — only the keyboard shortcuts can be utilized.

Here are the two things you cannot do to a type layer, unless you render the type layer and convert it to a regular layer (see more about this in the next section):

✔ You cannot use any of the painting and editing tools. When you hold the painting and editing tools over the type layer, you see a slashed circle symbol indicating "No can do!"

✔ You cannot apply filters under the Filter menu.

A type layer cannot be created for images in indexed color, bitmap, or multi-channel modes because these modes do not support layers of any kind — type or otherwise. Type created in these modes gets applied to the Background and cannot be edited. If you want type included in images you are preparing for the Web, for example, be sure and wait until you finish compositing your layers and editing your type to convert the image to indexed color. (For more on color modes, see Chapter 6.)

If you decide you don't want the type layer any longer, delete it by dragging the layer to the trash can icon at the bottom of the Layers palette (for help, see Chapter 15). Or just click on the layer name and then click on the trash can icon.

Rendering a Type Layer

In order to apply a filter or paint on a type layer, you must first do what Adobe calls rendering the layer. To render a type layer, choose Layer➪Type➪ Render Layer. Rendering basically converts the type layer to a regular layer. The type then acts as though it was created with the type mask tool. After rendering, the type will look the same; however, you will no longer be able to edit the type by double-clicking on the type layer icon. Notice that it isn't there anymore! So a word of advice — be sure the text is exactly like you want it before you render the type layer because editing capabilities go down the drain.

Declaring Open Season on Type Selection Outlines

If you created your type with the type mask tool and it's sitting there selected inside your image, you can do all kinds of things with it, including the following:

✔ To move a text selection outline, drag with the type mask tool or one of the other selection tools. Or press the arrow keys to nudge the selection outline this way or that.

✔ To move or clone the text selection, use the same techniques you use to move or clone any other selection (refer to Chapter 13). Drag with the move tool to move the text; Option-drag to clone the text.

In other words, selections that you create with the type mask tool work just like any other selection.

✔ You can paint inside the text. After you paint inside the letters, you can use the edit tools to smear the colors, blur them, lighten them, and so on.

✔ You can fill the text with the foreground color by pressing Option-Delete. To fill the text with the background color, press ⌘-Delete. To fill the text with a blend of colors, just drag across the text with the gradient tool. It just couldn't be easier.

✔ You can apply a border around your type by choosing Edit➪Stroke.

✔ Before you fill or stroke a selection outline, be sure that your text is positioned where you want it. You can't move the stroked text after you create it without leaving a hole in your image. Ditto with any other painting or editing commands you apply to a text selection outline. That's why it is a good idea to create a new layer before you create your text selection outline. It allows you to move the text without affecting the underlying image.

✔ If you want to delete text that was created with the type mask tool — and you didn't take my advice to create that text on its own layer — you need to undo your steps by using the History palette (see Chapter 11), to bring your image back to its pretext appearance.

Every one of these techniques can achieve some truly remarkable effects. Just to show you what I mean, in the following section, I show you how to create outline type and text with shadows, as I promised earlier. I also show you how to create translucent type. For full-color demonstrations of these techniques, see Color Plate 16-1.

Tracing outlines around your letters

Today's first set of steps shows how to create genuine outline type, like the stuff shown in the top example in Color Plate 16-1. You can see through the interiors of the letters, and you can make the borders as thick as you please.

1. **Create a new layer.**

   You don't have to put your text on its own layer, but doing so makes it simpler to edit the text later on if necessary. To create a layer, click on the new layer icon in the Layers palette, as discussed in Chapter 15.

2. **Use the type mask tool to create your text.**

   Click with the tool, type away into the text-entry area, format to your heart's content, and click on OK. Then move the text selection outline into the desired position by dragging it or nudging it with the arrow keys.

3. **Set the foreground color to white.**

   You can do this quickly by pressing D to get the default colors and then X to swap them.

4. **Make sure that the Preserve Transparency check box in the Layers palette is deselected.**

   In the next step, you apply a stroke to the center of your selection outline. If you don't deselect the Preserve Transparency check box, Photoshop doesn't let you paint outside the selection outline.

5. **Choose Edit⇨Stroke, select the Center radio button, and enter 12 as the Width value.**

   After making your selections in the Stroke dialog box, press Return. You now have a 12-pixel thick, white outline around your type.

6. **Make black or some other dark color the foreground color.**

   To create the top example in Color Plate 16-1, I changed the foreground color to red.

7. **Choose Edit⇨Stroke and enter** 4 **as the Width value.**

Then press Return. Congratulations! You have arrived at the effect shown in Figure 16-4 and the top of Color Plate 16-1. If you created your text on a layer, as I heartily recommended back in Step 1, you can use the move tool to reposition the text if needed. (Be sure to press ⌘-D to deselect the text first.) You can also play with the blend modes and Opacity slider in the Layers palette to change how the text blends with the underlying image.

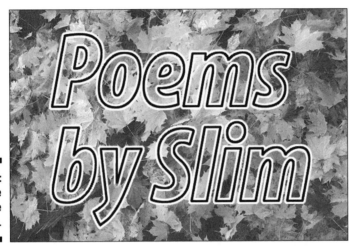

Figure 16-4:
Outline type
created the
right way.

Adding shadows behind your letters

In these steps, you create letters with shadows in Figure 16-5 and the second example in Color Plate 16-1. These kinds of shadows are commonly called *drop shadows* because they don't extend away from the letters; instead, they merely rest behind the letters. The new automated Layer Effects feature makes applying shadows quick and easy. See Chapter 15 for the comprehensive lowdown on Layer Effects (which can all be applied to type layers as well as regular layers).

1. **Set the foreground color to white. To do it quickly, type** D **and then** X.

2. **Create and format your text using the regular type tool.**

3. **Position the text with the move tool if necessary.**

4. **Choose Layer⇨Effects⇨Drop Shadow.**

A dialog box appears with various settings. Make sure that the Apply and Preview check boxes are on. Play with settings while previewing the effect on your type. I recommend leaving the Blend mode on the default of Multiply. For type, a 65% to 75% opacity is usually good.

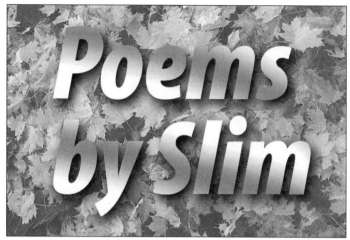

Figure 16-5:
Drop
shadows
help to set
text off
from the
background
and
otherwise
make it look
way cool.

Clicking on the right-pointing black arrow next to the numeric setting accesses a slider bar (as it does for the Distance, Blur, and Intensity settings). Angle lets you determine where your light source is coming from to create the shadow. Clicking on the right-pointing black arrow next to the numeric setting accesses a 360° slider. Distance determines how far the shadow offsets from your type. Keeping the shadow fairly close to the type usually results in a better effect. Blur and Intensity affect the softness and size and prominence of the shadow.

5. **Press Return when you are satisfied with the shadow's appearance.**

6. **Change the foreground color to medium gray or some other medium color.**

   In Color Plate 16-1, I used purple. This color is for the soft shading inside the letters.

7. **Choose Layer⇨Type⇨Render Layer.**

   This step allows you to paint on the type.

8. **Check on Preserve Transparency in the Layers Palette.**

   This step protects the transparent areas and allows only the paint to be applied to the type.

9. **Choose Window⇨Show Brushes and select a large, soft brush.**

10. **Paint a couple of streaks across the letters with the airbrush tool.**

    You now have something resembling the image shown in Figure 16-6 and in the middle of Color Plate 16-1.

Turning your letters into ghosts of their former selves

This last set of steps explains how to create translucent letters, which are just the ticket for creating *ghosted* or tinted text (see the third example in Color Plate 16-1). You may think that this effect would be rather difficult, but in truth, it's way easier than the previous techniques.

1. **Start with a light background.**

   I explain how to adjust the colors in your image in Chapter 18.

2. **Change your foreground color to something dark.**

   Note that in Color Plate 16-1, I opted for dark orange.

3. **Select the regular type tool and create your text.**

   Photoshop creates type in the background color and places it on a new type layer.

4. **Drag or nudge the text into position using the move tool.**

5. **Press a number key.**

   When you're working with a layer, pressing a number key changes the opacity of the layer. Higher numbers make the selection more opaque; lower numbers make it more transparent. Chapter 15 explains all of this in more detail, but for now, just press the number keys until you get the effect you want.

6. **Select the airbrush tool.**

7. **Choose Window⇨Show Brushes and select a large, soft brush.**

8. **Click on the Background layer.**

9. **Set the foreground color to white and take a couple of swipes at the background with the airbrush.**

   Ooh, isn't that pretty. I can't decide whether it looks more like the title for a wedding invitation, a soap opera, or a wake, but it sure is pretty.

Chapter 17
Forays into Filters

• •

In This Chapter

▶ Applying, reapplying, and fading filter effects

▶ Sharpening an image

▶ Using the Unsharp Mask command

▶ Blurring a background with Gaussian Blur

▶ Applying the Motion Blur command

▶ Randomizing pixels with Add Noise

▶ Creating images in relief by using Emboss

▶ Filling areas with flat colors by using Facet

▶ Averaging colors with Median

• •

*I*f you're a photographer or you've taken a photography course or two, you know how photographic filters work. They refine or refract light to modify the image as it comes into the camera. A daylight filter strains some of the blue out of the image; a polarization lens eliminates reflected light; a fish-eye lens refracts peripheral imagery into the photo.

But real-life filters present some problems. They take up a ton of room in your camera bag, and they generally bang around and get scratched. Also, you have to decide which filter you want to use while shooting the photo. Not only is it difficult to experiment through a viewfinder, but also whatever decision you ultimately make is permanent. If you go with a fish-eye lens, you can't go back and "undistort" the image later.

The Photoshop filters are another story:

  ✔ All filters reside under a single menu (surprisingly, called Filter).

  ✔ You can undo a filter if you don't like the results.

  ✔ You can preview the outcome of the most common filters.

  ✔ You can apply several filters in a row and even go back and revisit a single filter multiple times.

  ✔ Most Photoshop filters have no real-world counterparts, which means that you can modify images in ways that aren't possible inside a camera.

If you're a photographer, you may want to forego a few of your camera's filters and take up Photoshop filters instead. Granted, you may still want to use corrective lenses to adjust color and keep out reflected light, but avoid a special-effects filter that makes the image look like more than what your eyes can see. Such filters merely limit the range of effects you can apply later inside Photoshop.

If you aren't a photographer, filters open up a whole new range of opportunities that no other Photoshop function quite matches. Filters apply changes automatically, so there's no need to be an artist. Filters can make poor images look better and good images look fantastic. And you can use them to introduce special effects, such as camera movement and relief textures. Frankly, filters turn Photoshop into a lean, mean photo-munching machine.

Photoshop 4 generously brought you 48 new filters. Photoshop 5 brings only one new filter — the 3D Transform filter (see Chapter 20). But, hey, you have almost 100 filters to play with. This chapter doesn't even start to cover all the Photoshop filters, just those that you're likely to use on a regular basis. To see some of the others in action, check out Chapter 20.

A Few Fast Filter Facts

Before launching into explanations of Photoshop filters, check these facts:

- ✔ If some portion of your image is selected, the filter affects the selection and leaves the rest of the image unmodified. If no portion of the image is selected, the filter affects the entire image.

- ✔ To create smooth transitions between filtered and unfiltered areas in an image, blur the selection outline by choosing Select⇨Feather (see Chapter 13).

- ✔ After you apply a filter, you can reapply it in the same manner by choosing the first command in the Filter menu or by pressing ⌘-F.

- ✔ Some filters display a dialog box so that you can control how the filter is applied. If the last filter was one of these, press ⌘-Option-F to redisplay the dialog box and apply the filter again using different settings. *Note:* Chapter 10 explains how to use the preview options and other controls inside filter dialog boxes.

- ✔ To undo the last filter, press ⌘-Z. Unlike a canceled filter, the undone filter remains at the top of the Filter menu, so you can later apply it by pressing ⌘-F.

- ✔ Some filters take a few seconds or even minutes to apply. You can cancel such a filter in progress by pressing Esc. The name of the previous filter remains at the top of the Filter menu, so you can't press ⌘-F to apply a canceled filter.

✔ If you don't like the results of the filter or filters you've applied and you can't undo by pressing ⌘-Z, use the History palette to return to a source state — Photoshop's term for a previously saved step — that you are happy with (see Chapter 11 for details on the History palette).

✔ The Fade command is designed specifically for blending a filtered image with its unmolested twin. If you choose Filter⇨Fade or press ⌘-Shift-F immediately after applying a filter, the Fade dialog box appears, enabling you to play with the Opacity and blend mode of the filtered image. This command enables you to create all sorts of variations on a filter, as illustrated in Figure 17-1. In this example, I applied the Fresco filter once, then used the Fade command with a 60% opacity setting, and finally applied the Darken blend mode.

✔ Remember, you have to apply the Fade command *immediately* after you apply the filter. If you choose another command or apply a painting or editing tool to the image, you can't use the Fade command. The only alternative is to use the History palette and revert to the source state prior to applying the filter. You can reapply the filter and then choose the Fade command. (Again, for more on the History palette, see Chapter 11.)

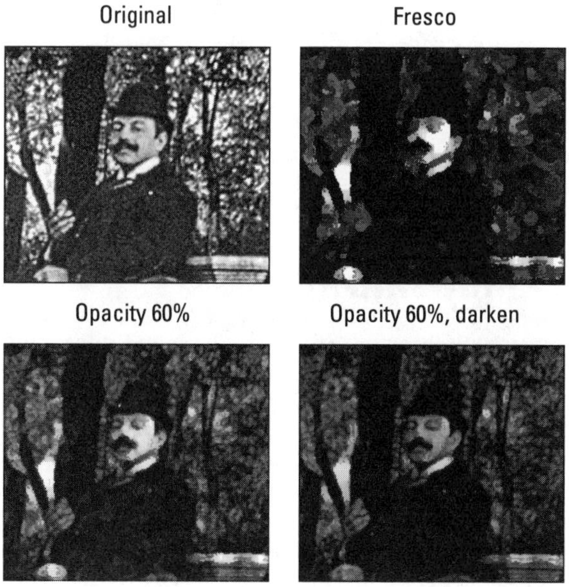

Original   Fresco

Opacity 60%   Opacity 60%, darken

Figure 17-1:
A dapper
gentleman
takes on a
new look.

How to Fortify Wishy-Washy Details

No matter how good an image looked before you scanned it, chances are better than even that it appears a little out of focus on-screen. The image in Figure 17-2 is an exaggerated example. Snapped around the time Stonehenge was built, this photo has suffered the cruel scourges of time.

Figure 17-2: Antique images such as this one are notoriously soft on focus.

The solutions to softness are the four commands under the Filter⇨Sharpen submenu. The following sections explain how these filters work and when — if ever — to apply them.

The single-shot sharpeners

The first three sharpening filters — Sharpen, Sharpen Edges, and Sharpen More — are what I call *single-shot filters*. You choose them, and they do their work without complex dialog boxes or other means of digital interrogation. These filters, with their straightforward names, are a breeze to use.

Unfortunately, when it comes to Photoshop, you get back what you put in — mentally, that is. In other words, if you don't have to work at it, it's liable to deliver rather mediocre results. As demonstrated in Figure 17-3, all three of these Sharpen filters sharpen, but none satisfactorily remedies the image's focus problems.

Figure 17-3 shows the results of applying each of the three single-shot sharpeners to a detail from the image. In each case, I applied the filter once — as shown in the middle row — and then a second time — as shown in the last row. For the record, here's what each of the filters do:

Figure 17-3: The effects of applying each of the single-shot sharpeners are shockingly shabby.

✓ Filter⇨Sharpen⇨Sharpen enhances the focus of the image very slightly. If the photo is already well focused but needs a little extra fortification to make it perfect, the Sharpen filter does the trick. Otherwise, forget it.

✓ The Sharpen More filter enhances focus more dramatically. Although it's easily the most useful of the three single-shooters, it's still fairly crude. For example, the center image in Figure 17-3 is not sharp enough, whereas the bottom image is so sharp that little flecks — called _artifacts_ — are starting to form in the woman's dress. Boo, hiss.

✓ The Sharpen Edges filter is a complete waste of time. It sharpens the so-called edges of an image without sharpening any of the neutral areas in between. In Figure 17-3, for example, the filter sharpens the outline of the guy's face but ignores the interior of his jacket. The result is an inconsistent effect that eventually frays the edges and leaves nonedges looking goopy by comparison.

As you may have gathered by now, I'm not a big fan of these filters. Still, you may want to go ahead and apply Sharpen or Sharpen More to an image to see whether it does the trick. If a single-shot sharpener turns out to be all you need, great. If not, undo the effect (press ⌘-Z) and try out the Unsharp Mask command, explained next. It's a little scarier, but it works like a dream.

Unsharp Mask: The filter with a weird name

If the Photoshop programmers had been in charge of naming Superman, they would have called him "Average Guy from Krypton." Rather than describing what the guy does, the programmers describe his origins. I say this because that's exactly what they did with Filter⇨Sharpen⇨Unsharp Mask. Rather than calling the filter "Supersharpen," which would have made a modicum of sense and may have even encouraged a few novices to give it a try, they named it after a 40-year-old stat camera technique that a few professionals in lab coats pretend to understand in order to impress members of the opposite sex.

So forget Unsharp Mask and just think "Supersharpen." To use the "Supersharpen" command, choose Filter⇨Sharpen⇨Unsharp Mask. The "Supersharpen" dialog box appears, as shown in Figure 17-4.

Figure 17-4:
Experts
agree that
the Unsharp
Mask dialog
box really
should be
called the
Supersharpen
dialog box.

Inside the "Supersharpen" dialog box

Like the Dust & Scratches dialog box (see Chapter 10), the Unsharp Mask dialog box in Figure 17-4 allows you to preview what happens when you change the values in the three option boxes. You can preview the filter inside the dialog box and in the main image window. If you can't quite remember how these previewing functions work, check out Chapter 10. To sharpen an image, use the three slider bars like so:

- ✔ Change the Amount value from 1% to 500% to change the amount of sharpening. This may strike you as obvious, but just to be sure, higher Amount values produce more sharpening.

- ✔ Adjust the Radius value to specify the width of the edges you want to sharpen. If the image is generally in good shape, use a Radius of 0.5. If the edges are soft and syrupy, like the ones in Figure 17-2, use a Radius of 1.0. And if the edges are almost nonexistent, go with 2.0. Generally, you don't want to go any lower than 0.5 or any higher than 2.0 (though 250.0 is the maximum).

- ✔ You don't have to enter 1.0 or 2.0 into the Radius option box. A simple 1 or 2 will suffice. It's just that you can enter $^1/_{10}$ values — such as 1.1 and 1.9 — if you're in a particularly precise mood.

- ✔ As with the Threshold option in the Dust & Scratches dialog box, the Unsharp Mask Threshold option determines how different two neighboring pixels must be to be considered an edge. (See Chapter 10 for a review of this concept.) The default value of 0 tells Photoshop to sharpen everything. By raising the value, you tell Photoshop not to sharpen low-contrast pixels.

- ✔ This idea is great, but the implementation by Photoshop leaves something to be desired. The filter creates an abrupt transition between sharpened and ignored pixels, resulting in an unrealistic effect. Therefore, I recommend that you leave Threshold set to 0.

Some sharpening scenarios

Figure 17-5 demonstrates the effects of several different Amount and Radius values on the same detail to which I applied the piddly little Sharpen More command in Figure 17-3. Throughout Figure 17-5, the Threshold value is 0.

Figure 17-5 is organized into two rows. To create the images in the top row, I started with an Amount value of 200% and a Radius of 0.5. Then I halved the Amount value and doubled the Radius in each of the next two images. Though the effect is similar from one image to the next, you can see that the right image has thicker edges than the left image. (The differences are subtle; you may have to look closely.)

The bottom row of Figure 17-5 features more pronounced sharpening effects. Again, I started with one set of Amount and Radius values — 500% and 0.5 — and progressively halved the Amount and doubled the Radius. Notice that the edges in the right image are thicker, and the left image contains more artifacts (those little flecks in the jacket and hat).

After experimenting with a few different settings, I decided that my favorite setting was an Amount of 250% and a Radius of 1.0. The final image sharpened with these settings is shown in Figure 17-6.

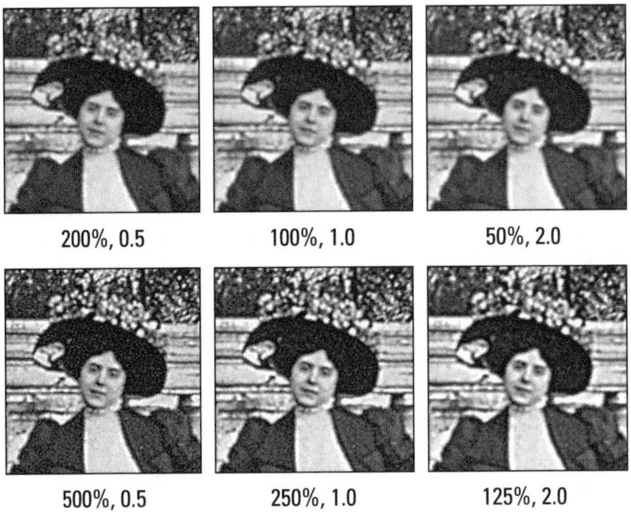

Figure 17-5:
The effect
of a whole
bunch of
Amount and
Radius
values on
detail from
an ancient
photo.

200%, 0.5   100%, 1.0   50%, 2.0

500%, 0.5   250%, 1.0   125%, 2.0

Figure 17-6:
The image
from Figure
17-2
sharpened
with an
Amount
value of
250% and
a Radius
value of 1.0.

Myopia Adds Depth

If you want to make a portion of your image blurry instead of sharp, you can apply one of the commands under the Filter⇨Blur menu. Right off the bat, you quick thinkers are thinking, "Blurry? Why would I want my image to be blurry?" This is a classic problem. You're thinking of blurry as the opposite of sharp. But blurry and sharp can go hand in hand inside the same image. The sharp details are in the foreground, and the blurry stuff goes in the background.

Take Figure 17-7, for example. In this image, I selected and blurred the background. The scene becomes a little more intimate, as though the background were far, far away. It also has the effect of making the foreground characters seem more in focus than ever.

To make the effect complete, I selected the lower-right corner of the image, which represents the ground coming toward us. I feathered the selection (using Select⇨Feather set to a value of 30) and then blurred it. The result is a gradual blurring effect, as though the ground were becoming progressively out of focus as it extends beyond our field of vision.

Figure 17-7:
Blurring the background as well as a small tip of the foreground (bottom right) brings the family up close and personal.

For the most part, then, blurring is a special effect. Unlike sharpening, which has the effect of correcting the focus, blurring heightens reality by exaggerating the depth of an image. In other words, you never have to blur an image — and you probably won't do it nearly as frequently as you sharpen — but it's a lot of fun.

Choosing your blur

The first two commands under the Filter⇨Blur submenu — Blur and Blur More — are the Dumb and Dumber of the blur filters. Like their Sharpen and Sharpen More counterparts, they produce predefined effects that never seem to be quite what you're looking for.

The "Superblur" command — the filter that offers the powers you need to get the job done right — is Filter⇨Blur⇨Gaussian Blur. The filter is named after Karl Friedrich Gauss, a dusty old German mathematician who's even older than the photograph from Figure 17-2. But just think "Superblur" — or, as Mr. Gauss would have put it, *Ueberblur*.

When you choose Filter⇨Blur⇨Gaussian Blur, Photoshop displays the dialog box shown in Figure 17-8. The Radius value determines the number of pixels that get mixed together at a time. You can go as high as 250.0, but any value over 10.0 enters the realm of the legally blind. In Figure 17-7, I blurred the background with a Radius value of 4.0 and the lower-right patch of ground with a Radius of 2.0.

Figure 17-8:
Specify the exact amount of blur you want in the *Ueberblur* dialog box, a.k.a. the Gaussian Blur dialog box.

Creating motion and puzzle pieces

The Filter⇨Blur submenu contains three additional filters — Motion Blur, Radial Blur, and Smart Blur — all of which are exclusively special-effects filters. The Motion Blur filter makes an image appear to move in a straight line; the Radial Blur filter can be used to move the selection in a circle or to zoom it outward toward the viewer. The Smart Blur option finds the edges in your image and then blurs only between the edges — it's as though Photoshop is carving your image up into puzzle pieces and then blurring each piece. If you apply the effect in heavy doses, the result is an image that resembles a watercolor painting and isn't too far removed from the effect created by the Filter⇨Artistic⇨Watercolor filter.

Of the three filters, Motion Blur is the filter you're most likely to use. First, the dialog box offers the standard previewing options, making this filter accessible and predictable. Second, it's much easier to use. Finally, when compared with Radial Blur, it takes a lot less time to use; Radial Blur is one of the slowest Photoshop filters.

When you choose Filter⇨Blur⇨Motion Blur, Photoshop displays the Motion Blur dialog box. The filter smears pixels at a specified angle and over a specified distance. Enter the angle and distance into the appropriately named option boxes. You can also drag the spoke inside the circle on the right side of the dialog box to change the Angle value.

By way of example, Figure 17-9 shows a couple of discrete applications of the Motion Blur filter. To blur the boy, I selected him, feathered the selection, and applied the Motion Blur filter with an Angle value of 90° — straight up and down — and a Distance of 30 pixels. To blur his sister's arm — the one nearest her beaming brother — I used an Angle of 45° and a Distance of 6 pixels. As you can see, Distance values over 20 smear the image into oblivion; smaller Distance values create subtle movement effects.

Filter Potpourri

The Filter⇨Sharpen and Filter⇨Blur submenus contain the filters you use most often. In fact, if you like, you can blow off the rest of the chapter without being much the poorer for it. But if you have five minutes or so to spare, I'd like to show you a few other interesting commands scattered throughout the Filter menu.

Figure 17-9:
Two
unlikely
applications
of the
Motion Blur
filter.

Giving your images that gritty, streetwise look

For starters, you have the Add Noise command. Not to be confused with the as-yet uncompleted Adenoids filter, Add Noise randomizes the colors of selected pixels. The result is a layer of grit that gives smooth images a textured appearance.

Choose Filter⇨Noise⇨Add Noise to display the Add Noise dialog box. Here's how to use the options found therein:

✔ Drag the Amount slider triangle or enter a value between 1 and 999 to control how noisy the image gets. Low values — such as the default value 32 or lower — permit a small amount of noise; high values permit more. Anything over 100 pretty much wipes out the original image.

✔ Select a Distribution radio button to control the color of noise. The Uniform option colors pixels with random variations on the shades it finds in the original image; the Gaussian option — which should be labeled High Contrast — colors pixels with more exaggerated light and dark shades. Therefore, Gaussian produces a noisier effect, about twice as noisy as Uniform. For example, an Amount value of 32 combined with Gaussian produces a similar visual effect to an Amount value of 64 combined with Uniform.

✔ The Monochromatic check box adds grayscale noise to full-color images. When the option is turned off, Photoshop adds all colors of noise. (The option has no effect on grayscale images except to shift the pixels around a little.)

To rough up the dark areas in the mother and son detail shown on the left side of Figure 17-10, I used Select⇨Color Range to select the dark areas in the image and then applied the Add Noise filter. By changing the Amount value to 100 and selecting Gaussian, I arrived at the effect shown in the middle example in the figure. To achieve the far-right image, I applied Filter⇨Blur⇨Motion Blur with an Angle value of 45° and a Distance of 6 pixels. Photoshop creates an etched metal effect that suits these two characters to a T.

| Original | Add Noise | Motion Blur |

Figure 17-10:
I selected the dark portions of the image on the left and applied the Add Noise filter (middle) followed by Motion Blur (right).

Color Plate 17-1 shows the same Add Noise and Motion Blur effect applied to the dark portions of a full-color image. But there's a slight twist. In the top image, I applied the Add Noise filter with the Monochromatic check box turned off; in the bottom image, the check box is turned on. As a result, the top image contains color streaks, and the bottom image contains black-and-white streaks.

Stamping your image in metal

Another intriguing and sometimes useful filter is Emboss. This filter makes your image appear as though it were stamped in metal. The edges in the image appear in relief, and the other areas turn gray.

When you choose Filter⇨Stylize⇨Emboss, Photoshop displays the dialog box shown in Figure 17-11. You enter the angle of the light shining on the metal into the Angle option box. The Height value determines the height of the edges, and the Amount value determines the amount of contrast between blacks and whites.

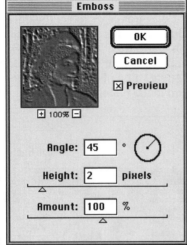

Figure 17-11:
Use the
Emboss filter
to stamp
images into
sheets of
metal
(figuratively,
of course).

I'm breezing over these options because they aren't the most useful gang in the world. From personal experience, I can tell you the following:

- How you set the Angle value doesn't matter. Feel free to drag the spoke on the circle until you get what you want, but don't expect big differences between one angle and another.

- Set the Height value to 1 or 2. Any value over 2 can impair detail.

- Okay, the Amount value is useful. Enter 50% for a very subtle effect, 100% for a medium Emboss effect, and 200% for added drama. You can go as high as 500%, but higher values make the contrast between blacks and whites too abrupt (in my humble opinion).

Like Add Noise, Emboss isn't the kind of filter you go around applying to an entire image. I mean, after you've done it once or twice, it gets a little old. Rather, you want to apply it to selected areas.

In the first example of Figure 17-12, I selected the dark areas in the mother and son image and applied the Emboss filter with an Angle of 45°, a Height of 2, and an Amount of 200%. In the middle example, I blurred the selection using the Gaussian Blur filter set to a Radius of 2 pixels. Then I applied Unsharp Mask with an Amount of 500% and a Radius of 2 pixels, arriving at the thrilling mottled metal effect on the far right.

Emboss　　　　　　Gaussian Blur　　　　　Unsharp Mask

Figure 17-12:
After selecting the dark portions of the image, I embossed it (left), blurred it (middle), and sharpened it (right), creating a soft relief.

TIP

Your reaction may be one of, "Whoa, hold up a minute here. First you blur, and then you sharpen? What kind of crazy logic is that?" Well, pretty sound logic, actually. After I applied Gaussian Blur, the image turned overly gray, as you can see in the second example in the figure. Luckily, one of the properties of Unsharp Mask is that it increases the amount of contrast between dark and light pixels. So, to bring the blacks and whites back from the dead, I set the Radius value inside the Unsharp Mask dialog box to the exact value I used in the Gaussian Blur dialog box — that is, 2.0. Using this value ensured that Unsharp Mask was able to correctly locate the blurred edges and boost their contrast. It's a great technique.

Merging colors in flaky images

The last two filters I cover in this chapter — Facet and Median — average the colors of neighboring pixels to create areas of flat color. Both throw away detail, but they're great for smoothing out the imperfections in old, cruddy images such as the one that keeps popping up in this chapter.

Filter⇨Pixelate⇨Facet is a single-shot command that roams the image looking for areas of similarly colored pixels and then assigns the entire area a single color. In Figure 17-13, I started with the elder daughter from way back in Figure 17-2, before she was sharpened. In the middle example, I applied Filter⇨Pixelate⇨Facet. See how the image is now divided into a bunch of globby areas of color? To make the image clearer, I applied the Unsharp Mask filter to the far-right example, using an Amount value of 250% and a Radius value of 0.5.

Filter⇨Noise⇨Median averages the colors of so many neighboring pixels. To tell Photoshop the "so many" part, choose the Median command and enter a value anywhere between 1 to 16 into the Radius option box.

Original   Facet   Unsharp Mask

Figure 17-14 shows the result of applying various Radius values to the elder daughter. The top row shows the effects of the Median command; the bottom row shows what happened when I applied Unsharp Mask to each image. Notice how higher values melt away more of the image's detail. A Radius value of 3 makes the image gooey indeed; any higher value is pure silliness.

You can use Facet and Median to blur background images, just as I did earlier with Gaussian Blur. Or you can combine them with the Add Noise and Emboss filters to create special effects.

Keep in mind that the real beauty of these more specialized filters is in combining them and applying them to small, selected portions of your image.

Radius: 1   Radius: 2   Radius: 3

Chapter 18

Drawing Color from a Dreary Wasteland

· ·

· ·

*H*ere's a common scenario for you: You get some pictures or slides back from the photo developer — I'm talking regular photos here, not the digital kind — and one of them catches your eye. The color is great, the composition is fantastic, everyone's smiling; it ranks among the best pictures you've ever shot. It's not 100 percent perfect, but you figure you can fix the few glitches with Photoshop.

A few days later — after you've had the photo scanned to Photo CD — you open the image inside Photoshop, and your heart sinks to the pit of your stomach. The image is dark, colorless, and generally a big, fat disappointment. That little picture on the cover of the CD jacket looks better than this murky mess on-screen.

In a perfect world, this would never happen. The service bureau that scanned the image would have corrected the colors so that they would look the way they did in your photo. But in practice, even the best service bureaus let a few duds fall through the cracks, and some don't bother with color-correction at all. It's a pickle.

Take Color Plate 18-1, for example. The original slide looked something like the example on the right, but when I opened the image in Photoshop, the image appeared as shown on the left. Sure, it's an old slide — that's me in the striped shirt, so you know that a couple of years have passed — and the composition leaves something to be desired. (I have a fake tree growing out of my shoulder and my sister seems to be balancing a flower-adorned globe on her head.) But, come on, it didn't look this bad. I mean, are we auditioning for the remake of *20,000 Leagues Under the Sea* here or what?

If you run into a similar problem, never fear — you have cause to be optimistic. The colors may not look like much now, but chances are better than even that you have enough colors to get by. Though it may be hard to believe, your image very likely contains a few million colors; it's just that they're all squished toward the dark end of the spectrum. Your job is to bring these colors back to life.

Want proof? The image on the right side of Color Plate 18-1 isn't a different scan, it's just a color-corrected version of its neighbor on the left. In fact, I revived the color by using only two commands — Levels and Variations. I didn't touch a painting or editing tool; I didn't draw a selection outline; I didn't do anything to add colors to the image. I merely took the existing colors and stretched them across the spectrum.

Photoshop offers several color-correction commands, but you need only three of these — at the most — to get the job done. In this chapter, I show you how these miracle commands work and encourage you to ignore the rest. I also explain how to use adjustment layers, which let you do some of your color correcting on an independent layer, thereby providing you with extra flexibility and safety.

The Color-Correction Connection

The Photoshop color-correction commands are located in one central spot, under the Image⇨Adjust submenu. Of these commands, only three should be of the least concern to you at this stage in your mastery of Photoshop: Levels, Auto Levels, and Variations.

Your friends — Auto Levels, Levels, and Variations

Choose Image⇨Adjust⇨Auto Levels or press ⌘-Shift-L to automatically correct the contrast of an image. For example, Figure 18-1 shows a typically low-contrast image composed entirely of cheerless grays. The inset squares show the lightest and darkest colors in the image as well as some sample shades in between. If I apply the Auto Levels command, Photoshop automatically makes the lightest gray white and the darkest gray black and stretches out the colors in between. Figure 18-2 shows the result.

Figure 18-1: What a dismal scene: Come to this gas station and get your tank filled with depression. The grim reaper will change your oil.

Unfortunately, Auto Levels doesn't always do the trick. Figure 18-2, for example, contains strong blacks and whites, but the grays appear overly dark (as witnessed by the shades in the inset squares). The solution is Image⇨Adjust⇨Levels, which you can access from the keyboard by pressing ⌘-L. The Levels command takes some getting used to, but it lets you adjust the darkest and lightest colors as well as the medium gray. (I explain the command in detail later in this chapter, in the section "Leveling the Contrast Field.") Figure 18-3 shows the Gulf station running in tip-top condition, thanks to the Levels command. See how much clearer the details in the cars now appear?

Unlike Auto Levels and Levels, which serve grayscale and color images equally well, Image⇨Adjust⇨Variations is specifically designed to correct full-color images. (You can use the command on grayscale images, but it merely duplicates some of the options inside the Levels dialog box.) You can increase or decrease the intensity of colors or tint the image to remove a color cast. For example, if an image is too yellow, you can add blue to it, as in the first example in Color Plate 18-2. If the image is too blue, add yellow, as in the second example. In both cases, Variations preserves non-blue and non-yellow colors. Throughout, for example, the Christmas tree remains true to its natural color of pink.

Figure 18-2:
The Auto Levels command brings out some strong blacks and whites, but the grays remain dark and dreary.

Figure 18-3:
A nice, even transition of grays makes a day at the gas station seem like a walk through the park.

Upcoming sections explain how to use Levels, Auto Levels, and Variations in detail. But just for the record, here's the general approach to take when color correcting an image in Photoshop:

1. **Apply the Auto Levels command.**

   Regardless of whether you're editing a grayscale or color image, this is a good first step.

If you like what you see, you can skip all the other steps. If you think some more tweaking is in order, proceed to Step 2.

2. **Apply the Levels command.**

   Use this command to change the contrast of the image and to lighten or darken the medium colors.

   If you're editing a grayscale image, this command is the end of the line. If your full-color image looks a little drab, however, keep correcting.

3. **Choose the Variations command and select the Saturation radio button.**

   The options inside the Variations dialog box let you boost the intensity of colors in an image, as discussed in the section "Variations on a Color Scheme," later in this chapter.

   If the colors now look the way you want, press Return and get on with your life. Continue only if you want to tint the image with a certain color or remove a color cast.

4. **Still inside the Variations dialog box, select the Midtones radio button and adjust the colors in the image.**

   Note: The section, "It sure feels good to remove that color cast," at the end of this chapter tells all.

The other color correctors (boo, hiss)

The other color-correction commands in the Image⇨Adjust submenu range from useful but very complex to simple but completely inept. Just in case you're chock full of curiosity, here's the rundown:

- ✔ The Curves command is even more capable than the Levels command, allowing you to change every one of the possible 16 million colors to a different color. Unfortunately, this feature is also very difficult to use.

- ✔ The Brightness/Contrast command is utterly and completely worthless. I'm serious. If you've never used it, don't start. If you have used it, stop — you're hurting your images.

- ✔ Color Balance is another loser. You keep thinking that it's going to produce some kind of useful results, but it never does. Worthless and irritating — what a combination.

- ✔ Hue/Saturation is good, and even improved in Photoshop 5. It lets you change the color, intensity, and lightness of an image using three slider bars. However, the Variations dialog box provides these same controls and is easier to use.

- ✔ Desaturate is just the thing for draining the color from a selected area and leaving it black and white. But if you want to convert an entire image to grayscale, see Chapter 5.

✔ The Replace Color command is a combination of Select⇨Color Range and the Hue/Saturation command. What's the point?

 ✔ The Selective Colors command lets you modify a range of colors using CMYK slider bars. Not a terrible command, but not a particularly useful one either.

 ✔ The new Channel Mixer command lets you redefine your channels by mixing them together. Very useful for repairing bad channels or special effects, but an advanced feature.

 ✔ The other commands on the Adjust menu — Invert, Equalize, Threshold, and Posterize — are typically used for creating special effects. Invert, for example, makes all white pixels black and all black pixels white, creating a photo-negative effect. Fun to play with, but not the sort of tool you can use to brighten up a dingy gas station.

Leveling the Contrast Field

Not one image in this book — except the gloomy-looking Figure 18-1 — has escaped a thorough going-over with the Levels command. I consider this command to be one of the most essential functions inside Photoshop. In fact, if an image displays any of the following symptoms, you can correct it with Levels:

 ✔ The image is murky, without strong lights and darks, like the one in Figure 18-1.

 ✔ The image is too light.

 ✔ The image is too dark.

 ✔ The image is gaining weight, losing hair, and developing bags under its eyes.

Whoops, that last item sneaked in by mistake. If an image gains weight, loses hair, and develops baggy eyes, you have to send it on a three-week cruise in the Caribbean.

Leveling on a layer

Photoshop offers a feature to use in conjunction with the Levels command (and, in a roundabout way, the Auto Levels command): adjustment layers. Adjustment layers are just like the layers discussed in Chapter 15, except that you use them expressly to apply color-correction commands.

At any rate, adjustment layers offer several advantages:

✔ The color-correction affects all the underlying layers in the image. If you don't use an adjustment layer, the color-correction affects only the active layer.

✔ You can create as many different adjustment layers as you want. So, if you want a few layers to use one set of color-correction settings and the rest of the image to use another set, you just create two different adjustment layers.

✔ Because the color-correction "exists" on its own layer, you can experiment freely without fear of damaging the image. If, at some point, you decide that you don't like the effects of the color-correction, you can edit the adjustment layer or just delete it entirely and start fresh.

✔ You can blend the adjustment layer with the other layers using the Opacity and blend mode settings in the Layers palette, just as you can with any layer. These features give you even more control over how your image appears.

To create an adjustment layer, do the following:

1. **In the Layers palette, click on the top layer that you want to color correct.**

   When you create an adjustment layer, Photoshop places it directly on top of the active layer in the Layers palette. This adjustment affects the layer or layers underneath, depending on what setting you choose in the New Adjustment Layer dialog box in Step 2.

   If you select a portion of your image before creating the adjustment layer, the color-correction affects the selected area across all underlying layers.

2. **Choose Layer⇨New⇨Adjustment Layer from the Layers palette pop-up menu or ⌘-click on the new layer icon at the bottom of the Layers palette.**

   The dialog box shown in Figure 18-4 appears. Here's a field guide to your options: If you want to give your adjustment layer a specific name, enter the name into the top option box. The Type pop-up menu lists all the different color-correction commands you can select — the only one you need to worry about is Levels, which is selected by default.

   Although the Auto Levels command isn't available in the Type pop-up menu, you can apply the Auto Levels command on an adjustment layer by choosing the Levels option from the pop-up menu. This option leads you to the Levels dialog box, which has an Auto button that works just like the Auto Levels command.

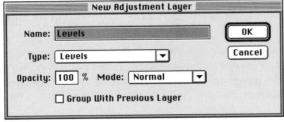

Figure 18-4:
The New Adjustment Layer dialog box enables you to do your color correcting on an independent layer.

Skip the Opacity and Mode pop-up menus; if you want, you can change these settings later in the Layers palette. Skip the Group With Previous Layer check box, too.

3. **Press Return.**

Photoshop adds the adjustment layer to the Layers palette and displays the Levels dialog box, which is explained in the next section.

Remember that an adjustment layer works just like any other layer in the Layers palette. You can vary the effects of the adjustment by playing with the Opacity slider and blend modes, you can move the layer up or down in the Layers palette to affect different layers, and you can merge the layer with an underlying layer to permanently fuse the color-correction to the image. (You can't, however, merge an adjustment layer with another adjustment layer.)

If you ever want to change the color-correction settings for an adjustment layer, just double-click on the adjustment layer name in the Layers palette. Photoshop redisplays the Levels dialog box, where you can modify the settings. To delete the adjustment layer, drag it to the trash icon in the Layers palette.

You can flip back and forth between a view of your corrected image and your uncorrected image by clicking on the eyeball icon next to the adjustment layer name in the Layers palette. When the eyeball is present, the layer is visible, showing you the color-corrected image. When the eyeball is hidden, so is the layer, giving you a "before" view of your image.

Making friends with the Levels dialog box

To apply the Levels command, you can create a new adjustment layer, as described in the preceding section, or choose Image⇨Adjust⇨Levels, or press ⌘-L. If you choose the command from the Image menu or press the keyboard shortcut, the color-correction is applied directly to the image and affects only the active layer.

Either way, the dialog box shown in Figure 18-5 appears. Luckily, you don't need to address all the options that inhabit this dialog box. So, before you break into a cold sweat, shriek at the top of your lungs (or do whatever it is you do when you see terrifying sights like Figure 18-5), let me try to distinguish the important options in this dialog box from the stuff you won't use in a month of Sundays:

Histogram

Figure 18-5:
The complicated-looking Levels dialog box contains a lot of options that you don't need to worry about.

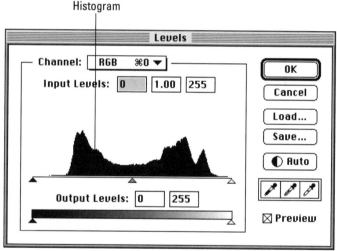

✔ The options in the Channel pop-up menu let you adjust one color channel in a full-color image independently of the other channels. These options are helpful if you know what you're doing, but they're not terribly important.

✔ The three Input Levels option boxes control the settings of the darkest, medium, and lightest pixels in your image, in that order. These options are important, which is why I cover them thoroughly in the next section.

✔ That black birthmark in the middle of the dialog box is called a *histogram*. It shows you how the colors in your image are currently distributed. It also rates the Seal of Importance.

✔ The slider bar beneath the histogram provides three triangles, one each for the darkest, medium, and lightest pixels in your image. These triangles are the most important options of all.

✔ The Output Levels option boxes and the accompanying slider bar let you make the darkest colors lighter and the lightest colors darker, which is usually the exact opposite of what you want to do. Mark these options Not Particularly Important.

✔ The OK and Cancel buttons are as important as always. One applies your changes, the other doesn't. No news here.

✔ Press the Option key to change the Cancel button to a Reset button. Click on the button while pressing Option to reset the settings to the way they were when you entered the dialog box. Very helpful.

✔ Click on the Save button to save the settings in this dialog box to disk. Click on the Load button to later load and reapply them. Unless you're color correcting about 20 images in a row, all of which require exactly the same treatment, these buttons are about as important to your health and well-being as lava lamps. Ignore them.

✔ Click on the Auto button to automatically change the darkest pixels to black and the lightest ones to white, exactly as though you had chosen Image➪Adjust➪Auto Levels. The only time you need to use this button is when you want to apply the Auto Levels command on an adjustment layer, as discussed earlier. Otherwise, just choose the command from the Image➪Adjust menu or press ⌘-Shift-L and save yourself some work.

✔ When you press the Option key, the Auto button changes to an Options button. I tell you about this feature only because I'm afraid that you may notice it for yourself when you press the Option key to access the Reset button. But whether you notice it or not, the Options button is totally unimportant. And if you do notice it, don't muck with the settings that become available to you when you click on the button.

✔ The three eyedropper icons let you click on colors in your image to make them black, medium gray, or white. If I were you, I'd steer clear of these icons except to stamp them Not Important, Ditto, and Doubly So.

✔ The Preview check box lets you view the effect of your edits inside the image window. It's very important that you turn this option on.

Figure 18-6 shows the Levels dialog box as it appears after you strip it down to its most important components. As you can see, the Input Levels options — which include the three option boxes, the histogram, and the slider bar — represent the core of the Levels command. The other options are just icing on the cake.

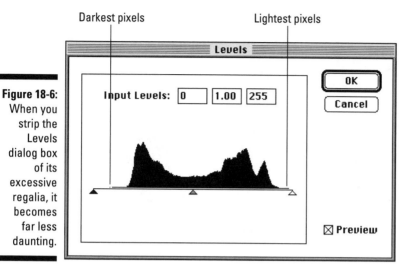

Darkest pixels   Lightest pixels

Figure 18-6:
When you
strip the
Levels
dialog box
of its
excessive
regalia, it
becomes
far less
daunting.

Levels

Input Levels: [0] [1.00] [255]

OK

Cancel

☒ Preview

Brightness and contrast as they should be

The histogram in Figure 18-6 is a graph of the color in the uncorrected image in Figure 18-7. (I didn't even choose the Auto Levels command.) The graph is organized from darkest colors on the left to lightest colors on the right. The peaks and valleys in the histogram show the color distribution. If the darkest colors were black, the histogram would start on the far-left edge of the slider bar. If the lightest colors were white, it would continue to the far-right edge. But as it is, the left and right edges taper off into flatlands. This means that the darkest and lightest pixels in the image are not as dark or light as they could be.

If some of that information went a little over your head, not to worry. Some folks understand graphs, while other folks think that they're in a board meeting and start to nod off the second they see anything resembling a graph. Either way, remember that the histogram is provided for your reference only. All that matters is how you adjust the slider triangles beneath the histogram:

✔ To make the darkest pixels black, drag the left slider triangle to the right so that it rests directly under the beginning of the first hill in the histogram. Figure 18-8 shows the dragged triangle and its effect on the image.

✔ To make the lightest pixels white, drag the right-hand triangle to the left so that it lines up directly under the end of the last hill in the histogram, as in Figure 18-9.

Figure 18-7:
Though they lived in a time when Photoshop was not available, these uncorrected characters still managed to find something to smile about.

Figure 18-8:
Dragging the first triangle affects the darkest pixels in the image.

Input Levels: 45 | 1.00 | 255

REMEMBER

✔ If you already chose the Auto Levels command or the Auto button in the Levels dialog box, you most likely won't have to change either the left or right slider because Photoshop has already done this automatically. (You may want to adjust the sliders slightly, but that's up to you.) Instead, just concentrate on positioning the middle slider, described next.

Figure 18-9:
The image lightens up when I drag the white triangle to the left.

✔ The most important triangle is the middle one. Called the *gamma point* — just in case you get stuck in an elevator with the guys from R&D and find yourself scraping for something to talk about — this triangle lets you change the brightness of the medium colors in your image. Drag to the right to make the medium colors darker. But more likely, you want to drag to the left to make the medium colors lighter, as demonstrated in Figure 18-10.

Figure 18-10:
Dragging the middle triangle brings out the detail in an image.

The values in the three option boxes above the histogram update as you drag the slider triangles. The left and right values are measured in color levels. Just like the values in the Color palette — where you define colors (see Chapter 5) — 0 is black and 255 is white. So if the left value is 45, as it is in Figures 18-8 through 18-10, any pixel that is colored with a level of 45 or darker becomes black. The gamma value — the middle one — is measured as a ratio . . . er, forget it, it doesn't make any sense, and it matters even less. The point is, a value of more than 1 lightens the medium colors; a value less than 1 darkens them.

The old stock photo featured in Figures 18-7 through 18-10 is a wonderful example of a work of art that takes on new meaning the more you look at it. Three of the subjects are proudly displaying unlighted tobacco products, the fourth guy is using a paper cup for a megaphone, and all four have feathers in their caps (figure that one out). Meanwhile, you can see their shadows on the wall in back of them. Call me picky, but it sort of ruins the illusion that they might be outdoors enjoying a chilly sporting event.

If you want to see the effect of the Levels command on a full-color image, you need look no further than Color Plate 18-3. Nestled in this quiet corner of the book is a homemade Italian gate. Starting with the uncorrected image in the upper-left corner, I adjusted each of the slider triangles, eventually arriving at the much superior color balance shown in the lower-right image. It just goes to show you, Levels is bound to be good for any image.

If you notice a loss of color in your image after you apply the Levels command, don't worry. You can get that color back by using the Variations command, discussed in the next section.

Variations on a Color Scheme

One negative effect of the Levels command is that it can weaken some of the colors, particularly if you lighten the medium colors by dragging the gamma point in the Levels dialog box to the left. To bring the colors back to their original intensity, call on Image➪Adjust➪Variations.

The Variations command can also cure color casts, in which one color is particularly prominent in the image. A photograph shot outdoors, for example, may be overly blue; one shot in an X-rated motel room may be a shade heavy in the reds. Whatever color predominates your image, the Variations command can tone it down with elegance and ease.

Turning plain old color into Technicolor

To bolster the intensity of colors in your image — for what it's worth, color intensity is called *saturation* in image-editing vernacular — follow these pleasant steps:

1. **Choose Image⇨Adjust⇨Variations.**

   The enormous Variations dialog box erupts onto your screen, filled with about a million small previews of your image.

2. **Select the Saturation radio button in the upper-right corner of the dialog box.**

   Most of the small preview images disappear. Only five remain, as shown in Figure 18-11. The three previews in the middle of the dialog box represent different color intensities. The top two previews show the image as it appeared before you chose the Variations command and how it looks now, subject to the changes in the Variations dialog box.

Saturation radio button

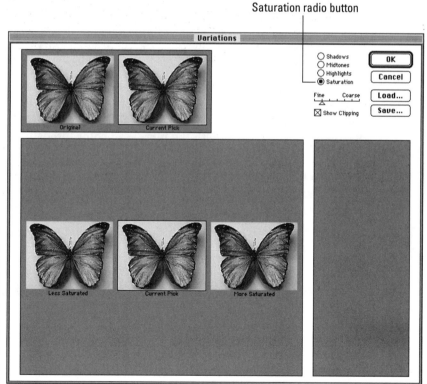

Figure 18-11: Click on the More Saturated preview to boost the intensity of the colors in an image.

3. Drag the slider triangle in the upper-right corner to the left, toward Fine.

This slider controls the extent of the changes made inside the Variations dialog box. If you drag the triangle toward Coarse, the changes become more drastic; drag it toward Fine, and they become more gradual. The setting is reflected inside the left and right previews in the middle of the dialog box. The changes become more subtle.

Because color intensity is a very sensitive function inside Photoshop, it's best to set the slider to one of the first two notches so that you can make gentle, incremental changes.

4. To increase color intensity, click on the preview labeled More Saturated.

Clicking once increases the intensity by a gradual amount, owing to the slider bar setting. To add more intensity, click again. Each time you click, the Current Pick previews update — one in the middle and one at the top — to reflect your latest change.

If inconsistently colored pixels begin to emerge, Photoshop is telling you that these colors are outside the CMYK color range and will not print. Don't worry about it until the weird pixels take over a third or more of your image. (If you don't care whether the colors will print correctly or not, turn off the Show Clipping check box to view the pixels normally.)

If at any time you want to reset the Current Pick preview to the original image, just click on the preview labeled Original in the upper-left corner of the dialog box.

5. When you're satisfied with the increased color intensity, press Return.

Photoshop applies your settings to the original image, just as they were shown in the Current Pick preview. No surprises with this dialog box.

Changes you make via the Variations dialog box affect only the active layer. Unfortunately, you can't apply the Variations command using an adjustment layer as you can the Levels and Auto Levels commands.

Color Plate 18-4 shows the difference between a butterfly whose splendor I completely destroyed using the Levels command and that same butterfly restored to its original luster and brilliance via the Variations command. To achieve this radical transformation, I set the slider bar inside the Variations dialog box to the second notch over from the left and clicked on the More Saturated preview a total of six times.

It sure feels good to remove that color cast

Images are like people in that they hate to wear casts. When your image is encumbered by a color cast, it becomes uncomfortable and downright crotchety. Take the first image in Color Plate 18-5, for example. To the inexperienced eye, this image may appear happy and at peace with itself. But in truth, its life is a living heck, made miserable by a decidedly yellow color cast.

To remove the color cast once and for all, revisit the Variations command:

1. **Choose Image⇨Adjust⇨Variations.**

   The Variations dialog box takes over your screen.

2. **Select the Midtones radio button in the upper-right corner of the dialog box.**

   This option lets you edit the medium colors in your image. (You can also edit the dark or light colors by selecting Shadows or Highlights, but these options produce extremely subtle effects and have little impact on your image.)

   After you select Midtones, the central portion of the dialog box fills with seven previews, as shown in Figure 18-12. These previews let you shift the colors in the image toward a primary color — green, yellow, red, magenta, blue, or cyan. As usual, the Current Pick preview in the center of the cluster updates to show the most recent corrections applied to the image.

   The three previews along the right edge of the Variations dialog box let you lighten and darken the image. But because they're less capable than the gamma point control in the Levels dialog box, you can feel free to ignore them.

3. **Click on one of the More previews to shift the colors in the image toward that particular color.**

   First, identify the color cast. Then click on the preview opposite to that color. In the case of the horse image from Color Plate 18-5, the cast is clearly yellow and, to a lesser extent, green. To eliminate the yellow cast, I clicked on More Blue. To eliminate the green cast, I clicked on More Magenta.

   Check out Color Plate 5-3, which shows that yellow ink filters out blue light and magenta ink filters out green light. This filtering means that yellow and blue are direct opposites, as are magenta and green. Such opposite colors are termed *complementary.* I'm not sure why. I guess it's like a marriage of opposites in which each spouse complements the other. If they don't kill each other first, of course.

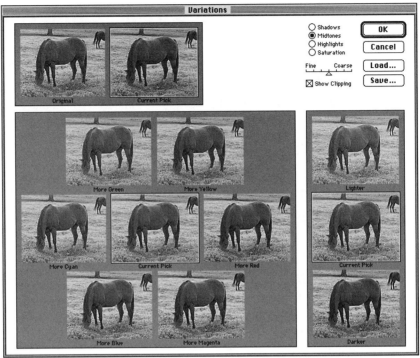

Figure 18-12:
Click on the
More Blue
preview to
add blue
and remove
yellow in an
image. Click
on More
Magenta
to add
magenta
and remove
green.

4. **If you go too far toward one color, just click on the opposite color to step backward.**

   In Color Plate 18-5, for example, I clicked on the More Blue preview twice, clicked on More Magenta twice, and then clicked on More Blue again. But after some concerted soul searching, I decided that I had gone too far. The resulting image — shown in the bottom-right corner of the color plate — was too blue and too magenta. So I clicked on the More Yellow button to remove the last application of blue and clicked on More Green to remove the last application of magenta. The lower-left example in the color plate shows the result.

As when you adjust color saturation, you can vary the impact of the previews on the image by dragging the slider triangle toward Fine or Coarse. The images in Color Plate 18-5 were all created with the triangle set right in the center, as it is by default.

If your image has more than one layer, your color-cast manipulations affect only the active layer.

Part VI
The Part of Tens

The 5th Wave   By Rich Tennant

ATTEMPTING TO SAVE MONEY ON FAMILY PHOTOS, THE DILBRANTS SCAN THEIR NEWBORN INTO A PHOTO IMAGING PROGRAM WITH PLANS OF JUST DITHERING THE CHILD INTO ADOLESCENCE.

Nope! She must have moved again! Run the scanner down her once more.

In this part . . .

Some say that there's magic in the number three. Bears, pigs, Musketeers, and Stooges regularly cavort about in groups of three. But I say that the real magic is in tens. The Ten Commandments, the ten amendments that make up The Bill of Rights, and the ten ingredients in a Big Mac — if you count both all-beef patties and the three sesame seed buns — are items that we can count on the ten fingers of our hands (or the ten toes of our feet when we're at the beach). Top ten lists abound in newspapers, magazines, books, and late-night TV shows. And I say, why buck a trend? If everyone else is doing it, I for one am happy to mindlessly follow along.

But then I thought, "What ho, if there's magic in threes and in tens, why not do both?" So, that's what I did. This part contains three chapters, each of which contains ten factoids. Ten great shortcuts that you'll want to assign to memory, ten great ways to wreak havoc on a loved one's face, and ten things you can do with your image after you finish messing it up in Photoshop.

As if that's not enough, the last chapter of this book — Chapter 21 — is divisible not only by 3, but also by the lucky number 7. We are talking major number magic at work here, the kind of stuff that numerologists, fortune tellers, and lottery fanatics would give their eyeteeth for. And this book costs you only $19.99, a number whose only claim to fame is that it's slightly cheaper than $20.

Chapter 19

Ten Tricky Techniques
to Assign to Memory

. . . .

. . . .

Some guy named Odell Shepard said, "Memory is what makes you wonder what you've forgotten." I don't know anything about this Odell fellow — he was just lucky enough to get picked up by one of those books of quotations that are supposed to make you sound like a halfway intelligent human being without really trying. Not having met Odell — Odie, we call him — I can only hazard the guess that he was talking about that feeling you get — usually, when you're in bed, trying to sleep, or when you're on the way home from work and it's too late to turn back — that you've forgotten something that's pretty much going to send your life spinning into a state of absolute chaos. In fact, I believe that feeling is known as the Odie Syndrome.

Well, I can't help you with every aspect of your life, but I can help you with Photoshop. Say, for example, that you wake up at 2 a.m. one morning with the dread suspicion that you've forgotten an important Photoshop shortcut. Normally, of course, your life would be forfeit. You'd just have to give up on your technological pursuits and take up beet farming. But thanks to this chapter, people like you can again live happy and productive lives because all of the most important Photoshop shortcuts are contained in these pages. A few minutes of reading, and order is restored. (By the way, did you notice that there are 11 tricks. Consider it a "buy one get one free deal.")

Displaying and Hiding the Toolbox and Palettes

Tab

I'm ashamed to admit this, but there was a time when I wanted to view an image on-screen all by itself, without the toolbox. I had no idea how to do it. I even called the Photoshop product manager and asked him how to do it. He told me it was impossible.

Naturally, he was wrong. It was possible then, and it's possible now. Just press the Tab key. The toolbox and all the palettes disappear, leaving just you and the image. To bring the toolbox and palettes back, press Tab again. To make the toolbox and palettes flash crazily on-screen and off, press Tab over and over again until your finger gets numb. I'm not sure why you'd want to do this, but I like to spell out all the options.

If you want to hide the palettes but keep the toolbox visible, by the way, press Shift-Tab. Press Shift-Tab again to bring the palettes back.

 If you have a dialog box open or an option in a palette is active (highlighted), Tab and Shift-Tab take you to the next option box or move you back one option box, respectively. But after you close the dialog box or press Return to apply the palette option, Tab and Shift-Tab control your palettes and toolbox once again.

F5, F6, F7, F8

Press F5 to hide or display the Brushes palette, F6 to hide or display the Color palette, and F7 to hide or display the Layers palette. To display the Navigator palette, press F8, which brings up the Info palette. Then click on the Navigator palette tab. Press F8 twice to hide the palette.

Changing the Way a Tool Works

Return

After selecting a tool in the toolbox, press Return to bring up the Options palette for that tool. If the palette contains an option box, the value inside the option box becomes highlighted, allowing you to change it.

Up arrow, down arrow

Enter a new value in the option box or use the up or down arrow key to raise or lower the value by 1. Press Shift-↑ or Shift-↓ to raise or lower the value by 10, respectively. Then press Return again to accept the new value.

Scrolling and Zooming

Spacebar

Press the spacebar to temporarily access the hand tool. As long as the spacebar is down, the hand tool is available. Spacebar-drag to scroll the image.

⌘-spacebar, Option-spacebar

To get to the zoom in cursor, press both ⌘ and spacebar. Pressing Option-spacebar gets you the zoom out cursor. This means that you can magnify the image at any time by ⌘-spacebar-clicking. To zoom out, Option-spacebar-click. You can also ⌘-spacebar-drag to marquee an area and magnify it so that it takes up the entire image window.

⌘-plus, ⌘-minus

Another way to magnify or reduce the image is to press ⌘-+ (plus sign) to zoom in or ⌘-– (minus sign) to zoom out.

Double-click on the hand icon

To zoom the image so that you can see the whole thing on your monitor, double-click on the hand tool icon in the toolbox. Or press ⌘-0 (zero).

Double-click on the zoom icon

To restore the image to the 100% (Actual Pixels) zoom factor, double-click on the zoom tool icon or press ⌘-Option-0 (zero).

Shift-Return

When you change the zoom factor by using the magnification box in the lower-left corner of the image window, press Shift-Return instead of Return after you enter a new zoom value. That way, the option box remains active after Photoshop zooms your image. If you need to further magnify or reduce your image, just enter a new zoom value from the keyboard. When you have the image at the magnification you want, press Return to finalize things.

This trick also works when you're using the magnification box in the Navigator palette.

Changing the Brush Size

Left bracket ([)

Press [(left bracket) to reduce the brush size to the next smallest one in the Brushes palette. If you're using the smallest fuzzy brush, pressing [selects the largest smooth one.

Right bracket (])

Press] (right bracket) to select the next brush size up. If you're using the largest smooth brush, pressing] selects the smallest fuzzy one.

Shift-[, Shift-]

Shift-[(left bracket) selects the first brush size in the Brushes palette, which is the single-pixel brush. Shift-] (right bracket) selects the last brush size. By default, this is the 100-pixel fuzzy brush, but if you've created some custom brushes of your own, Photoshop selects the last one in the Brushes palette.

Changing Opacity

1, . . . , 9, 0

To change the Opacity setting for a selected painting or editing tool, just press a number key — 1 equals 10% Opacity, 9 equals 90%, and 0 equals 100%. To enter a more specific value — say, 82 — just type the number quickly.

If a selection tool or the move tool is active, pressing a number key changes the opacity of the active layer.

Creating Straight Lines

Shift-click

To create a straight line with any of the painting or editing tools, click at one end of the line and Shift-click at the other. Photoshop connects the two points with a straight line.

Click with polygon lasso, Option-click with regular lasso and magnetic lasso

The new polygon lasso creates straight-sided selections; you just click to set the first point in your selection and keep clicking to create additional points.

When working with the regular lasso tool, you can temporarily switch to the polygon lasso by Option-clicking. Option-click to set the first point in the selection and keep Option-clicking until you finish drawing the desired outline.

When working with the magnetic lasso, press Option and click with the mouse to get the polygon lasso. Release the Option key and drag momentarily to reset to the magnetic lasso.

However, don't use this approach when you want to add or subtract from an existing selection marquee. When you have an active selection marquee, pressing Option subtracts from the selection instead of switching you between lasso tools. So use the polygon tool to add or subtract straight-sided areas from a selection.

Click with the pen tool

To create straight segments with the pen tool, click at the beginning of the path to create the first anchor point and keep clicking until the path is complete. To end the path, press the ⌘ key to access the direct selection tool and click away from the path.

Option-click with the freeform and magnetic pen tools

To create straight segments with the freeform pen, press the Option key, making sure to keep the mouse button pressed, and then click to create a point. Keep clicking until you finish drawing the straight segments. Release the Option key, then the mouse, to return to the freeform pen.

When working with the magnetic pen, Option-click to set anchor points for the straight segments. To return to the magnetic pen, release the Option key, click again, and continue moving the mouse.

Adding to, Subtracting from, and Reselecting Selection Outlines

Shift-drag, Shift-click

To select an additional area of your image without deselecting the part that is currently selected, Shift-drag around the new area with a lasso or marquee tool or Shift-click with the magic wand. You can also press Shift and choose Select⇨Color Range.

Option-drag, Option-click

To deselect an area of the selection, Option-drag around it with a lasso or marquee tool or Option-click with the magic wand. You can also press Option and choose Select⇨Color Range.

Shift-Option-drag, Shift-Option-click

To retain the intersection of the existing selection and the new outline you draw with a lasso or marquee tool, Shift-Option-drag with the tool. To retain an area of continuous color inside a selection, Shift-Option-click with the magic wand.

⌘-Shift-D

To reselect your last selection, press ⌘-Shift-D.

Moving, Nudging, and Cloning

⌘ key

To move selections and layers, use the move tool. To temporarily access the move tool, when any tool except the pen or hand is active, press and hold ⌘.

Arrow key

To nudge a selection one pixel, press one of the arrow keys with the move tool selected. Or press ⌘ and an arrow key with any tool except the hand or pen tool.

Shift-arrow key

To nudge a selection ten pixels, select the move tool and press Shift with an arrow key. Or select any tool but the pen or hand tool and press ⌘-Shift with an arrow key.

Option-dragging, Option-arrow key, Shift-Option-arrow key

To clone a selection and move the clone, Option-drag the selection with the move tool. You can also press Option with an arrow key to clone a selection and nudge it one pixel or press Shift-Option-arrow key to clone and nudge ten pixels.

When any other tool but the hand or pen tool is selected, you can accomplish the same cloning feats by pressing and holding the ⌘ key with the other keys. (Pressing ⌘ temporarily accesses the move tool, remember?)

Drag with a selection tool

To move a selection outline without moving anything inside the selection, just drag it with a marquee tool, lasso tool, or the magic wand. You can also press the arrow key or Shift-arrow key to nudge the selection outline in 1-pixel and 10-pixel increments, respectively.

Filling a Selection

⌘-Delete

To fill a selection with the background color, press ⌘-Delete. If the selection exists on the Background layer, you can also press Delete to accomplish the same thing. However, if the selection is on a layer or is floating on the Background layer, pressing Delete wipes out the selection instead of filling it. So, it's a good idea to always press ⌘-Delete instead of Delete to fill your selections.

Option-Delete

To fill any selection with the foreground color, press Option-Delete.

Shift-Delete

Press Shift-Delete to bring up the Fill dialog box, which lets you fill a selection with all kinds of stuff, including the saved version of that portion of the image.

⌘-Option-Delete

Press ⌘-Option-Delete to fill the selection with the source state identified in the History palette.

Making, Switching, and Selecting Layers

⌘-J, ⌘-Shift-J

To clone a selection and place the clone on a new layer, press ⌘-J. To cut a selection and place the selection on a new layer, press ⌘-Shift-J.

Option-[, Option-]

To activate the layer below the one that is currently active, press Option-[(left bracket). To activate the next layer up, press Option-] (right bracket).

Control-Option-click with the move tool

To activate the layer belonging to a certain image, Control-Option-click on that image with the move tool. Or ⌘-Control-Option click on the image with any other tool except the pen or hand tool.

⌘-click on layer name

To generate a selection outline from the contents of a layer, ⌘-click on the layer name in the Layers palette. You can use any tool to do the job.

Stepping through the History palette

⌘-Option-Z, ⌘-Shift-Z

To step backward one history state at a time, press ⌘-Option-Z. To move forward one state at a time, press ⌘-Shift-Z.

So Many Shortcuts, So Little Time

The preceding tips don't address all of the many Photoshop shortcuts. For some additional time-savers, be sure to check out the Cheat Sheet at the front of this book.

Chapter 20

Ten Amusing Ways to Mess Up a Loved One's Face

• •

• •

*N*ormally, we're all pretty fond of our loved ones. But on that one day when a loved one gets kind of pesky — or two days during leap years — it's nice to have Photoshop within easy reach. So, are you mad at your boyfriend for going to Paris with a childhood sweetheart? Just scan his face and while away the hours modifying it in a way he won't soon forget. Peeved at your sister for snagging all of Aunt Rowena's multimillion-dollar inheritance? Open Sis in Photoshop and distort her as you please. No need to get angry. Just warp your loved one's face, print it, and send it off to your local newspaper or tack it on neighborhood telephone poles.

But, alas, I'm one of those rare people who has never experienced anger or resentment. So instead, I'll take a stab at the absolute strangers shown in Figure 20-1, who, as I understand it, were actresses, captured in the moment of auditioning for a commercial. Although I'm not sure they were actually cast in parts, in tribute to their obviously stirring performances, I'm going to trod heavily upon them in the following sections.

Figure 20-1:
Two faces
that cry out
"Muck me
up in
Photoshop!"

Pinching the Face Inward

Here's how to get the effect applied to the surprised character in Figure 20-2:

1. **Select the face using the elliptical marquee tool.**

   You can use some other tool, but an oval selection outline gives the best results. No need to be precise; an approximate selection is adequate.

2. **Feather the selection.**

   Choose Select⇨Feather, enter **6** or thereabouts as the Feather Radius value, and press Return. This step ensures a smooth transition between the distorted and undistorted areas.

3. **Choose Filter⇨Distort⇨Pinch.**

   The Pinch dialog box appears, allowing you to collapse the selected image toward its center.

4. **Enter** 50 **as the Amount value and press Return.**

   The face pinches slightly, as shown in the first example in Figure 20-2. This is a dangerous step in the process because the face may actually look better. Typically, the forehead, jaw, and chin grow, while the nose shrinks — all ingredients that might be misconstrued as indications of beauty. So whatever you do, don't stop now.

Figure 20-2:
Pinch the
face once
(left) and
then pinch
again
(right).

5. Press ⌘-F to reapply the filter.

The second example in the figure shows the result. Now, we're looking at some extreme distortion.

You may be wondering why I didn't just tell you to raise the value in Step 4 rather than apply the filter twice. After all, the Pinch dialog box accepts values as high as 100. However, thanks to the way the filter works, it's better to apply it multiple times using a low value rather than once with a high value.

Bending the Face Outward

The opposite of the Pinch filter, Filter➪Distort➪Spherize, bends the face outward, as shown in Figure 20-3. Here's how to create a similar effect:

1. Select the face using the elliptical marquee tool.

Make your selection just as instructed in the preceding steps.

2. Feather the selection.

Again, you're just doing the same thing you did before.

Figure 20-3:
Bend the
face once
(left), then
select a
different
area and
bend it
outward
some more
(right).

3. **Choose Filter⇨Distort⇨Spherize.**

Now this part is different. The Spherize filter brings up the Spherize dialog box, which reflects the image on the back of a spoon so that it curves outward. (Remember staring sleepily at your spoon before diving into the Lucky Charms or Count Chocula? Even in those remote years, the Spherize filter was at work.)

4. **Enter** 100 **and press Return.**

Unlike the Pinch filter, Spherize works just fine at the maximum setting. (Better algorithm, don't you know.) The first example in Figure 20-3 shows the nose-expanding, chin-contracting results.

5. **Select a different area inside the first selection.**

One swipe of the Spherize filter is never enough, but you can't apply the filter twice to the same area without losing detail. The eyes may start sliding off the face, for example. So select an area inside the first selection to do more damage. (Shift-Option-drag with the elliptical marquee tool to get the job done.)

6. **Feather the selection.**

Choose Select⇨Feather or press ⌘-Shift-D and press Return. Whatever value you use the first time does well the second time around.

7. **Press ⌘-F to reapply the Spherize filter.**

Ooh, isn't that nice? The second example in Figure 20-3 shows what happened to my image. A couple more swipes, and I bet we can see right up her nostrils.

Twisting the Face around a Taffy Pull

To twist a face so that it looks like it's being put through a blender — as demonstrated in Figure 20-4 — follow these steps:

 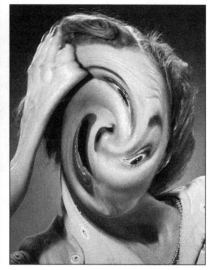

Figure 20-4:
The Twirl filter applied at 100 degrees (left) and 200 degrees (right).

1. **Select the face with the rectangular marquee tool.**

   For this effect, a rectangular selection outline works best.

2. **Choose Filter⇨Distort⇨Twirl.**

   The Twirl dialog box lets you do the twisting.

3. **Enter an Angle value between 100 and 200 and press Return.**

   The first example in Figure 20-4 shows the effect of a 100-degree twist; the second example shows a 200-degree twist. Any value over 200 eliminates too much detail for our purposes. Negative values between –100 and –200 are also acceptable.

4. **Sharpen the image.**

   The Twirl filter tends to blur the detail. To make it sharp again, choose Filter⇨Sharpen⇨Unsharp Mask. Enter an Amount value of 50%, a Radius of between 0.5 and 1.0, and press Return.

Giving the Face a Bath

If you're only slightly piqued at your loved one, you may want to make the face appear under water, as shown in Figure 20-5. Here's how to submerge the image:

Figure 20-5:
What happens when you apply the Ripple filter with an Amount value of 300 (left) and 999 (right).

1. **Select the image any which way you want.**

   No special constraints this time.

2. **Choose Filter⇨Distort⇨Ripple.**

   I bet you're beginning to think that all the great face-mucking features are under the Filter⇨Distort submenu. As it turns out, Ripple is the last one that is.

3. **Select Medium from the Size pop-up menu in the Ripple dialog box.**

   The Small option isn't enough, and the Large option is too much. As with the baby bear in the famous story — I believe Snow White and the three little pigs is the one — Medium is just right.

4. **Enter any old Amount value you want and press Return.**

   In Figure 20-5, I applied an Amount value of 300 to the first image and 999 — the maximum setting — to the second image.

Stretching the Face This Way and That

Why don't you and I take a little break from the commands under the Filter⇨Distort submenu and try out some manual distortion techniques? Figure 20-6 shows how to distort an image using Transform and Free Transform commands. The following steps tell you what the figure leaves out.

Figure 20-6: The Free Transform command lets you bend, pull, rotate, and otherwise stretch a selection in whatever way you please.

1. **Select something.**

   Again, select what you want. I can't make all the decisions for you. But you have to select something or you can't access the command I'm about to instruct you to use. If you want to apply the command to your entire image, press ⌘-A or choose Select⇨All.

2. **Press ⌘-H.**

   Photoshop hides the selection outline. Otherwise, the outline just gets in your way.

3. **Choose Edit⇨Free Transform or press ⌘-T.**

   The Free Transform command surrounds the selection with a box and displays square handles on the sides and at the corners. With the Free Transform box, you can resize, rotate, skew, distort, and apply perspective effects to your selection.

To scale (resize) the selection, drag any handle. Shift-drag to scale proportionately, and Option-drag to scale symmetrically around the center of the selection. To rotate the selection, move the cursor outside the marquee until you see a curved, double-headed arrow, and then drag. To move the selection, drag inside the marquee.

But to really have some fun, use the following techniques: ⌘-drag any handle to distort the image freely. ⌘-Shift-drag a side handle to skew the image. And ⌘-Shift-Option-drag a corner handle to apply perspective effects.

Be patient when working with the Transform command — Photoshop sometimes takes a while to generate the effects of your drags. If you don't like the outcome of a drag, just press ⌘-Z to undo it.

4. **When you've distorted the image to your satisfaction, press Return.**

Figure 20-6 shows two lovely effects created by tugging this way and that on my crying woman. In the left example, I skewed and distorted the image, giving Miss Crocodile Tears shoulders that a linebacker would envy. In the right example, I ⌘-Shift-Option-dragged to create an infant-looking-up-from-a-crib view.

The Edit➪Transform submenu contains individual commands for distorting, skewing, scaling, rotating, and adding perspective to the image. When you choose one of these Transform commands, you get the transform box as you do when using Free Transform. Just drag the handles to apply the effect — no Option, ⌘, Shift key combinations required. If you want to apply a different effect, you can choose the desired effect from the Edit➪Transform submenu. I usually prefer the Free Transform command — it's one-stop-shopping for transforming.

You can choose the Flip Horizontal and Flip Vertical commands, also found in the Transform submenu, when you are in the process of transforming your image using the Free Transform command.

Applying the Nuclear Sunburn Effect

Phew, that's enough of that manual stuff. You're entitled to automation, and automation is exactly what you're going to get. This next effect takes a different approach. Rather than moving the pixels around, the Nuclear Sunburn effect relies on commands that change the pixels' colors. As you can see in Figure 20-7 the face takes on a kind of eerie luminescence.

1. **Select your image.**

Make your selection as detailed or as imprecise as you like.

Figure 20-7:
Choose the
Solarize
filter and
the Auto
Levels
command
(left) and
then press
⌘-I.

2. **Choose Filter➪Stylize➪Solarize.**

   Sounds like an exciting command, huh? Actually, by itself, Solarize is pretty dull. It makes the black pixels black, the medium pixels medium, and the white pixels black again. Big whoop. But have no fear, we're going to spruce things up a little.

3. **Choose Image➪Adjust➪Auto Levels.**

   Photoshop lightens the gray pixels and makes them white, as shown in the first example in Figure 20-7. The areas that were previously either dark or light are now dark; the medium areas are now light.

4. **Choose Image➪Adjust➪Invert or just press ⌘-I.**

   This command inverts the image, turning the black pixels white and the white pixels black, as in a photo negative. The finished result is shown in the second example of Figure 20-7.

Applying the Cubist Look

This effect was created with the new 3D filter. This filter isn't the greatest; for example, it doesn't map all sides of the shape. But, hey, this isn't a 3D drawing program either! Take it for whatever it's worth. You can check it out in Figure 20-8.

Figure 20-8:
The 3D
Transform
filter gives a
new
meaning to
the saying,
"She's kind
of square."

1. **Select your image.**

   In this case, I used the lasso (see Chapter 12) to select the face and hand which now looks like it was surgically attached to her face. Ah, the wonders of modern plastic surgery.

2. **Double-click the Background in the Layers palette to convert it to a layer.**

3. **Choose Select⇨Inverse and then press Delete.**

   This gets rid of the background and leaves the area around the selection transparent.

4. **Choose Select⇨Deselect.**

5. **Choose Filter⇨Render⇨3D Transform.**

   A dialog box containing a small toolbox appears enabling you to choose various mapping types — sphere, cube, or cylinder.

6. **Select the cube tool in the toolbox and drag a cube around the whole image.**

   You can resize the cube by dragging on the cube's handle with the white arrow. To move the cube itself, drag on a side of the cube.

7. **When the cube is positioned the way you want, select the Trackball tool (black circle with a curved arrow) in the toolbox and drag the cube to rotate it.**

8. **Use the pan camera tool (to the left of the Trackball) to move the image if needed.**

   You can also use the Field of View and Dolly sliders to adjust how large the image appears against the background.

9. **Press Return.**

   Photoshop may take a couple of minutes to render the image, so be patient.

Stamping the Face in a Marble Haze

Again, this is a fairly weak name for a wonderful effect. The following steps alternatively lighten and darken the image, utilizing a cloud pattern that ends up looking a lot like marble, as you can see in Figure 20-9.

1. **Select your image.**

Figure 20-9: The result of choosing the Difference Clouds command once (left) and five times (right).

2. **Choose Filter⇨Render⇨Difference Clouds.**

   Of the two Clouds filters, this one is the more exciting. It blends Photoshop-generated clouds with the selected image using the Difference mode. The first example in Figure 20-9 shows the result of this single-shot filter.

3. **Press ⌘-F to reapply the Difference Clouds filter.**

   Photoshop blends the clouds with the image. Things are getting more mottled.

4. **Repeat Step 3 three times.**

5. **Choose Image⇨Adjust⇨Auto Levels.**

   Looking a little dark? Auto Levels brings the colors back to life.

6. **Apply the Unsharp Mask filter.**

   An Amount value of 50% and a Radius of 0.5 should bring back some of the detail. The second example of Figure 20-9 shows how the face now appears emblazoned on a dense, marble wall. At least, that's what the image looks like to me. Feel free to draw your own conclusions.

Effecting a Total Molecular Breakdown

This technique reduces your image to a bunch of colored shapes and then blends them with the original image to form something truly other-worldly, as shown in Figure 20-10.

 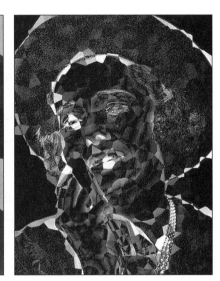

Figure 20-10: After applying the Crystallize command to my image, I used the Fade command to mix the new image with the original using the Difference mode (right).

1. **Select your image.**

2. **Choose Filter➪Pixelate➪Crystallize, enter** 30, **and press Return.**

   Nice words, Pixelate and Crystallize, but what do they mean? Like most of the commands under the Filter➪Pixelate submenu, Crystallize subdivides the image into blocks of color. In this case, the blocks resemble little particles of stained glass, as in the first example in Figure 20-10.

3. **Choose Filter➪Fade Crystallize.**

   The Fade command lets you mix the filter effect with the unfiltered original by using the same blending modes and Opacity slider you find in the Layers palette.

4. **Choose the Difference option from the Mode pop-up menu and press Return.**

   Photoshop uses the stained-glass pattern to invert the face.

5. **Press ⌘-L and use the options in the Levels dialog box to lighten the image.**

   As things stand now, the image is way too dark to print. I lightened the image on the right side of Figure 20-10 by setting the three Input Levels values to 0, 2.30, and 170, respectively. Press Return to apply the changes.

6. **Apply the Unsharp Mask filter.**

   I used an Amount value of 100% and a Radius of 0.5, but I encourage you to sharpen according to your personal tastes.

Framing the Goofy Pose

Sometimes, you're lucky enough to dig up a photograph of your unruly loved one that's embarrassing all on its own — no special effects required. In that case, all you need to do is add a little finishing touch, such as the wood frame or vignette effect shown in Figure 20-11.

The Actions palette contains prerecorded macros (sets of commands) that apply the effects shown in Figure 20-11. Here's how to create the wood frame effect using the Actions palette:

1. **Make sure your image is at least 100 pixels wide and tall.**

   If you aren't sure, choose Image⇨Image Size and check the dimensions. (For more info on sizing, see Chapter 4.)

Figure 20-11:
You can easily create a wood frame or vignette effect using the Actions palette.

2. **Choose Window⇨Show Actions to display the Actions palette.**

3. **Click on the right-pointing gray triangle next to the Default Actions folder to display list of actions.**

4. **Select the Wood Frame action.**

5. **Choose Play from the Actions palette pop-up menu or click on the white triangle at the bottom of the Actions palette.**

   Photoshop automatically starts applying the steps to create a wood frame around your image.

6. **When you see the dialog box saying your image must be a minimum of 100 pixels wide and tall, press Return.**

7. **If you see a dialog box saying changing modes will affect layer compositing, choose Don't Flatten.**

   Photoshop creates the faux wood frame and places it on a separate layer.

To create a rectangular vignette, as shown in the right-hand example in Figure 20-11, follow similar steps:

1. **Select the face with the rectangular marquee tool.**

2. **Select and play the Vignette action from the Actions palette.**

3. **When you see a dialog box, press Return.**

   As Photoshop applies the vignette effect, a dialog box appears enabling you to apply more or less of a feather radius. Just press Return to accept the default settings. Photoshop creates the vignette and places it on a separate layer.

Photoshop places the wood frame or vignette effect on a separate layer. If you don't like what you see, drag the layer to the trash can icon at the bottom of the Layers palette. You can't undo the wood frame or vignette using ⌘-Z because Photoshop has actually applied a series of commands to create the effect. You can undo only the last command in the series, which doesn't get you back to your original image.

Well, that should do it. If you don't have the anger worked out of your system by now, I suggest counseling. Or better yet, you kids kiss and make up. That's what my wife and I always do.

Chapter 21

Ten Things to Do with Your Photoshop Masterpiece

After you finish creating your image in Photoshop, you may experience a hint of letdown. I mean, now that you're done with the image, what do you do with it? You can't just sit there and look at it on your screen for the rest of your life.

Well, that is an option, I suppose, but certainly not your only option. Photoshop is one of the key programs used by graphics professionals, and only a few of said professionals create images just to sit around and stare at them all day. More often, these images have specific purposes and are used in specific ways.

This chapter examines a few options. Some of them cost money, and some involve the use of other programs that I don't explain in this book. All of the following options provide food for future thought.

Printing and Dispersing

Just about everyone who has a computer also owns a printer. Assuming that you do too, make sure that the image fits onto a sheet of paper and print it out (refer to Chapter 7 if you need help). Then you can photocopy the image and hand it out to everyone you know or stick it in an envelope and mail it to your grandmother. Digital images are a welcomed gift any time during the year.

Framing Your Work of Art

Okay, the preceding option was obvious. This one isn't, and it's expensive to boot. If you've created just about the best-looking image you could possibly imagine, you can actually print it and frame it. The image needs to have a resolution of at least 150 ppi, and you probably want it to be fairly large to justify the expense (although many classic works of art are only a few inches tall). And, of course, the image should be full color, RGB. (See Chapter 5 for more on RGB and other color modes.)

When the image is ready to go, call around to a few service bureaus in your neck of the woods and find one that can print to a dye-sublimation printer. A dye-sub printer creates images that look just like photographs — no little dots, like you see in newspaper photos, just smooth colors. You can't reproduce from dye-sub prints, but they look great. If you think your masterpiece deserves an even better print, look into Iris prints. They are a bit more expensive than dye-sub prints, but the quality is top notch. Images to be printed on an Iris printer should be 300 ppi and CMYK color. (See Chapter 5 for more on CMYK and other color modes.) Professionals use them for proofing to make sure that the colors in the printed image look the way they want.

A dye-sub printout will probably cost you from, say, $10 to $20. An Iris print will run $25 to $40. But provided the image looks good, the results for both prints can be fantastic.

When you go to get the image framed, make sure to ask for UV-protected glass, which also runs around $20 to $30. Most service bureaus spray Iris prints with UV spray to protect them. Dye-sub prints are very sensitive and can fade when exposed to direct or even indirect light, so hang the piece away from a window.

Placing the Image into PageMaker or QuarkXPress

Adobe PageMaker and QuarkXPress are two popular page-layout programs. They allow you to combine text and graphics to create multipage documents such as brochures, newsletters, reports, catalogs, magazines, and even books. This book, for example, was laid out in PageMaker; the color plates were laid out in QuarkXpress. (For more information on these two programs, check out *PageMaker 6 For Macs For Dummies,* 2nd Edition, by Galen Gruman and yours truly; and *QuarkXPress 4 For Dummies,* by Barbara Assadi and Galen Gruman, with John Cruise — both published by IDG Books Worldwide.)

If you want to use a Photoshop image in one of these programs, save it in the TIFF format with LZW compression. (See Chapter 6 for more on file formats.) Then import the file from disk into PageMaker by choosing the Place command (⌘-D), found under the File menu, or into XPress using the Get Picture command (⌘-E), also found under the File menu. (Both commands are found inside the respective programs, not inside Photoshop.)

You can move the image on the page, run text around it, and print the final pages, all inside PageMaker or QuarkXPress. So, unless you want to further modify the image, you have no reason to return to Photoshop. Although you can change the dimensions and rotate or skew the image in PageMaker and QuarkXpress, it is always best to do this in Photoshop rather than in your page layout program. Your file prints much faster and has less potential for snafus.

Whatever you do, don't copy the image in Photoshop and paste it into PageMaker or XPress. To do so is the same as importing the image in the PICT format, and neither PageMaker nor XPress works well with PICT.

Placing the Image into Illustrator or FreeHand

Adobe Illustrator and MacroMedia FreeHand are graphics programs like Photoshop, but instead of enabling you to edit images, they let you create smooth-line artwork. Information graphics, logos, maps, architectural plans, general artwork, and single-page documents, such as flyers and ads, are all projects ideally suited to Illustrator and FreeHand.

Both programs let you import images. In the case of Illustrator, save your Photoshop image in the EPS format. Then import it from disk by choosing File➪Place from inside Illustrator. For FreeHand, go ahead and save the image as a TIFF file. Then choose File➪Place (⌘-Shift-D) from inside FreeHand. Again, do not copy the image in Photoshop and paste it into either program.

After placing the image, you can combine it with smooth-line artwork or integrate it into a single-page document. The IDG Books Worldwide, Inc., production staff used FreeHand to label Figure 2-1 (see Chapter 2) and the other figures that required labels in this book. It's not possible to label the figures inside Photoshop — which is where they all originated — because small text in Photoshop is jagged and illegible. PageMaker, meanwhile, is great for creating long text documents but not so good at handling little bits of text here and there.

Here's how labeled figures such as Figure 2-1 got onto their respective pages:

1. **I saved the image in the TIFF format.**

   Then I copied the TIFF file to disk and sent it to IDG Books Worldwide, Inc., in Indiana.

2. **A member of the IDG crackerjack production staff placed the images into FreeHand.**

   A production artist then created all the labels and saved the FreeHand document in the EPS format. (See Chapter 6 for more on file formats.) EPS is the best format for smooth-line artwork and high-resolution text. It also retains the image.

3. **Inside PageMaker, another production artist imported the FreeHand EPS graphic.**

   The layout artist then positioned the EPS graphic and ran the text around it, as you see the page now.

4. **The final PageMaker document was saved to disk and shipped to the commercial printer.**

   The printer printed the pages and reproduced the pages onto the paper you're reading now.

How's that for a start-to-finish examination of how this process works? And, just in case you thought I was spilling out some trade secrets, just about every publisher creates books this way these days. It's a desktop world.

Pasting the Image into PowerPoint

Microsoft PowerPoint is a popular presentation program used for creating slides and on-screen presentations for board meetings, product demonstrations, and kiosks. Photoshop is a great tool for creating backgrounds for these presentations or refining head shots that may appear on the slides.

Because PowerPoint does most of its work on-screen, it's perfectly acceptable to transfer the image from Photoshop via the Clipboard. While inside Photoshop, just select the portion of the image you want to use, copy it by pressing ⌘-C, switch to PowerPoint, and paste the selection by pressing ⌘-V.

However, this recommendation holds only if you're creating an on-screen presentation or plan to print the presentation on a non-PostScript printer. If you want to print overheads on a color PostScript printer, don't use the Clipboard to place the images into your presentation program. Instead, import the image into PowerPoint as a TIFF file.

As you can in PageMaker, you can move the image around, change the dimensions, and wrap text around it. If you plan on displaying the presentation on-screen, you want to give some thought to the file size of the image. For example, if you intend for the image to serve as a background for a presentation that takes up an entire 13-inch monitor, the image should be 640 x 480 pixels. A good size for a head shot may be 300 x 200 pixels. Experiment to find the file sizes that work best for you.

Making a Desktop Pattern

You know that pattern that appears in the background behind all the icons at the Finder? It may be plain gray or some kind of colored dot pattern. Well, using Photoshop and System 7.5 or higher, you can change this pattern.

First, go to the Finder and check which version of the system you're using (if you don't already know). Choose the About This Macintosh (or About This Computer for System 8) command from the Apple menu. A dialog box appears, listing the version number of your system. If it says System 7.5 or later, you're in luck. Here's what you do:

1. **Find the Desktop Patterns (called Desktop Pictures in System 8) program.**

   This program could be anywhere on your hard disk. If you're having problems finding it, press ⌘-F, enter Desktop Patterns or Desktop Pictures, depending on your operating system, and press Return.

2. **Double-click on the Desktop Patterns or Desktop Pictures program.**

   This displays a window with a scroll bar that lets you scroll through various predefined patterns.

3. **Switch to Photoshop.**

4. **Open an image.**

5. **Crop it to 128 x 128 pixels.**

   Use Image⇨Canvas Size or the crop tool. This file size — 128 x 128 pixels — is the maximum size of desktop patterns/pictures.

6. **Press ⌘-A, ⌘-C.**

   This selects the image and copies it.

7. **Switch back to the Desktop Patterns or Desktop Pictures program.**

8. **Press ⌘-V to paste the image from the Clipboard.**

   If you get an insufficient-memory error, you have to increase the amount of memory devoted to Desktop Patterns or Desktop Pictures, like so: Quit the program and select the program icon at the Finder level. Next, press ⌘-I to display the Info dialog box and enter a higher value in the Preferred Size option box. Close the Info dialog box and relaunch the Desktop Patterns or Desktop Pictures program by double-clicking on it. Then press ⌘-V again.

9. **Click on the Set Desktop Pattern (or Set Desktop for System 8) button.**

   The background fills with the pattern.

You may want to return to Photoshop and work on making the left edge of the image match the right edge and the top edge match the bottom edge. This feat takes some experimenting, of course, but it helps to eliminate the harsh edges that divide one tile from the next. If you decide to edit the image in Photoshop, just repeat Steps 6 through 9 to reapply it to the Finder background.

Making a Start-Up Screen

Another way to modify your working environment is to create a start-up screen. The start-up screen is the image that displays when your computer is starting up. Normally, you see a little box that says "Welcome to Macintosh," but you can make it say anything you want. Here's how:

1. **Create a screen-size image.**

   Again, if you're working on a 13-inch monitor, make sure that the image measures 640 x 480 pixels. The resolution doesn't matter.

2. **Choose File⇨Save As.**

   Up pops the Save dialog box.

3. **Select the PICT Resource from the Format pop-up menu.**

   The PICT Resource format is designed especially for start-up screens.

4. **Navigate to the System Folder.**

   If you've forgotten how to motor around your hard disk from inside the Save dialog box, check out Chapter 3.

5. **Name the image** StartupScreen **and press Return.**

   Be sure the exact name is StartupScreen. A second dialog box, PICT Resource Options, appears.

6. **Enter** SCRN **into the Name option box.**

   It's very important that you enter SCRN in all caps.

7. **Select None from the Compression radio button.**

   Oh, my goodness, is this step ever important! If you select any of the JPEG options, you really mess things up.

8. **Press Return.**

   Photoshop saves the file to disk.

9. **Quit Photoshop and restart your computer.**

   As the computer starts up, you get to see your awesome start-up screen. Kind of fun, huh?

Engaging in Tag-Team Editing

Just because you're an electronic artist doesn't mean that you have to work alone. If you want to give another artist or a friend a whack at one of your images, copy it to disk and mail it off. Then have the associate or friend mail the disk back when he or she is done. Or, if you're hooked into the Internet or some other online service that offers e-mail, just send the file back and forth using e-mail.

You didn't have nearly this range of give-and-take editing options back in the days before computers. I mean, you can keep trading images for years. It's like a long-distance chess game — whoever comes up with the craziest editing trick wins.

Posting the Image over the Internet or an Online Service

Both the CompuServe and America Online electronic information services have Photoshop forums, and subscribers can connect to either service using a modem. You can then upload images to the forums to make them available to other subscribers. You have to pay for the time it takes to upload the image — and so does the person who downloads the image — so keep the images fairly small and save them in the JPEG or CompuServe GIF format. (See Chapter 6 for more about these formats.)

Also, tons of Photoshop-related sites are on the World Wide Web, accessible to anyone with a modem and an account with an Internet Service Provider. If you do a search for the word Photoshop, you'll be surprised at the number of matches.

If you happen to have your own Web page — or know someone who does — you can also add your image to the page, thereby making it available to Web surfers worldwide. As discussed in Chapter 6, you can use JPEG or the CompuServe GIF format to post images on the Web.

Just in case you haven't gotten enough of me through the course of reading this book, by the way, you can check out my Web page at the following URL: `www.dekemc.com`. It offers some Photoshop tips and tricks along with a bunch of other stuff, including lots of shameless self-promotion. But, hey, what's the point of having a Web page if you can't brag a little, right?

Adding It to Your Private Collection

No one says that you have to produce artwork for public consumption. I do plenty of stuff just for my own amusement and edification. What you see in this book, for example, represents about half of what I came up with; the other images are working files, experiments, or just too hideous for publication.

So share the stuff you're proud of, keep the random experiments to yourself, and try to learn from your inevitable mistakes. Oh, yeah, and don't beat the computer when it crashes.

Photo Credits

The following pages list every figure and color plate that features a photograph (or partial photograph) and the collection or photographer from which the photograph comes. My sincere thanks to the generous folks who contributed photos for inclusion in this book.

Figures	Photographer/Product	Company
Figure 1-1 (frame)	Signature Series #4, "The Painted Table"	PhotoDisc
Figure 1-2 (text)	Kent Knudson, Signature Series #2, "Urban Perspectives"	PhotoDisc
Figure 1-2 (eyes & mouth)	Vol. 11, "Retro Americana"	PhotoDisc
Figures 1-3 through 1-6	Vol. 11, "Retro Americana"	PhotoDisc
Figures 2-2, 2-3 (flower)	"Natural World"	Digital Stock
Figure 3-2	"Southern California"	Digital Stock
Figure 3-3	"Active Lifestyles 2"	Digital Stock
Figures 3-4, 3-5	"Children & Teens"	Digital Stock
Figure 3-6	"Active Lifestyles 2"	Digital Stock
Figure 3-8	"Southern California"	Digital Stock
Figure 4-1	"Children & Teens"	Digital Stock
Figures 4-3, 4-4, 4-5	Frederick Shussler, Signature Series #3, "Children of the World"	PhotoDisc
Figures 5-2, 5-9, Color Plate 5-1	"Indigenous Peoples"	Digital Stock
Color Plate 5-1 (background)	"Natural Textures"	Digital Stock
Color Plates 5-2, 5-3 (background)	"Conceptual Backgrounds"	Digital Stock
Figure 5-3	"Natural World"	Digital Stock
Figure 7-2	"Space Exploration"	Digital Stock

Figures	*Photographer/Product*	*Company*
Figure 7-6	"Southern California," "Space Exploration," "Natural World," "Children & Teens," "Active Lifestyles 2"; *and* "The Painted Table"	Digital Stock and Photo Disc, respectively
Insert Figure 7-8, Color Plate 7-1	"Indigenous Peoples"	Digital Stock
Color Plate 7-1 (background)	"Natural Textures"	Digital Stock
Color Plates 8-1, 8-2 (background)	"Conceptual Backgrounds"	Digital Stock
Figure 8-9	Robert Yin, "Undersea Textures"	Digital Stock
Figures 9-1, 9-2, 9-3	"Space Exploration"	Digital Stock
Figures 9-5, 9-6, 9-7, 9-10, 9-11, and Color Plate 9-1	"Undersea Life"	Digital Stock
Color Plate 9-1 (background)	"Urban Textures"	Digital Stock
Figures 10-1 through 10-4; 10-6, 10-7, 10-8	"Space & Spaceflight"	Digital Stock
Color Plate 10-1	"Indigenous Peoples"	Digital Stock
Color Plate 10-1 (background)	"Urban Textures"	Digital Stock
Figures 11-2, 11-3, 11-4	"Undersea Life"	Digital Stock
Figures 12-2, 12-3, 12-4	Eric Wunrow, "Sampler One"	ColorBytes
Figure 12-5	"Animals"	Digital Stock
Figures 12-6, 12-7, Color Plates 12-1, 12-2, 12-3	"Animals"	Digital Stock
Figure 12-10	"Natural World"	Digital Stock
Color Plate 12-1 (background)	"Urban Textures"	Digital Stock
Color Plates 12-2, 12-3 (background)	"Conceptual Backgrounds"	Digital Stock

Figures	Photographer/Product	Company
Figures 13-1, 13-3	"Buildings & Structures"	Digital Stock
Figure 13-4	Frederick Shussler, Signature Series #3, "Children of the World"	PhotoDisc
Figure 13-6	"Skylines of North America"	Digital Stock
Figures 14-1, 14-2, 14-4, 14-5, 14-6, 14-9, Color Plate 14-1	Signature Series #4, "The Painted Table"	PhotoDisc
Color Plate 14-1 (background)	"Conceptual Backgrounds"	Digital Stock
Figures 15-1, 15-2, 15-4, 15-5	"Undersea Life"	Digital Stock
Figures 15-6, 15-7	Stephen Schafer	SCHAF PHOTO
Color Plate 15-1 through 15-4 (fish and kelp)	"Undersea Life"	Digital Stock
Color Plates 15-1 through 15-4 (cathedral)	"Buildings & Structures"	Digital Stock
Color Plates 15-1, 15-2 (Neptune, comet, astronaut, and nebula)	"Space & Spaceflight"	Digital Stock
Color Plates 15-1, 15-2 (lily)	"Flowers"	Digital Stock
Color Plates 15-1, 15-2 (background)	"Antistock"	Digital Stock
Color Plates 15-3, 15-4 (background)	"Natural Textures"	Digital Stock
Figures 16-4, 16-5 (leaves)	Hans Wiesenhofer, Signature Series #1, "Colors"	PhotoDisc
Color Plate 16-1 (trees)	Hans Wiesenhofer, Signature Series #1, "Colors"	PhotoDisc
Color Plate 16-1 (background)	"Natural Textures"	Digital Stock
Figures 17-1 through 17-14	Vol. 13, "Italian Fine Art, Prints, & Photographs"	PhotoDisc
Color Plate 17-1	"Western Scenics"	Digital Stock

Figures	Photographer/Product	Company
Color Plate 17-1 (background)	"Tranquility"	Digital Stock
Figures 18-1, 18-2, 18-3	Vol. 11, "Retro Americana"	PhotoDisc
Figures 18-7 through 18-10	Vol. 11, "Retro Americana"	PhotoDisc
Color Plates 18-1, 18-2	Daniel McFarland	
Color Plates 18-1, 18-2 (background)	"Conceptual Backgrounds"	Digital Stock
Color Plate 18-3	Denise McClelland	
Color Plate 18-3 (background)	"Antistock"	Digital Stock
Figure 18-11, Color Plate 18-4	"Animals"	Digital Stock
Figure 18-12, Color Plate 18-5	"Animals"	Digital Stock
Color Plates 18-4, 18-5 (background)	"Conceptual Backgrounds"	Digital Stock
Figures 20-1 through 20-11	Vol. 11, "Retro Americana"	PhotoDisc

Index

(continued)

(continued)

Discover Dummies Online!

The Dummies Web Site is your fun and friendly online resource for the latest information about ...*For Dummies*® books and your favorite topics. The Web site is the place to communicate with us, exchange ideas with other ...*For Dummies* readers, chat with authors, and have fun!

Ten Fun and Useful Things You Can Do at www.dummies.com

1. Win free ...*For Dummies* books and more!
2. Register your book and be entered in a prize drawing.
3. Meet your favorite authors through the IDG Books Author Chat Series.
4. Exchange helpful information with other ...*For Dummies* readers.
5. Discover other great ...*For Dummies* books you must have!
6. Purchase Dummieswear™ exclusively from our Web site.
7. Buy ...*For Dummies* books online.
8. Talk to us. Make comments, ask questions, get answers!
9. Download free software.
10. Find additional useful resources from authors.

Link directly to these ten fun and useful things at
http://www.dummies.com/10useful

For other technology titles from IDG Books Worldwide, go to
www.idgbooks.com

Not on the Web yet? It's easy to get started with *Dummies 101*®: *The Internet For Windows*® *95* or *The Internet For Dummies*®, 5th Edition, at local retailers everywhere.

IDG BOOKS WORLDWIDE

Find other ...*For Dummies* books on these topics:
Business • Career • Databases • Food & Beverage • Games • Gardening • Graphics • Hardware
Health & Fitness • Internet and the World Wide Web • Networking • Office Suites
Operating Systems • Personal Finance • Pets • Programming • Recreation • Sports
Spreadsheets • Teacher Resources • Test Prep • Word Processing

IDG BOOKS WORLDWIDE
BOOK REGISTRATION

Register This Book and Win!

We want to hear from you!

Visit **http://my2cents.dummies.com** to register this book and tell us how you liked it!

- ✔ Get entered in our monthly prize giveaway.

- ✔ Give us feedback about this book — tell us what you like best, what you like least, or maybe what you'd like to ask the author and us to change!

- ✔ Let us know any other *...For Dummies*® topics that interest you.

Your feedback helps us determine what books to publish, tells us what coverage to add as we revise our books, and lets us know whether we're meeting your needs as a *...For Dummies* reader. You're our most valuable resource, and what you have to say is important to us!

Not on the Web yet? It's easy to get started with *Dummies 101*®: *The Internet For Windows*® *95* or *The Internet For Dummies*,® 5th Edition, at local retailers everywhere.

Or let us know what you think by sending us a letter at the following address:

...For Dummies Book Registration
Dummies Press
7260 Shadeland Station, Suite 100
Indianapolis, IN 46256-3945
Fax 317-596-5498

BUSINESS AND
**GENERAL
REFERENCE
BOOK SERIES
FROM IDG**

COMPUTER
**BOOK SERIES
FROM IDG**